We Improved Your Course

The hallmark of thriving schools has always been their willingness to make adjustments based on student feedback. Global University's Undergraduate School of Bible and Theology is committed to designing and redesigning its curriculum according to your needs.

To that end, we have replaced the Student Packet with an Essential Course Materials section at the back of this Independent-Study Textbook. It contains all the items formerly found in the Student Packet:

- Checklist of Study Methods
- Student's Planner and Record
- Question/Response Forms
- Service Learning Requirement (SLR) and SLR Report
- Undergraduate Writing Assignment Guidelines
- Project Instructions
- Collateral Reading Assignment (CRA) Instructions
- Answers to Self-Tests
- Unit Progress Evaluations (UPEs) and UPE Answer Keys
- Student's Request to Take Final Examination

The changes within this streamlined format will aid your study while also helping Global University fulfill its calling to wise stewardship.

Please remember that your feedback concerning your undergraduate experience is valuable to us. May God bless you as you continue your studies.

GLOBAL UNIVERSITY

1211 S. Glenstone • Springfield, Missouri 65804-0315 • USA

www.globaluniversity.edu

PH: 800-443-1083• FAX: 417-862-0863

NEW TESTAMENT LITERATURE

Sixth Edition

NEW TESTAMENT LITERATURE
A Study Guide
by Jesse K. Moon

Sixth Edition
Based on the Textbook
NEW TESTAMENT SURVEY
by Merrill C. Tenney

Developed in Cooperation With
the Global University Staff

1211 South Glenstone Avenue
Springfield, Missouri 65804
USA

What is new in this printing?

- The objectives in the introductory material for each lesson now match the objectives in the lesson content.

Global University
Springfield, Missouri, USA

TO BE USED WITH:
   Grading Packet, Sixth Edition
      (For Grader's Use Only)

PN 06.14.01

ISBN 978-0-7617-0906-0

Previously published as BL1103, BIB1023 *New Testament Survey*
© 1975 ICI University, USA

Printed in the United States of America

Table of Contents

The Degree Program

This Study Guide is one of the courses that comprise the Degree Program. Majors are offered in Bible and Theology, Christian Education, and Intercultural Studies. For additional information regarding the various programs available for study, write to your enrollment office.

Study materials in the Degree Program are designed in a self-teaching format for ministers and Christian workers who want to engage in systematic Bible study at the post-secondary level. These courses will provide many of the necessary tools for practical ministry and Christian witness.

Students may enroll in either individual courses or in a program of study leading to academic certification. However, you should be aware of the possibility that some courses may not fit into a specific study program. When satisfactorily completed courses are applied toward a study program, only those that meet the requirements of the selected program will receive credit toward certification. Therefore, it is important for you to select courses that contribute to your program requirements.

The Degree Program curriculum is under constant evaluation. Revisions and additions will be made in keeping with the goal of providing students with the best possible independent-study learning experiences.

Attention

We have prepared this Study Guide to help you successfully complete the course. Please read the course introduction very carefully. By following the instructions, you should be able to achieve your goals for the course, and you should not have difficulty preparing for your final examination.

Address all your correspondence concerning the course to your local enrollment office at the address stamped below. If no address is stamped there, and you do not have the address of the office in your area, then please write to the following address:

Global University
1211 South Glenstone Avenue
Springfield, Missouri 65804
USA

The address of your local office is:

Course Introduction

A New Revelation

Throughout history, humankind has pondered the mysteries of God. Where does He dwell? What is He like? What is His relationship to humankind? In the Old Testament, His presence was manifested by a pillar of fire, or by a cloud. But He remained a mystery.

The New Testament is God's revelation of Himself to humankind through His Son, Jesus Christ. Jesus Himself said, "I and my Father are one" (John 10:30). "He that hath seen me hath seen the Father" (John 14:9). Jesus' earthly ministry was a continual revelation of the love and compassion of the Father. He implanted the truths of God's love and holiness in the hearts of His disciples. His entire ministry was one of giving. The Father gave the Son. The Son gave Himself as a sacrifice for the sins of the world, thus making possible again the fellowship between the Father and all humanity.

When Jesus had completed His earthly ministry, He passed it on to His disciples. He told them, "As my Father hath sent me, even so send I you" (John 20:21). It was His disciples who recorded the events of Jesus' life in the Gospels. All of the writers of the New Testament, except the apostle Paul and Luke, lived and walked with Jesus. But Paul also had a personal encounter with Jesus, and it transformed his life. No longer was he a persecutor of Christians, because He had seen the Son. From that moment his life was dedicated to manifesting Jesus Christ to a lost and dying world. God chose this zealous, educated, self-giving Jew to take the gospel to the Gentile world. It was Paul who gave us the fullest exposition of Christian doctrine and instruction in his Epistles to new converts in the early church.

The New Testament begins with the revelation of Christ, the Son of God, who became man. His earthly kingdom was not lofty or glorious in humanity's eyes. His crown was a crown of thorns. He had no palace or other possessions. But the final book of the New Testament gives us a new revelation of Christ—high and lifted up, seated at the right hand of the Father in honor and glory. In His earthly kingdom people mocked Him, spat on Him, placed a crown of thorns upon His head, and crucified Him. But in His heavenly kingdom, we shall gather around His throne and sing with all the saints of all the ages, "Worthy is the lamb that was slain!" That will be the complete revelation of God to man.

In this survey of the New Testament, may you catch a greater vision of what the Father is like, as seen through His Son, so that you may be more like Him—and as did the apostle Paul, you can manifest Him to a lost and dying world.

Course Description

New Testament Literature LIT1303 (Credit: 3 hours)

This course seeks to introduce a panoramic view of the New Testament by presenting the following:

1. The chronological sequence of the writing of its books and its events.

2. Its significant geographical information.

3. Its principal characters.

4. An outline and a synopsis of the content of its books.

5. Its outstanding doctrines, passages, terms, and events.

An effort is made to integrate the messages of the various New Testament books, doctrines, and personalities. This is accomplished by analyzing their individual contributions to the corporate message. This integration is made in the context of basic introductory information about authorship (including biographical data), dates written, purpose, literary style, recipients (including cultural, historical, political, and religious background), and location of each writing.

Course Learning Outcomes

The general aims of this course are threefold:

1. At the head—to impart knowledge to you as the student (objective for understanding).

2. At the heart—to bring change in you as the student (objective for experience).

3. At the hand—to induce action by you as the student (objective for service).

Please read the following more specific statements of objectives and pray with me that they may be fulfilled as we study the New Testament together.

Objectives for Understanding

1. To enable you to do effective biblical studies. You will accomplish this by studying the guidelines given for effective Bible study and by practicing effective Bible study throughout the lesson assignments.

2. To enable you to gain a better understanding of the message of each New Testament book. For this reason we have provided basic introductory information about authorship, dates, purpose, literary style, recipients, and place of writing for you to learn.

3. To enable you to achieve a panoramic view of the whole New Testament. You will be able to establish the chronological sequence of the writing of the New Testament books and the occurrence of its events; learn its significant geographical information; become acquainted with its principal characters; study an outline and a synopsis of the content of each book; and study in greater detail the more outstanding New Testament passages, doctrines, terms, and events.

4. To enable you to develop an integrated understanding of the various New Testament books, doctrines, personalities, and problems. This task will be accomplished when you have analyzing their individual (special) contributions and their corporate relationships.

5. To enable you to see the Christocentric character of the New Testament. You will be able to recognize the Old Testament foundations for Christ's centrality; and identifying the contributions of each New Testament book, doctrine, and event toward the progressive fulfillment of Christ's redemptive work in the Church Age and in the ages to come.

6. To enable you to evaluate the importance of the inspired Word of God as the special revelation of His will for all mankind in all ages. You will accomplish this by discovering that the New Testament includes the saving revelation of God in Christ, and also, in conjunction with the Holy Spirit, providing both the guiding principles and the enabling dynamics of abundant life and of eternal life.

Objectives for Experience

1. To encourage you to prayerfully search out and accept the truths of the Bible in general and the New Testament in particular so that after affirming your conversion in Christ affirmed, you may mature in Christian experience. You will grow in love, holiness, and faith as the scriptural principles are practiced in your relationships with God, with others, and with yourself.

2. To inspire you to grow in love and dedication to the Lord Jesus Christ. You will discover in your New Testament studies that He is the *Alpha* and *Omega* of human experience.

3. To give you an experiential knowledge of the New Testament. This knowledge will be accomplished through meditation and through memorization of key Scriptures.

Objectives for Service

1. To equip you to be a diligent student of the Scriptures so that you may be effective in Christian service.

2. To enable you to memorize key Bible content which will provide you with ready inspiration, motivation, and confidence for Christian service.

3. To help you develop greater faith, power, vision, wisdom, and compassion for Christian service. This objective will occur as the Word of God which you have absorbed is demonstrated in your own life situations and in the lives of those to whom you minister.

4. To challenge you through exposure to biblical truths to prayerfully seek spiritual growth so that a rich anointing and the gifts of the Spirit will accompany your preaching and teaching of the Word of God.

Resources

You will use *New Testament Literature,* a Study Guide by Jesse K. Moon, with the textbook it was written to accompany: *New Testament Survey,* revised, by Merrill C. Tenney. *The Holy Bible* is the only other requirement. Bible quotations in this Study Guide are from the King James (Authorized) Version (KJV) unless otherwise noted. Some assignments require you to access the Global University Library website or other academic sources. Instructions for accessing the Library website are provided in the Undergraduate Writing Assignment Guidelines (UWAG) in the Essential Course Materials.

Content Specialist for the Course

Jesse K. Moon was the Bible college dean and campus pastor of Southwestern Assemblies of God University in Waxahachie, Texas, where his teaching responsibilities included homiletics, church administration, pastoral counseling, and Bible.

He received his bachelor's degree from Southwestern Assemblies of God University (Waxahachie, Texas, USA), and holds a Master's of Divinity (MDiv) and Doctorate of.Ministry (DMin) from Texas Christian University (Fort Worth, Texas, USA).

Dr. Moon combines a scholarly approach to the Scriptures with a warm personal interest in the student to make this Study Guide a most interesting and valuable guide to the student of the New Testament.

TIME SURVEY

This course has been selected for a special review that involves your cooperation. You are asked to log the time it takes you to complete various tasks:

- Reading the content of each lesson in the IST (or Study Guide)
- Completing each set of learn-by-doing exercises
- Completing and checking each self-test and unit progress evaluation (UPE)
- Completing the project, SLR, and CRA (if applicable)
- Studying for the final exam

Throughout the course we have included reminders to time yourself for these tasks as well as space for you to record the hours and/or minutes you spend on each one. At the end of the course, you are asked to add up the total number of hours and minutes for each task and log all the times on the "Time Survey" response form in your Essential Course Materials. Submit this form to your enrollment office with your Service Learning Requirement report.

Study Time

We recommend that you have a regular time for study. Of course, you may take advantage of spare moments to study when you have them, but there is no substitute for a regular study time. Try to complete at least one lesson each week. In a classroom, two or three class sessions would ordinarily be given to each lesson. Studying independently, you may expect to spend from three to six hours on a lesson.

How much time *you* actually need to study each lesson depends in part on your knowledge of the subject and the strength of your study skills before you begin the course. It also depends on the extent to which you follow directions and develop skills necessary for independent study. Plan your study schedule so you spend enough time to attain the objectives stated by the author of the course as well as your personal objectives.

Study Methods

The Essential Course Materials include two helpful tools. The "Checklist of Study Methods" and the "Student's Planner and Record" will help you know how to study a lesson, review for a unit progress evaluation on a group of lessons, and prepare for the final examination that covers all of the lessons. If you do not usually study as recommended, you will need to adapt your study methods to achieve the highest success in the course.

Ways to Study This Course

All of your course work except your final examination should be submitted by e-mail. If e-mail is not available, submit by mail or fax.

Although this course has been designed for individual study, there are limited opportunities to join in a study group or class. In that case, the adviser may give you additional instructions. If so, be sure to follow the adviser's directions.

Lesson Organization, Learning Tools, and Study Strategy

A recommended step-by-step procedure for approaching each lesson is presented as part of the introduction to each unit of this course. The procedure is a formula for getting the most out of the lesson. Each lesson includes specific components to help you learn the material: (1) introduction, (2) learning activities, (3) objectives, (4) outline, (5) content, (6) study questions and suggested answers, (7) defined words, and (8) self-test.

Introduction

Most lessons include an introduction that serves as a bridge between the previous lesson and the new material about to be presented. Read each introduction to review what you have learned thus far in preparation for being introduced to new concepts which build on that foundation.

Learning Activities

The learning activities are a brief summary of steps to successful study of the lesson. They let you know what to expect in the lesson and guide you in such a way as to help you achieve the lesson objectives.

Objectives

The key concepts presented in the lesson are derived from the objectives. Study each objective carefully as you begin each lesson. First, identify the key concepts presented in the objective, and second, identify what each objective is asking you to do with the key concepts. For example, in the objective *Assess the positive and negative ways that colonialism affected the spread of Christianity,* the key concept is *colonialism affected Christianity.* In this objective you are asked to assess positive and negative ways—or show the good and bad effects colonialism had on the spread of Christianity.

Outline

The outline gives a succinct picture of the lesson in a few words. It shows each main topic in relation to the content in subtopics. These offer helpful memory cues for acquiring and retaining the lesson content.

Content

The content presents the subject matter. To ensure the subject matter is learned effectively, the content incorporates several learning tools: objectives, headings, subheadings, and study questions.

As you study the content, (1) refer to the objective that relates to the section, (2) identify the key concepts presented in the objective, (3) identify what each objective is asking you to do with those key concepts, and (4) use the objective and study questions to direct your learning of the important concepts and perspectives. Use headings and subheadings to give you an idea of what will be discussed in each section. Having an idea of what to expect will improve your learning process.

The content is the substance of the lesson. You should underline, highlight, or otherwise mark it to help you remember the key points and significant statements of the author.

Study Questions

Study questions are included throughout the lesson content. Most study questions can be answered in the space provided; others require a notebook in which to write your responses. As you write the answers in your notebook, be sure to record the number and title of the lesson and to write them in correct numerical order. This will help in your review for the unit progress evaluations. You are not required to turn in your answers to the study questions.

Suggested answers to study questions are given at the end of each lesson. *Do not look ahead at the answers to study questions* until you have written your response. If you give your own answers first, you will retain what you study much better. After you complete each study question, check your answer with the one given. Then correct any mistakes you made.

These questions are important, as they will help you develop and improve your knowledge and Christian service. The suggested activities will also help you use your knowledge in practical ways.

Defined Words

The defined words help you understand unfamiliar and unique words used in the lessons. These words are identified in the text with an asterisk (*). You will find a definition in the left margin and again in the alphabetized glossary at the back of this Independent-Study Textbook or Study Guide. If you are in doubt about the meaning of any other word, you may look it up in a dictionary immediately or when you come across it again in your reading.

Self-Test

The self-test is typically comprised of an essay related to the lesson and approximately ten multiple-choice questions. (Some courses vary the number and type of self-test questions.) Always complete these questions before checking the answers in the Essential Course Materials. The self-test will reinforce your recall of key points.

Essential Course Materials

The Essential Course Materials at the end of this Independent-Study Textbook or Study Guide include instructions for taking the unit progress evaluations and the final examination. They also include the service learning requirement, undergraduate writing assignment guidelines (UWAG), project instructions, unit progress evaluations and answer keys, and other important forms. Use the checklist on the Essential Course Materials table of contents page to determine what materials you should submit to your enrollment office and when to submit them.

Form and Style Guide

The *Global University Undergraduate Form and Style Guide* defines the form, style, and documentation system for completing undergraduate writing assignments. The guide can be downloaded for free from http://www .globaluniversity.edu/PDF/UG-FormAndStyleGuide.pdf or is available as a stand-alone document.

Service Learning Requirement

The service learning requirement (SLR) instructs you to apply principles from the course content to ministry in the church and the community. This practical experience allows you to develop ministry skills while meeting real-world needs. You can find the SLR in the Essential Course Materials. The SLR report must be submitted to your enrollment office along with your project before you take the final examination. Course credit will be granted only after the SLR report is submitted and assessed as satisfactorily completed.

Project

The required project asks you to demonstrate an ability to apply the principles taught in the course. This work will give you valuable practical experience in using the knowledge you have gained. The project instructions are included in the Essential Course Materials. The project is worth 25 percent of your final grade and must be submitted to your enrollment office before you take the final examination. Submit the project by e-mail attachment. If e-mail is not available, submit by mail or fax.

Unit Progress Evaluations and Final Examination

Unit progress evaluation (UPE) scores are *not* counted as part of your final course grade. However, UPE scores indicate how well you learned the material and how well you may do on the final examination. After completing each UPE, check your answers with the answers provided in the Essential Course Materials. You can then review the information in your course text and Bible concerning points that were difficult for you. Reviewing the lesson objectives, self-tests, and UPEs will help you to prepare for the final examination. Instructions for taking the final examination are in the Essential Course Materials.

Credit for This Course

To obtain credit for this course, you must complete the assigned project and the service learning requirement (SLR). You must also pass the final examination. The examination must be written in the presence of an approved examining supervisor. Since we have examining supervisors in many countries, it most likely will not be difficult for you to meet with the one in your area. Your enrollment office will work out the details with you.

This course may also be taken for its practical value only and not for credit. In this case, you will not need to send in any assignments or take the final examination. The study of this course will enrich your life whether or not you take it for credit.

Course Grade

Your grade for this course is based on the final examination (75 percent) and the course project (25 percent). Although the service learning requirement (SLR) is not graded, you will not receive credit for this course until the SLR assignment is completed and the SLR report is submitted and evaluated as satisfactory.

Your course grade will be listed in one of the following categories: 97–100 percent, superior; 90–96 percent, excellent; 83–89 percent, good; 73–82 percent, satisfactory; 60–72 percent, poor; or 0–59 percent, failing.

Your Enrollment Office

Your enrollment office will be happy to help you in any way possible. Ask your adviser any questions you may have about arrangements for your final examination. Be sure to allow sufficient time so plans can be made accordingly. If several people want to study the course together, ask your adviser about special arrangements for a group study. May God bless you as you begin your study.

THE WORLD OF THE NEW TESTAMENT

Lessons... **1** Aspects of the New Testament World

                2 Other Religions, Judaism

Procedures...   **1** Read the lesson introduction and study the learning activities to know what to expect.

                       2 Reflect on the objectives for key concepts and expected outcomes.

                       3 Study the content, identifying key points by underlining or highlighting, and answer the study questions.

                       4 Answer the self-test questions to synthesize the lesson.

                       5 Review the lessons in this unit in preparation for the unit progress evaluation.

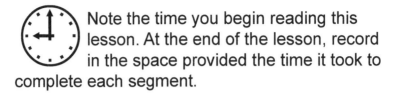

Note the time you begin reading this lesson. At the end of the lesson, record in the space provided the time it took to complete each segment.

Lesson 1

Aspects of the New Testament World

Start Time

_____

When you think about the New Testament it is important to understand the world at the time the New Testament was written. To do this, we will explore how the political, social, and economic aspects of the New Testament world all played a role in setting the stage for the coming of Christ into the world.

From the time of their Babylonian captivity in 586 BC, the nation of Judah was ruled by outside forces. They were in turn under the dominion of Babylon, then Persia, then the Greek Empire of Alexander the Great, and finally they became a part of the Roman Empire. While under Persian dominion, some of the Jews in exile returned to Palestine and rebuilt Jerusalem. Others chose to remain in Babylon or spread out to other areas of the empire. Consequently, during the time of the events recorded in the New Testament, God's chosen people were no longer a unified group. Many had adopted the customs and culture of their conquerors.

However, Judaism, their religion, was still very much alive and was to become the foundation for devout Jews who regularly read the Law and the prophets, and were looking for a coming Messiah. They expected that their Messiah would free them from the dominion of the Roman emperors. It was into this world that Jesus Christ was born at the right time, in the right place to fulfill His Father's plan of redemption. And the world has never been the same since.

the activities...

◇ Read the introduction to this Study Guide. Give particular attention to the sections that explain the lesson organization and study methods. This section contains instructions that are important to your success in this course. Notice the course learning outcomes for your study of the course. They all are important, but some may stand out to you. Underline those you feel would be particularly helpful to you. You may also want to list learning outcomes of your own.

◇ Study the lesson outline and lesson objectives. These will help you identify the things you should try to learn as you study this lesson.

◊ Work through the lesson development in this Study Guide. Be sure to read all Scripture references given, do the required exercises and check your answers. You will need a separate notebook for this course. Use the notebook to write answers to study questions when space is not provided in the Study Guide.

◊ Your reading assignments in this course are based on the textbook *New Testament Survey* by Merrill C. Tenney. We will refer to this book simply as Tenney. Each reading assignment is numbered, and you will find the readings indicated by the symbol ⊞ beneath various section headings throughout the lesson. Read the indicated pages when they are assigned. This will be your practice throughout the course. The readings for this lesson are

    Reading 1: Tenney, pages 3–45
    Reading 2: Tenney, pages 48–58
    Reading 3: Tenney, pages 58–62

◊ Develop and use a chart of the major Roman emperors, showing for each the dates of his rule, evaluation of his personality, description of his reign, and his significance to Judaism and Christianity.

◊ Take the self-test at the end of this lesson, and check your answers carefully with those given in the Essential Course Materials. Review any items you answer incorrectly.

the objectives...

1.1 *Name the major emperors of the Roman Empire, and describe their reigns and the effects of their reigns upon Judaism and Christianity.*

1.2 *Describe the two kinds of government in the Roman provincial system.*

1.3 *Describe the positive and negative influences of Hellenism upon Judaism and Christianity.*

1.4 *Make a list of the positive contributions of Judaism to Christianity.*

1.5 *Describe the social world of the first century, including the Jewish society, pagan society, cultural attainments, and standards.*

1.6 *Explain economic factors that dominated the Roman Empire and their effects on the spread of the gospel.*

The Political World

📖 Reading 1

When you read the textbook assignment, you may be a bit bewildered by all of the empires, emperors, dates, and cultures. We will follow the outline given at the beginning of the lesson. The textbook follows the same outline. This will help you locate the references to the textbook that are made in the Study Guide.

In this chapter you have read about two major empires and their subdivisions. Some parts of the rulerships were concurrent (occurring at the same time). Consequently, it is difficult to be sure about certain dates and influences. To get these empires in focus, a short outline will be helpful. They were approximately as follows:

GREEK EMPIRE (333–165 BC)—From Alexander's conquest of Persia to the Maccabean revolt.

Macedonian Rule	(333–322 BC)
Egyptian Rule	(322–198 BC)—The Ptolemies
Syrian Rule	(198–168 BC)—The Seleucidae

JEWISH INDEPENDENCE (168–63 BC)—From Maccabean revolt to conquest by Pompeii.

Maccabean Rule	(168–142 BC)
Hasmonean Rule	(142–37 BC)

ROMAN EMPIRE (63 BC–AD 70)—[From conquest to destruction of temple and Jerusalem.

Herodian Rule	(37 BC–AD 6)
Procurator's Rule	(63 BC to Constantine)
Priest's Rule	(142 BC–AD 70)

Study this outline to get an idea of the empires, subdivisions, scope of each rule, and the beginning and concluding events of each empire.

Objective

Name the major emperors of the Roman Empire, and describe their reigns and the effects of their reigns upon Judaism and Christianity.

The Empire of Rome

Read the first three paragraphs under this section and then turn to the map of "The Roman World in the Time of Jesus" located inside the front cover of your textbook. Study this map as you consider the information you have just read about the expansion of the Roman Empire. It was a great empire during the early years of Christianity.

1   To learn the essential information about the Roman emperors, develop a chart on the Roman rulers: Augustus, Tiberius, Claudius, and Nero. Make headings on your chart. Include only the most important material and state it briefly.

As an example for you to follow, look at the data about Augustus on the chart below; then do the others. After the chart is completed, review it a few times to get familiar with the facts; then keep it in your notebook for future reference in your ministry.

Emperor	Dates of Rule	Personality	Description of Reign and Accomplishments	Significance to Judaism and Christianity
Augustus	27 BC— AD 14	wise and well-liked by Romans	First emperor. Established empire. Ruled wisely and well. Made reforms. Revived state religion, worship of the state and himself. Attempted to restore family life.	Established the empire that politically influenced Christianity greatly.
Tiberius				

Relate these emperors to the time of major Jewish and Christian events by studying the chart of "The Roman Emperors of the First Century" in the appendix of your textbook.

Objective **1.2** *Describe the two kinds of government in the Roman provincial system.*

The Provincial Government

Under this section of study, try to get a clear understanding of the nature of the Roman provincial system.

2 After studying your textbook, answer these questions in your notebook.
  a What were the two types of provincial government?
  b Who governed each type?
  c What conditions called for the use of each type?
  d Under which type was Palestine at the time of Christ?
  e What liberties and restrictions were included in each type?

3 Carefully read the paragraph that lists the Roman provinces which appear in the New Testament. You will be seeing them again and again as you read the New Testament. Include this list in your notebook. Also examine the chart of "The Roman Procurators of Judea" in the appendix of the textbook. It will help to establish their relation to events in the New Testament.

Objective **1.3** *Describe the positive and negative influences of Hellenism upon Judaism and Christianity.*

The Hellenistic Kingdoms

Your study of this section will reveal that the culture of the Hellenistic* (Greek) kingdoms profoundly influenced Judaism and Christianity.

Hellenistic
relating to the spread of Greek influence as far as India and Egypt between the periods of Alexander the Great and the conquest of Rome

4 As you read through this section in the textbook, mark the positive contributions of Hellenism to Judaism and Christianity. In the same section mark with a different color the negative influences to highlight these elements. You will be impressed by their magnitude while learning them.

The Jewish State

As you read this section in the textbook, you will come to these important words: "The end of the Jewish state did not mean the end of Judaism." Judaism was to stay alive and become the foundation for Christianity.

5 Beginning with the above quotation and ending with "Under the Herods" in Reading 1, look for each incident, developing institution, literary production, and language development that eventually, greatly benefited Christianity. Make a list of those contributions and if possible, share them with a friend. Discuss the significance of each item on your list. Rank the items in the order of their importance to Christianity and see if your friend agrees with your evaluations. Do the written part of this exercise in your notebook. Perhaps the best way to get acquainted with the Herods is to read this section in the textbook. Turn to the chart of "The Herodian Family" (in the appendix of your textbook), note the Scripture references, and read them from your Bible.

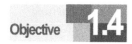

Make a list of the positive contributions of Judaism to Christianity.

The section in the textbook "Under the Priests to the Fall of Jerusalem AD 70" is very significant for understanding much of what happened in the New Testament, especially such momentous events as the religious and civil trials of Jesus. Among the other important data in this section, you will want to remember that the rule of the Jewish priests was concurrent with the rule of the Ptolemies, Seleucidae, Maccabees, Herods, and Procurators.

6 Circle the letter preceding each TRUE statement concerning the priesthood prior to the fall of Jerusalem in AD 70.

    a Under the various types of civil government throughout Israel's history, the word of the priest was final.

    b There was never a time that the priesthood was inactive.

    c Even under the foreign rulers, the Jewish people were considered to be under the control of the priests.

    d As long as the priests did not interfere with tribute or foreign policies, they were permitted by the rulers to function in their usual way.

    e At the time of the Maccabean revolt the priesthood was powerful and highly respected by the political rulers.

Describe the social world of the first century, including the Jewish society, pagan society, cultural attainments, and standards.

The Social World
📖 Reading 2

The author indicates in this section that the social world of the first century was essentially the same as that of our day. As you read this section see if you agree that the social situation in your country is comparable to that of the first century.

Jewish Society

7 In this section Tenney divides Jewish society into two broad categories.

    a What are the two categories? ....

    b Do these two categories exist in your country? ....

Pagan Society

8 In your notebook, list the five social classes mentioned in this section and give two characteristics of each.

Cultural Attainments

In this section you will gain an understanding of how the Roman and Hellenistic cultures affected the morals of the people through the activity carried on in the arena, and their use of literature, art, architecture, music, and drama.

9 Briefly describe how each of these aspects of Roman culture influenced the people.

a The arena: ....

....

b Literature: ....

....

c Music: ....

....

d Drama: ....

....

The sections on "Language, Schools, and Moral Standards" should be studied carefully as they relate so closely to the coming of the gospel.

10 In the following chart list the four chief languages and the major use of each one. Be sure to relate the significance of Aramaic and Greek to the spread of the gospel.

	Language	Major Use	Significance
a			
b			
c			
d			

Notice how God, in providential manner through the Greeks, furnished a learned culture and a universal language for the communication of the gospel. Also notice how God provided, through the Romans, roads for the travel of early Christians and a government that gave them reasonable protection and liberties to evangelize.

In the section on schools, you will discover that the educational system was not up to the level of the educational systems in most of our modern world. However, it was sufficient to have produced a fair degree of *literacy*, which reached well into the middle and lower classes of the first century world. In my opinion, this level of literacy produced a great *appetite* for knowledge that opened wide the door to the gospel. That the moral level was generally so low was evidence of the tremendous *need* of the gospel. Another clear evidence for the need of a gospel of power was the admission that teachings, like those of first century moralists such as Seneca, could furnish neither example nor *dynamics* for reaching the lofty ideals that they taught.

In the paragraph above I have tried to give you an example of how you can study a section of material that may seem rather ordinary and unimportant. You can draw the pertinent facts out of it, analyze them, and produce a significant outline or summary of the information. Look at the paragraph again. Those ordinary lines from the textbook have taken on important connotations for the first century Christians and the gospel. You might make these thoughts into a teaching or preaching outline at some time. It might look like this:

I. The need of the gospel
   Because of immorality.

II. The medium of the gospel
   Through the ability to read and communicate in a common language.

III. The door of the gospel
   Opened by an appetite for knowledge that literacy brings.

IV. The power of the gospel
   No moral ideal furnishes the dynamics to achieve its own lofty goals, *except* the gospel of Jesus Christ.

Moral Standards

11 In your notebook make two lists with the headings *Positive Moral Factors* and *Immoral Factors.* Read through the section on moral standards and write each factor given under the heading that describes it. Which is the longest list?

12 Now take a few moments to list some positive moral factors and immoral factors of your own country or town. How do they compare with those of the first century? Use your notebook.

Would you say that your community is more moral, or less moral, than the first-century world?

Objective 1.6 *Explain economic factors that dominated the Roman Empire and their effects on the spread of the gospel.*

The Economic World

📖 Reading 3

13 Read this section, then circle the letter preceding each TRUE statement below:

a The economic conditions of the first century had no influence upon the spread of the gospel.

b The land occupied by the Roman Empire was fertile and produced both fruits and vegetables.

c Goods were manufactured on a small scale mainly by independent craftsmen or were imported by sea.

d Because there were so many slaves, there could be low-cost mass production of goods.

e Most banking practices in effect today were in use during the first century.

f Roman roads were well-built, providing the means for better rule and better communication.

Now reread the objectives for this lesson, making sure you can fulfill them. Take the self-test and check your answers.

Total Time
(Read, answer
questions, check
answers)

Hr_____ Min_____

Self-Test 1

Start Time

Matching. Match the subjects or names (right) with the definitions (left).

.... **1** Launched the Greek Empire

.... **2** Completed the destruction of Jerusalem in AD 70

.... **3** Existed from 333–165 BC.

.... **4** Was the Roman procurator under whom Jesus died

.... **5** Was one of the chief languages of the Roman Empire in the first century AD

.... **6** Reached into Palestine with the conquest of Pompeii

.... **7** Ruled Palestine at the same time as the Ptolemies, Seleucidae, and Herods

.... **8** Brought the period of Jewish independence

.... **9** Was the emperor who blamed the Christians for the great fire in Rome in AD 64 with the result that many Christians were persecuted

.... **10** Demanded to be worshiped as a god, persecuted Christians, put John on Patmos isle

.... **11** Was the Roman emperor when the Jews were expelled from Rome

.... **12** Was on the throne at the time of Jesus' public ministry and death

.... **13** Was the first Roman emperor

.... **14** Was the language of the courts of law in the Roman Empire

.... **15** Degenerated under the influence of the Roman drama and arena

.... **16** Directly supervised the provinces which were turbulent

a) Greek Empire
b) Roman Empire
c) Maccabean revolt
d) Alexander's conquest
e) Priests
f) Augustus
g) Claudius
h) Nero
i) Titus
j) Domitian
k) Tiberius
l) Roman emperor
m) Pilate
n) Morality
o) Aramaic
p) Latin

Multiple Choice. Select the best answer.

17 The Roman emperor when Jesus was born was
a) Tiberius.
b) Augustus.
c) Nero.
d) Domitian.

18 The Roman emperors during the great period of missionary expansion were
   a) Claudius and Nero.
   b) Domitian and Nero.
   c) Tiberius and Nero.
   d) Claudius and Domitian.

19 The empire that influenced Christianity greatly through its culture was the
   a) Roman.
   b) Greek.
   c) Hebrew.
   d) Aramaic.

20 The language of Jewish theology at the time of Jesus was
   a) Greek.
   b) Latin.
   c) Hebrew.
   d) Aramaic.

21 The language of the Near East that was probably the common tongue of Jesus was
   a) Hebrew.
   b) Aramaic.
   c) Syriac.
   d) Greek.

22 The language of culture and the *lingua franca* of the majority of people from Rome eastward was
   a) Hebrew.
   b) Aramaic.
   c) Latin.
   d) Greek.

23 The people who furnished the roads for the spread of the gospel were the
   a) Romans.
   b) Parthians.
   c) Greeks.
   d) Jews.

24 The people who furnished the language in which the New Testament was circulated soon after its origin were the
   a) Syrians.
   b) Hebrews.
   c) Romans.
   d) Greeks.

25 The people who furnished a political system which gave liberty for the disciples to spread the gospel were the
   a) Greeks.
   b) Romans.
   c) Jews.
   d) Syrians.

Self-Test Time

Hr_____ Min_____

Answers to Study Questions

7 a Rich and poor.

b You probably answered *yes*.

1 Your chart should contain all the information you consider important for each emperor.

8 Your answers may include the following (in your own words):

a Aristocracy: (1) New aristocrats controlled public lands and bought up private lands at low prices. (2) Contractors and speculators became wealthy by exploiting provinces.

b Middle Class: (1) Wars and slave competition nearly eliminated the middle class. (2) After leaving their lands, members of the middle class became members of crowds in Rome—without homes, work, or food.

c Plebs: (1) The condition of these free persons was more pitiful than that of slaves, for they lacked steady work. (2) The unemployed followed any man who provided food and amusement (to gain the support of the plebs for his selfish ends).

d Slaves: (1) More than half of the people living in the Roman Empire are believed to have been slaves. Many slaves were better educated than their Roman masters. (2) Slavery debased morality and selfrespect. Corruption spread from slaves to owners.

e Criminals: (1) The unemployed persons in the society caused an increase in crime. (2) Many officials who were immoral committed many kinds of evil.

2 a Government under the senate; government under the emperor.

b Senate: proconsuls. Emperor: prefects, procurators, propraetors.

c Senate: Peaceful, loyal provinces. Emperor: Troublesome provinces.

d The emperor.

e City states were permitted to retain local sovereignty and to mint coins. Romans never interfered with worship. Roads were constructed, public edifices were erected, and commerce developed. Heavy taxation.

9 a It revealed glorified brutality with the sight of bloodshed.

b It showed the feeling against the emperor, and the manners of the day.

c It entertained the mob instead of the individual.

d It contributed to the moral decline.

3 Your list should include these Roman provinces: Spain, Gaul, Illyricum, Macedonia, Achaia, Asia, Pontus, Bithynia, Galatia, Cappadocia, Cilicia, Syria, Judea, Cyprus, Pamphylia, and Lycia.

10 a Language: *Koine* Greek (lingua franca). Major Use: Language in which Christian missionaries (Paul, for example) communicated the gospel in various countries. Significance: Language in which the entire New Testament was circulated.

b Language: Hebrew. Major Use: Language of Jewish Scriptures before their translation. Significance: Not of major importance to development of the church in the first century AD.

c Language: Latin. Major Use: Language of Roman law, literature. Significance: Eventual language of Christian theology because of clarity, preciseness.

d Language: Aramaic. Major Use: Predominantly spoken language of the Eastern Mediterranean area. Significance: Language of some of the earliest accounts of Jesus' life and teachings.

4 Your answer.

11 Your list; you probably found there are more *immoral* factors listed.

5 Your answer.

12 Your answer.

6 Statements **a**, **c**, and **d** are true.

13 Statements **b**, **c**, **e**, and **f** are true.

Note the time you begin reading this lesson. At the end of the lesson, record in the space provided the time it took to complete each segment.

Other Religions, Judaism

Start Time

_____

Christianity did not emerge in a world without religions. Men have always had an innate desire to know and worship God. Because they do not know the one true God, they have formed many other concepts of God, and these have become their religion.

In the New Testament world there were many religious beliefs and many gods. Eastern mystical religions, the occult, mythological gods, worship of emperors—all of these were much in evidence, along with Judaism, the religion of the Jews.

We have studied in Lesson 1 the political, economic, and social aspects of the New Testament world, and how each was a factor in preparing the world for the coming of Christ. The religious world, too, and particularly Judaism, influenced the hearts of the people to receive the Messiah. None of the religions or philosophies of that time could fully satisfy the deep longing of man to know God and worship Him. In Matthew 2:1–2 we read that wise men came from the east to Jerusalem seeking the newborn King, and saying, "Where is he that is born King of the Jews? for we have seen his star in the east, and [have] come to worship him."

This does not mean that all people easily accepted Christianity. Early Christians faced persecution, rejection, and misunderstanding as they struggled to spread the gospel of Christ. But the gospel could not be stopped! Today, 2000 years later, it has spread around the world, reaching men and women from every nation, every tribe, and every religion!

the activities...

◊ The readings for this lesson are
Reading 1: pages 65–78
Reading 2: pages 80–114

◊ Read the lesson development and complete each assignment. Then, take the self-test and check your answers with those in the Essential Course Materials.

◊ Review the key words. Be sure to look up the meaning of any key word that is unfamiliar to you.

◊ Review the lessons in this unit in preparation for your unit progress evaluation (UPE). Read the instruction page in your Essential Course Materials, then turn to Unit Progress Evaluation 1. When you have completed the UPE, check your answers with the answer key provided in your Essential Course Materials. Review any items you may have answered incorrectly. (Although UPE scores do not count as part of your final course grade, they indicate how well you learned the material and how well you may perform on the final examination.)

the objectives...

2 1   *Explain the religious situation in the first century including the worship of Greek and Roman gods, the occult, and the mystery religions.*

2.2   *Compare the major philosophies of the first century, including their main beliefs, chief good of each, and their relationship to Christianity.*

2.3   *Describe the unique features of Judaism, the temple, and the synagogue.*

2.4   *List the seven Jewish feasts, the month in which each occurs, and the significance of each feast.*

2.5   *Explain the importance of education to the Jews of the Dispersion.*

2.6   *Define the major writings in Jewish literature.*

2.7   *Compare the beliefs of the Pharisees and the Sadducees.*

the outline...

1   The Religious World (Other than Judaism)
   a   The Graeco-Roman Pantheon
   b   Emperor Worship
   c   Mystery Religions
   d   Worship of the Occult
   e   Philosophies

2   Judaism
   a   Origin
   b   Theology
   c   The Temple
   d   The Synagogue
   e   The Sacred Year
   f   The Educational System
   g   Literature
   h   Sects of Judaism
   i   Diaspora

Objective

Explain the religious situation in the first century including the worship of Greek and Roman gods, the occult, and the mystery religions.

The Religious World (Other than Judaism)
Reading 1

You have discovered that Christianity did not come into a neutral religious situation. Some aspects of the religious scene were assets to Christianity and some were liabilities. The textbook considers the five distinct types of religion that were a part of the culture in which Christianity developed. As you work through this chapter and the following one in the textbook, try to see the significance of these religions for both the first century and twenty-first Christianity. In many respects the scene is still the same. This dual perspective will help you relate your study both to the beginning of Christianity and to your life and ministry today.

The Graeco-Roman Pantheon

As the title of this section suggests, the Romans associated each of their deities with a Greek counterpart. The word *pantheon* is used to indicate that all of the gods of the people were represented. The word is a combination of *pan* meaning *all* and *theos* meaning *god*. *Pantheon* is also used to refer to a temple for *all gods*. Such a temple was built in Rome in 27 BC. This Roman pantheon later became the sanctuary for a Christian church.

1   You will notice that the worship of the Graeco-Roman pantheon was on the decline by the time of Christ. Two things contributed to this decline, according to the textbook. What were they?

    a ....

    b ....

Emperor Worship

We notice here that the practice of emperor worship developed gradually until it became a powerful instrument of state policy. And in the process it brought Christians into conflict with the state. Thus, the policy polarized people according to the ultimate loyalty: Christ or Caesar?

2   Answer the following questions based on your reading in the text.
    a   Who was the first emperor to be deified?

    ....

    b   What process was used?

    ....

    c   Who was the first Roman emperor to attempt to compel his subjects to worship him?

    ....

    d   How did the Christians react to the demands to worship the emperor?

    ....

We may be inclined to relegate worship of the emperor or the state to the ancient past, but this may not be realistic. Can you think of any governments of recent history that have approached this worship of the state or of its leader?

Mystery Religions

Tenney discusses several very definite similarities between the various Eastern mystery religions. However, he fails to note that there are some similarities between Christianity and the Eastern mystery religions. There are also several very pronounced contrasts.

3 Circle the letter preceding statements that show similarities between mystery religions and Christianity.

a A god who died and was either resurrected or resuscitated

b Secret initiation rites

c Belief in immortality

d Belief in equality of all men

e Belief in a personal religious experience

f Belief in more than one god

g Practice of purification ceremonies

What do you think about Christianity having points in common with religions that are basically in gross error? Can you explain this to your own satisfaction and to a nonbeliever who may ask you about it?

Worship of the Occult

In this section Tenney defines the worship of the occult as "the superstitious observances and regard of the masses for the powers of the universe, which they could not understand but which they could vaguely feel." You should learn this definition and learn the main aspects of this astrologically oriented religion because its influence reaches into our day in a pronounced way. There seems to be a tremendous revival of interest in the occult around the world today. See what the textbook has to say about the attitude of the following toward the occult:

The Scriptures (Old and New Testament)

The Jews (as compared with the Gentiles)

The Christians

Interest in the occult reportedly reached its peak in the time of the Roman emperor Tiberius who reigned at the time of Christ's public ministry and death. Is it possible that interest in the occult is greater today than when it reportedly peaked in Christ's day? Should the attitude of Christians today be the same as that of early Christians?

4 Circle the letter preceding each TRUE statement concerning the attitudes of Jews, Gentiles, the Scriptures, and the Christians of the first century with respect to the occult.

a The majority of Jews and Gentiles were superstitious and interested in magic.

b Gentiles were more involved in magic than were the Jews.

c Both the Old and New Testaments strictly forbid believers to be involved with demonic powers or the occult.

d Astrology is an occult belief acceptable to Christians as a guide for their lives.

e Christians refused to have anything to do with the occult.

Objective **2.2**

Compare the major philosophies of the first century, including their main beliefs, chief good of each, and their relationship to Christianity.

Philosophies

philosophy
the attempt to correlate all existing knowledge about the universe into systematic form and to integrate human experience with it; the general beliefs, concepts, and attitudes of an individual or group

As you study this section, learn Tenney's definition of philosophy.* In teaching philosophy I have preferred this definition to any that I have found in philosophy books. Also, all of the philosophies discussed in the textbook are based upon premises that are in contrast to the basic premises of Christianity. I suggest you learn the important points of these philosophies.

5 Make a chart in your notebook like the following example. Include these headings:

a Name of philosophy

b Name of founder or most prominent teacher

c Brief definition of the philosophy

d The main beliefs (be brief)

e The chief good for which the philosophy strives

f The philosophy's relationship to Christian truth

PHILOSOPHIES

Name	Founder or Teacher	Definition	Main Beliefs	Chief Good	Relationship to Christian Truth

Objective 2.3 *Describe the unique features of Judaism, the temple, and the synagogue.*

Judaism
📖 Reading 2

This chapter is of great importance to your understanding of the New Testament and Christianity. In the previous lesson we noted that Judaism was destined to live beyond all attempts to exterminate it, and provided the foundation of Christianity. As a religion, Judaism is unique both in its tenacity and in its beliefs.

Below are listed the unique features of Judaism. Almost all of the questions listed under each feature can be answered either yes or no. Write your answers in the blank at the end of each question. Notice the contrast between Judaism and other religions when you have finished. In a paragraph in your notebook, summarize the aspects of other religions.

6 Judaism was a national religion in origin but was not restricted to Jews.

    a Did other religions originate in one nation?

    ....

    b Were other national religions restricted to people of that nation?

    ....

    c Did religious leaders in other nations have as much leadership in their governments as the priests had in Judaism?

    ....

7 Judaism was intensely monotheistic (one God).

    a How many gods did polytheistic religions have?

    ....

    b Did polytheistic religions accept worship of gods of other religions?

    ....

8 Judaism was significant because of the importance attached to the temple and the degree of allegiance given to it.

    a Did other religions sacrifice animals in temples?

    ....

    b Did other religions have images (statues or sculptures of persons and animals) in their temples?

    ....

    c Did these other religions have the exclusive allegiance of as many people as Judaism had?

    ....

9 Judaism's ethics were inherent in the nature of its worship. Did other religions relate ethical living to the sacrifices offered in the temple as Judaism did?

....

10 Judaism's ethics were rigidly enforced upon all of its followers. Did some of the philosophies have ethical ideals about how their followers should live and treat each other?

....

....

11 Judaism was founded upon a self-attesting revelation from God. To what type of beginning did the ethnic religions (other than Judaism) in the first century AD trace their origin?

....

12 Tenney states, "Christianity is the child of Judaism." List four contributions of Judaism to Christianity as noted in the early paragraphs of Chapter 4.

    a ....

    b ....

    c ....

    d ....

Origin

The Jewish exile in Babylon made two outstanding contributions to Judaism: (1) the development of the synagogue, and (2) the origination of the order of the scribes. Although Babylonian influence caused some cultural change, these two developments helped Judaism to retain its basic principles.

Theology

As you read through this section in Tenney, you probably noticed how Jewish exclusiveness contributed toward the isolation of Jews within the larger Gentile communities. While this attitude had a positive effect in helping to maintain theological purity, it did not enable Jews to make the kind of impact for good that God intended. This spiritual impact would be made later, not by traditional Judaism but by the gospel, as we shall see.

13 In spite of the pressures of the cultures surrounding Judaism, Jews maintained their theology with very little change. In your notebook, list the eight tenets of Jewish faith that came down to the first century AD.

14 In your notebook analyze and briefly describe how each of the above doctrinal statements is foundational to Christian doctrine.

The Temple

While we noted the unique place of the temple in Jewish worship earlier in the lesson, you should know that there was more than one temple. In fact, there were three:

1. The temple built by Solomon and later destroyed by Nebuchadnezzar in 586 BC.

2. The restoration temple completed by Zerubbabel in 516 BC and partially destroyed several times between 168 and 37 BC.

3. The elaborate temple rebuilt by Herod the Great and finished between AD 62 and 64, and completely destroyed by Titus in AD 70.

We have included sketches of both temples so that you can compare Solomon's temple with Herod's. Study these sketches thoroughly (especially Herod's) in order to get a good understanding of the temple dimensions, furnishings, and functions. Keep the sketch of Herod's temple before you as you read its description in the textbook.

Figure 2.1 An Exterior Sketch of Solomon's Temple

See the photograph of a model of Herod's temple and its environs in the textbook on page 89.

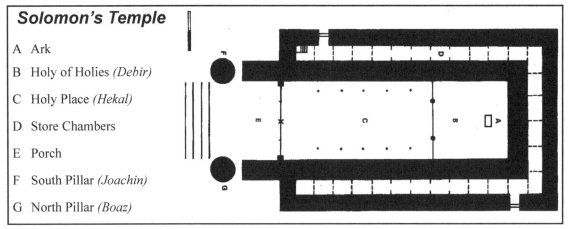

Solomon's Temple

A Ark

B Holy of Holies *(Debir)*

C Holy Place *(Hekal)*

D Store Chambers

E Porch

F South Pillar *(Joachin)*

G North Pillar *(Boaz)*

Figure 2.2

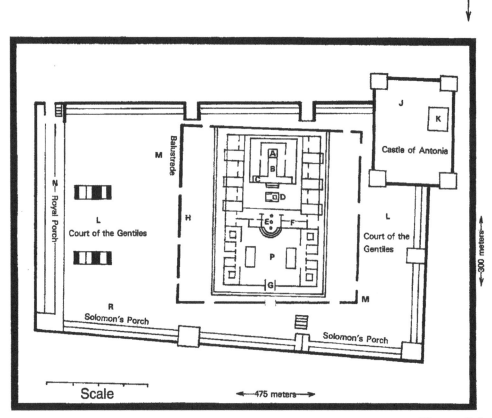

Figure 2.3

Herod's Temple

A Holy of Holies (Inner Sanctuary 20 cubits square

B Holy Place (20 cubits wide, 40 cubits long)

C Priests'Court

D Altar

E Court of Istael

F Porch (100 cubits wide)

G Beautiful Gate (Where Scribes held school and debates)

H Gentiles could not pass

J (Held a garrison of soldiers to subdue temple disorders. Priest's robes stored there as a sign of subjection to Romans.)

K Procurator's residence in Jerusalem

L Court of the Gentiles

M Wall of large stores (about 1x5 meters)

N Royal Porch

P Court of Woman

R Solomon's Porch

Here Tenney observes that Christians continued to use the temple until the Gentile branch of the church developed. Thus, the temple had a profound and lingering effect upon the church.

The Synagogue

The synagogue had a great influence upon the church, as this section will show. As you study this section, you will learn about the furnishings of the synagogue and its elements of worship. You will find that the synagogue influenced Christian worship, giving the church both an emphasis on the Scripture and on the sermon. Along with this influence, the church utilized the Jewish synagogues themselves for a period of time.

15 Read the description of the synagogue in the textbook, and study the sketches of the synagogues in this Study Guide.

    a   How did the Christian use of the synagogue resemble its use by Jews?

    ....

    b   Which Christians used the synagogues?

    ....

Figure 2.4 The Capernaum Synagogue, AD Third Century

The Beth-Alpha Synagogue

A Apse

B Ark

C Base of pillars

D Nave

E Stone Benches

F Gateway

G Raised platform

H Contained scrolls of Law

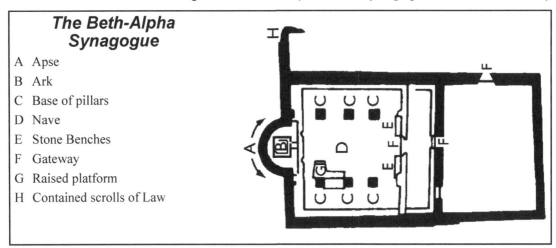

Figure 2.5

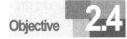

Objective **2.4** *List the seven Jewish feasts, the month in which each occurs, and the significance of each feast.*

The Sacred Year

You will be well-advised to take ample time as you study this section because of the obvious relationship between the special days of the Jewish sacred year and Christianity. Study the chart of "The Sacred Year" in the textbook. Also, be sure to read the New Testament references to these special days given in the textbook in order to get a better understanding of their relationship to the church.

16 In your notebook make a list of the seven feasts, the Jewish month in which each occurs, the present month in which each would occur, and the significance of each feast. This should help you to remember them.

Objective 2.5 *Explain the importance of education to the Jews of the Dispersion.*

The Educational System

As Tenney observes, education was a chief characteristic of Jewish life. And while it was narrow, it was precise. Moreover, it included the entire people as it sought to inculcate and preserve religious values. In addition, vocational education added a practical element as it prepared young men to be useful and to support themselves. Paul's lifestyle and teaching are powerful examples.

17 Choose one of the following to complete the sentence so that it is a true statement. Education was very important to the Jews of the Dispersion mainly because it was
   a) their means of providing training in the Law which was essential to their survival as a nation.
   b) through education that they could become more powerful than their rulers.
   c) their only way of becoming rich and famous.
   d) the only way they could learn to adapt to the customs of their new environment.

Objective 2.6 *Define the major writings in Jewish literature.*

Literature

A good knowledge of the literature of Judaism is essential to a clear understanding of much that you will read in the New Testament. This is true because of the considerable amount of material from the Old Testament that is quoted in the New. Turn to the chart of "Old Testament Quotations in the Gospel Accounts" in Appendix A of this Study Guide. You will be impressed by the extent to which the New quotes the Old.

Another reason for needing to know about the literature of Judaism relates to the Talmud. You cannot possibly understand the full implications of some of Jesus' and Paul's references to the traditions of the Jews—or the encounters of Jesus and His disciples with the Scribes, Pharisees, and Sadducees—without a knowledge of the content and use of the Talmud. Do not leave this section of study until you understand the relationship of other Jewish literature to the Old Testament Scriptures.

18 Match each element of Jewish literature (right) with its appropriate description (left).

.... **a** Works which sounded biblical or religious, but were not accepted as authoritative

.... **b** The canonical Jewish Scriptures which were quoted by Jesus and New Testament writers

.... **c** A collection of Jewish traditions with comments by early rabbis

.... **d** The Law, or first five books of the Hebrew canon, to which were added oral interpretations

1) Old Testament
2) The Torah
3) The Apocrypha
4) The Talmud

Objective *Compare the beliefs of the Pharisees and the Sadducees.*

Sects of Judaism

Each of the Jewish sects discussed in this section of the textbook, except the Essenes, are mentioned in the New Testament. New Testament writers mention the Pharisees and Sadducees repeatedly. Be sure that you can distinguish between the Pharisees and the Sadducees on the basis of their beliefs. You will find that, if you list the beliefs of each in a column and place them side by side, many of the beliefs of one group are in direct contrast with those of the other.

19 Compare the sects of the Pharisees and the Sadducees by describing them in the areas listed below:

		Pharisees	Sadducees
a	Basis of their theology		
b	Attitude toward the Law		
c	Angels and spirits		
d	Immortality		
e	Resurrection		
f	Have they survived?		

Diaspora

You will note, in studying this section, that even though the Jews have been widely scattered from Palestine into many countries, beginning with the captivity of Israel in 721 BC, they have retained their Jewish distinctiveness. Everywhere they went they built synagogues in an effort to maintain their religious heritage. You discovered previously that the early Christians used the synagogues as places to preach the gospel. Synagogues were providentially arranged to help the Jews retain their faith and also to aid in Christian evangelism.

In Lessons 1 and 2, we have seen how God used the Roman, the Greek, and the Jew to launch the church and to spread the gospel of Christ. This understanding of the world into which the New Testament came will enable you to get the most out of your study of the New Testament to which we turn in the next lesson. Before proceeding to the unit progress evaluation, take the self-test for this lesson and check your answers.

Total Time
(Read, answer
questions, check
answers)

Hr_____ Min_____

Self-Test 2

True-False. Write T in the blank space preceding each statement that is TRUE. Write F if it is FALSE.

.... **1** Romans worshiped many Greek mythological gods in the Graeco-Roman pantheon.

.... **2** By the time of Christ, the Greek pantheon worship was not so popular because the philosophers of the day ridiculed the practice.

.... **3** Most of the early emperors of the Roman Empire insisted that their subjects worship them.

.... **4** Emperor worship points out the danger of men exalting the position of another human being.

.... **5** The Eastern mystery religions in no way resembled Christianity.

.... **6** The Eastern religions allowed for emotional experiences in worship.

.... **7** Interest in the occult was strong among the Greeks and Romans.

.... **8** The Jews never became interested in the occult.

.... **9** The use of astrology to predict the future helps individuals to make plans and set goals.

.... **10** Many philosophers believe that man is adequate to understand his own world and decide his own fate.

.... **11** Many people, other than Jews, had accepted Judaism by the time of Christ.

.... **12** Study of the Law was an important part of the religious practices of the Jews.

.... **13** Judaism presented God as a personal and knowable being.

.... **14** Jewish theology included belief in individual responsibility, resurrection, future judgments of God, and the coming of a deliverer or Messiah.

.... **15** During the time of Christ, the synagogue was the main center of worship in Jerusalem.

.... **16** Many synagogues were established by the time of Christ.

.... **17** The synagogues were used only for religious services.

.... **18** Education was important to the Jews because it was the means of giving instruction in the Law.

.... **19** To the Jew, the Torah represented the voice of God.

.... **20** The Torah, the Talmud, and the Apocrypha are three different Jewish translations of the Old Testament.

Matching. In each of the following exercises, follow the specific instructions given.

21–27 Match the philosophies (right) with the description of each (left).

. . . . **21** This belief holds that the greatest good is to have no wants or desires.

. . . . **22** Because we live in a world with no purpose or design, the highest possible good is pleasure.

. . . . **23** The real world is the world of ideas of which the material world is only a shadow.

. . . . **24** Because knowledge depends on experience, there can be no final standard; thus, everything is relative.

. . . . **25** Because the world is controlled by an Absolute Reason, conformity to reason is the highest good.

. . . . **26** The spirit of man is good, and the body is evil; thus, all bodily desires must be eliminated.

. . . . **27** This philosophy promised salvation by knowledge and denial of the material world.

a) Platonism
b) Gnosticism
c) Neo-Platonism
d) Epicureanism
e) Stoicism
f) Cynicism
g) Scepticism

28–34 Match the feasts (right) with the definition of each (left).

. . . . **28** This day was really a fast day, in which the high priest offered the annual sacrifice for a sin offering.

. . . . **29** It was the most important feast day, the anniversary of deliverance from Egypt.

. . . . **30** This was the day on which the book of Esther was read in the synagogue.

. . . . **31** The Feast of Weeks, or the Day of the First-fruits, was the day in which a wave offering was presented.

. . . . **32** This Feast of Dedication honored the Maccabees for cleansing the temple.

. . . . **33** This Feast of the New Year was observed by the public reading of the Law and by rejoicing.

. . . . **34** It celebrated the wandering in the wilderness and the close of the harvest.

a) The Passover
b) Pentecost
c) The Feast of Trumpets
d) The Day of Atonement
e) The Feast of Tabernacles
f) The Feast of Lights
g) The Feast of Purim

Short Answer. Answer the following questions by naming the sect described in each.

35   Which sect of Judaism was the separatists, or Puritans, who obeyed both the oral and written Law?

....

36   Which sect was a closed brotherhood whose members did not marry and who held common property?

....

37   Which sect was the governing group in the civil life of Judaism and followed the Torah closely?

....

Self-Test Time

Hr_____ Min_____

Unit Progress Evaluation 1

Now that you have finished Unit 1, review the lessons in preparation for Unit Progress Evaluation 1. You will find it in your Essential Course Materials. Answer all of the questions without referring to your course materials, Bible, or notes. When you have completed the UPE, check your answers with the answer key provided in your Essential Course Materials, and review any items you may have answered incorrectly. Then you may proceed with your study of Unit 2. (Although UPE scores do not count as part of your final course grade, they indicate how well you learned the material and how well you may perform on the final examination.)

Answers to Study Questions

10 Yes. (But they lacked the inward dynamic to enable their followers to live up to the ethical ideals.)

1 a Gross immoralities and petty squabbles of gods.
   b Failure of gods to protect believers.

11 Tradition or mystic intuition.

2 a Augustus.
   b By Senate Vote.
   c Domitian.
   d They refused to participate.

12 In any order.
   a Jews wrote all but two books of the New Testament.
   b The roots of doctrines in the New Testament are in the Old Testament.
   c There are many quotations from the Old Testament in the New Testament.
   d Jesus was a Jew.

3 Answers **a**, **c**, **d**, and **e** show similarities.

13 In any order.
   a The unity and transcendence of one God.
   b A personal relationship between God and Israel.
   c Man, a being created by God and endowed with freedom to choose to obey or disobey his Creator.
   d Sin, failure to obey the will of God which is expressed in the Law.
   e Responsibility of man for the consequences of his choices.
   f Punishment and reward for individual and nation on the basis of obedience or disobedience.
   g Personal existence after death in Sheol.
   h Expectation of a Messiah.

4 Statements **a**, **c**, and **e** are true statements.

14 Your analysis.

5 Your chart. This chart will help you to see the similarities and differences in the various philosophies and remember the teachings of each.

15 a They followed to some degree the same procedures.
    b The community in the Epistle of James.

6 In this order:
   a Yes.
   b No.
   c No.

16 Your answer. Compare it with the list found in Reading 12 in your textbook.

7 a Some had many.
   b Yes.

17 a) their means of providing training in the Law which was essential to their survival as a nation.

8 a Some did. (Molech worship included sacrifice of human infants.)
b Yes.
c No.

18 a 3) The Apocrypha.
b 1) Old Testament.
c 4) The Talmud.
d 2) The Torah.

9 No.

19 Pharisees:
a Entire Old Testament, plus the oral Law.
b Complete obedience to both written and oral Law.
c Believed in them.
d Believed in immortality.
e Believed in resurrection.
f Yes.

Sadducees:
a The written Torah only.
b Obeyed the written Law by a literal interpretation of it.
c Denied their existence.
d Denied immortality.
e Denied resurrection.
f No.

THE GOSPELS: THE RECORDS OF THE LIFE OF CHRIST— THE PERIOD OF INCEPTION: 6 BC–AD 29

Lessons...

Procedures...

1. Read the lesson introduction and study the learning activities to know what to expect.
2. Reflect on the objectives for key concepts and expected outcomes.
3. Study the content, identifying key points by underlining or highlighting, and answer the study questions.
4. Answer the self-test questions to synthesize the lesson.
5. Review the lessons in this unit in preparation for the unit progress evaluation.

Lesson 3

Note the time you begin reading this lesson. At the end of the lesson, record in the space provided the time it took to complete each segment.

The New Testament Gospels: An Overview

Start Time

_____

It is not amazing that, although the New Testament was written over a period of about seventy years, by at least eight men of differing backgrounds and education, there is a remarkable unity in organization, theme, and message! Peter, the fisherman; Luke, the physician; James, the brother of Jesus; John, the beloved disciple; Paul, the scholar; and others of varying backgrounds contributed to the recording of the gospel story and its meaning for all believers.

The principal character of the New Testament is Jesus Christ, the Incarnate One, who became flesh and dwelt among us. Through His ministry, death, and resurrection, He brought hope to a hopeless world. The Gospels record His life and ministry; the book of Acts reports the impact of His message through the growth of the early church; the Epistles make application of His teachings in the lives of all believers; and the book of Revelation reveals to us the eternal promise that He will come again to receive us unto Himself. What a glorious message!

In our last lesson, we compared Christianity with other religions of the New Testament world. In this lesson we will see the relationship of the Old Testament to the New—of the old covenant to the new covenant. The central figure of the entire Bible is Jesus Christ. As we look at the structure of the New Testament and study the historical background of Jesus' life and ministry, I hope you will develop a new appreciation for this written Word of God, whose message has brought redemption to lost humanity.

the activities...

◇ The readings for this lesson are
   Reading 1: pages 129–135
   Reading 2: pages 137–145
   Reading 3: pages 203–226

◇ As you work through the lesson development, pay particular attention to the study questions. You will retain what you study much better if you will write your own answers before looking at the answers provided at the end of the lesson.

◇ Be sure to look up and read any Scripture references that are not quoted in full in the lesson development.

◇ Take the self-test at the end of the lesson and check your answers.

the objectives...

3.1 *Explain the significance of the name "New Testament."*

3.2 *Classify each book of the New Testament according to its character, and the period in which it was written.*

3.3 *Explain the synoptic problem and the proposed solution to it.*

3.4 *Give three attitudes about Jesus revealed in secular literature of the first century.*

3.5 *Analyze the outline concerning the harmony of the life of Christ in the Gospels.*

3.6 *Write on a map the names and location of important places in the life of Jesus.*

3.7 *Identify examples of teaching methods Jesus used.*

the outline...

1 The New Testament Introduced
  a Name
  b Content

2 The Gospels as Literary Works
  a The Synoptic Problem
  b Proposed Solution

3 The Life of Christ
  a Secular Sources of Information
  b Periods of Jesus' Life
  c Geography of Jesus' Life
  d Teaching of Jesus

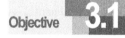 Objective **3.1**

Explain the significance of the name "New Testament."

The New Testament Introduced
📖 Reading 1

In the previous lesson you discovered that there were three historical preparations for the New Testament era. One preparation was *cultural* and was represented basically by the Greek world. The second was *political* and was represented basically by the Roman world. The third was *religious* and was represented by the Hebrew world. Each of these historical preparations contributed to the New Testament, but the Hebrew influence was by far the most important. And, of course, the greatest contribution of the Hebrews was the Hebrew Scriptures that we refer to as the *Old Testament*. You have already considered what the Old Testament contributed to the New Testament through the Old Testament quotations in the New Testament.

Now let us note the relationship between the Old Testament and the New Testament. I believe that Christ is the central and uniting theme of the whole Bible. The Old Testament is the foundation and the New Testament is the structure. The Old is the prediction and the New is the performance. The Old is the commencement and the New is the completion. The Old Testament constitutes the preparation for and prophecy of Christ's humanity, divinity, and ministry. The New Testament constitutes the revelation, realization, and propagation of Christ's humanity, divinity, and ministry.

We can clearly see the centrality of Christ in the Hebrew Scriptures if we look at the Old Testament prophecies about Christ's *humanity, divinity,* and *ministry*. In the chart on the following page, notice the references in the New Testament where each prophecy is fulfilled. Read the chart, select a few prophecies that interest you, and read the Old and New Testament references to them. You will have occasion throughout your ministry to use this chart of messianic prophecies.

The central theme of the New Testament is easily seen to be Christ—His humanity, divinity, and ministry. He is presented *historically* in the Gospel accounts and Acts, *doctrinally* in the Epistles, and *prophetically* in Revelation.

Name

As we begin this study, we see that the name *New Testament* has various shades of meaning. You can see what the term *covenant* includes in Tenney's treatment and how the new covenant compares with the old. You will benefit from reading and rereading this section in the textbook.

1   The word *testament* comes from the Latin word.

....

2   Circle the letter preceding the statement below that best defines the Latin word for *testament* as it relates to the Bible's New Testament.
    a)   A last will or testament
    b)   A binding agreement, or covenant, between two parties

3   Explain the difference between the old covenant and the new covenant. Use your notebook.

Old Testament Messianic Prophecies
Fulfilled in the New Testament

SUBJECT	*PROPHECY*	*FULFILLMENT*
THE MESSIAH'S HUMANITY		
Of the woman's seed	Genesis 3:15	Matthew 1:18, 21; Galatians 4:4
Born of a virgin	Isaiah 7:14	Matthew 1:22–23
Of line of Abraham	Genesis 12:3, 7; 17:7	Galatians 3:16; Romans 9:3–5
Of tribe of Judah	Genesis 49:10	Hebrews 7:14; Revelation 5:5
Of house of David	2 Samuel 7:12–13	Luke 1:30–33; Romans 1:3
To be born at Bethlehem	Micah 5:2	Matthew 2:6; Luke 2:4, 15
To be called Immanuel	Isaiah 7:14	Matthew 1:23
Called out of Egypt	Hosea 11:1	Matthew 2:15
Anointed by the Holy Spirit	Isaiah 11:2–3; 61:1	Luke 3:22; 4:18; John 3:34
His forerunner	Isaiah 40:3; Malachi 3:1	Matthew 3:1–3; Mark 1:2–3
THE MESSIAH'S DIVINITY	Psalm 2:7–12	John 1:1–2; Matthew 3:17; 16:16
To be the Eternal Son	Isaiah 9:6	Luke 2:11–12
To be incarnated	Isaiah 53:3–12	Matthew 16:21; Philippians 2:7–8
To be the Suffering Servant	Psalm 118:22	Matthew 21:42; Acts 4:11; Eph. 2:20
To be the Cornerstone	Numbers 24:17	Revelation 22:16
To be the Morning Star	Genesis 14:18	Hebrews 7:1, 14–17
To be the Priest-King	Zechariah 6:12–13; Psa. 110:4	Hebrews 5–5, 10; 7:11–28
To be the Greatest Priest	Deuteronomy 18:18	Acts 3:22
To be the Greatest Prophet	Jer. 23:5–6; Zech. 3:8, 6:12;	Matthew, Mark, Luke, John
To be the Branch	Isa. 4:2	Revelation 19:15
To be the Scepter	Number 24:17; Psalm 2:9	Matthew 2:2
To be worshiped by Gentiles	Isaiah 60:3, 6, 9	Ephesians 2:14–18
To be the Prince of Peace	Isaiah 9:6	Revelation 2:26–27
To rule the nations	Psalm 2:8	Acts 2:34–35; Revelation 17:14
To be the Universal King	Zechariah 14:9	Luke 1:33; Hebrews 12:28
To have an everlasting kingdom	Daniel 2:44; 4:34; 7:13–14, 27	

Old Testament Messianic Prophecies Fulfilled in the New Testament		
SUBJECT	*PROPHECY*	*FULFILLMENT*
THE MESSIAH'S MINISTRY	Isaiah 61:1–2	Luke 4:16–19; 7:22
The criteria of His ministry	Isaiah 35:5–6	Matthew 11:4–5
To be a worker of miracles	Isaiah 9:2; 42:6	Luke 2:32; Acts 13:47–48
To enlighten the Gentiles	Isaiah 11:10	Romans 15:9–12
To bless the Gentiles	Isaiah 53:3	Heb. 2:18; 4:15; Luke 18:31–33
To be sorrowful	Psalm 69:8; Isaiah 53:3	John 1:11; 7:5; 15:25
To be rejected	Zechariah 13:7	Matthew 26:31
To be deserted	Psalms 22:7–8; 109:25	Matthew 27:39–40; Mark 15:29–30
Surrounded by enemies	Isaiah 1:6; 50:6	Matthew 26:67; 27:26; Mark 14:65
Spat upon and scourged	Psalm 69:21	Matthew 27:34, 48
Given vinegar to drink	Psalm 22:16; Zechariah 12:10	Luke 23:33; John 20:25, 27
Pierced with nails	Psalm 22:15	John 19:28
To agonize in thirst	Psalm 22:18	Luke 23:34; John 19:23–24
Garments to be distributed	Psalm 34:20	John 19:33–36
No bones to be broken	Isaiah 53:12	Mark 15:28; Luke 22:37
Numbered with transgressors	Psalm 22:1	Matthew 27:46
To be forsaken by God	Psalm 31:5	Luke 23:46
To commend His spirit to God	Isaiah 53:9	Matthew 27:57–60
To be buried with the rich	Psalm 16:9–10	Acts 2:27, 31; 13:33–35
To be resurrected	Psalms 68:18; 24:7–10	Acts 1:9; Ephesians 4:8
To ascend to glory		

Figure 3.1

Objective **3.2**

Classify each book of the New Testament according to its character, and the period in which it was written.

Content

As you study this section, notice the three ways of classifying the New Testament, by

1. Literary character

2. Author

3. Period

Tenney classifies the New Testament by author and by period in Reading 1. In order to help you see all three classifications on one chart, I have added to Tenney's chart of classification by period, a column for author and one for literary character. Study Figure 3.2 carefully and be able to classify the books in the periods indicated.

4 After you have studied the chart, try to do the following exercises in your notebook without looking at the chart.

   a List the books that are *historical* in nature, and the author of each.

   b List the books that are *doctrinal* in nature, and the author of each.

   c List the books that are *personal* in nature, and the author of each.

   d List the book that is *prophetic* in nature, and its author.

   e Classify each book according to the period in which it was written: inception, expansion, or consolidation.

Objective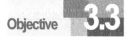

Explain the synoptic problem and the proposed solution to it.

The Gospels as Literary Works
📖 Reading 2

Read this section in the textbook and note the emphasis on both the diversity and unity of the Gospel accounts. Do these statements agree with your own understanding of the reason for our having four Gospel accounts? Did you notice that I said, "four Gospel accounts"? I did not say "four Gospels" because we have only one gospel and four reports or accounts of that gospel written from four perspectives. To quote the textbook, we have "four separate works, written at different times and in different places for distinct constituencies." "Each Gospel was selective according to the purpose of the author, and is complete in the sense that it carries out his intent."

The Synoptic Problem

As you study this section, learn what the word *Synoptic** means. You will get acquainted with what is referred to as the *Synoptic problem* if you read the Bible references given in the textbook. Also turn to the "Harmony of the Life of Christ" (Reading 3) and notice the overlaps and the gaps in the narratives.

Synoptic
of or relating to the first three Gospel accounts of the New Testament, affording a general view of a whole, manifested or characterized by comprehensiveness or breadth of view

The New Testament Classified						
Period	*Date*	*Event*	*History*	*Publication*	*Author*	*Literary Character*
Inception	6 BC 4 BC	Birth of Jesus Death of Herod				
6 BC to AD 29			Matthew Luke		Matthew, Apostle Luke, Gentile	Historical Historical
	AD 26 AD 29	Baptism Crucifixion	Mark John		John Mark John, Apostle	Historical Historical
Expansion	AD 31–33	Paul's Conversion				
			Acts		Luke, Gentile	Historical
				James	James, Jesus' Brother	Doctrinal
AD 29 to AD 60	AD 45 AD 49	Council of Jerusalem		Galatians (Mark) 1, 2 Thessalonians	Paul, Apostle Paul, Apostle	Doctrinal Doctrinal
	AD 52			1 Corinthians 2 Corinthians	Paul, Apostle Paul, Apostle	Doctrinal Doctrinal
	AD 54 AD 55 AD 56	Paul's First Imprisonment	Pauline Epistles	Romans Colossians, Ephesians Philemon	Paul, Apostle Paul, Apostle Paul, Apostle	Doctrinal Doctrinal Personal
	AD 60			Philippians	Paul, Apostle	Doctrinal
Consolidation				1 Timothy Titus 1 Peter	Paul, Apostle Paul, Apostle Peter, Apostle	Personal Personal Doctrinal
		Paul's Second Imprisonment		2 Timothy 2 Peter	Paul, Apostle Peter, Apostle	Personal Doctrinal
	AD 68 AD 70	Destruction of Jerusalem		Hebrews	Paul, Apostle	Doctrinal
AD 60 to AD 100				Jude	Jude, Jesus' Brother	Doctrinal
			General Epistles			
	AD 85			1 John 2, 3 John	John, Apostle John, Apostle	Doctrinal Personal
	AD 95		Revelation	Revelation		
					John, Apostle	Prophetic

Figure 3.2

Proposed Solution

You will need to learn the four theories of sources for the Synoptics that are presented in this section of the textbook. (The textbook discusses a fifth theory, but you will not need to learn this fifth theory.) Also, you should be able to explain, in your own words, what each theory involves, and what its strengths and weaknesses are. Imagine that you will be teaching a class on the Synoptic

Gospels and need to explain these theories to the class. You may practice by explaining the synoptic problem to one of your friends.

To help you understand the supposed flow of material under the documentary hypothesis, we could sketch a flow chart as follows:

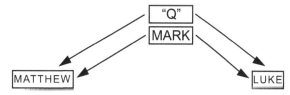

Figure 3.3

5 Circle the letter preceding each TRUE statement.
   a The Gospels are a complete account of everything Jesus said and did.
   b According to the textbook, the Gospels are four separate works written at different times.
   c The first three Gospels are called the Synoptic Gospels because they resemble each other closely.
   d It is clear that the writers of the Synoptic Gospels worked together in their writing.

6 Briefly summarize the following four theories of sources for the Synoptics.

   a *Oral tradition:* ....
   ....

   b *Mutual interdependence:* ....
   ....

   c *Documentary hypothesis:* ....
   ....

   d *Formgeschichte theory:* ....
   ....

7 Circle the letter beside the ending that BEST completes the following sentence: To summarize the conclusions of these theories, we could say that the Gospels should be considered as
   a) the independent writings of four men who did not have any contact with one another.
   b) collections of different writings that were put together in a later period by various scholars.
   c) honest attempts to arrange and record events in the life of Jesus, under the inspiration of the Holy Spirit, in the framework of each author's purposes.
   d) writings of four independent authors using the same notes from a fifth source, but organized and arranged according to the personal choices of each author.

Objective 3.4 *Give three attitudes about Jesus revealed in secular literature of the first century.*

The Life of Christ
📖 Reading 3

The lesson outline calls for us to consider the life of Christ at this point. It seems logical to do so immediately following the introduction to the New Testament and the study of the synoptic problem. Thus, studying the life of Christ comes before the individual study of the Gospel accounts, which makes for a good overview.

Secular Sources of Information

As you read this section, you will learn that there was little mention of Christ or of Christianity in the secular literature of the first few decades after Christ's death.

8 In the last paragraph under this section, the textbook indicates that these brief notices in secular literature reveal three things about Christianity. List these three things on the lines provided.

a ....

....

b ....

....

c ....

....

Objective 3.5 *Analyze the outline concerning the harmony of the life of Christ in the Gospels.*

Periods of Jesus' Life

The author of the textbook has generously furnished a "Harmony of the Life of Christ" in outline form. Spend some time analyzing this harmony. Go over the material several times (especially the main divisions marked by Roman numerals) in order to get a general picture of the major divisions of the life of Christ.

9 Circle the letter preceding each TRUE statement.
  a The most complete biography of the life of Christ is found in Luke.
  b Each Gospel presents a chronological report of events in Jesus' life.
  c The Gospels are more concerned with the significance of events recorded than they are with giving complete accounts of the events.
  d All of the Gospels report the resurrection of Jesus from the dead.

Objective **3.6**

Write on a map the names and location of important places in the life of Jesus.

Geography of Jesus' Life

Read this section in the textbook with special interest. Many of the places mentioned will come to life in the Gospel accounts as you continue the study in Lessons 4–7. After reading, go back to the last two paragraphs and take note of these places since they are significant to the life of Jesus.

10 On the Map of "Places Significant to Jesus" and on the map of "Jerusalem and Its Environs," (Figures 3.4 and 3.5, next page) write the names and mark the locations of the places mentioned in these last two paragraphs. You can check your work with the maps on pages 174 and 261 in your textbook. Transferring them as accurately as you can will help fix their locations in your mind. Practice this exercise several times on a separate sheet of paper; then, from memory, fill in the maps (Figure 3.4 and 3.5).

Objective **3.7**

Identify examples of teaching methods Jesus used.

Teaching of Jesus

Tenney discusses the communication skills of Jesus and His ability as a master teacher. You should note that what impressed Jesus' contemporaries was not His pedagogy (the science or art of teaching),* although He was doubtless familiar with all the current teaching strategies and learner characteristics. Rather, it was His ability to use the familiar events of daily life, for example—to relate spiritual truth and apply it in a meaningful way to people's lives. He challenged people's thinking and He used devices that spoke powerfully to people's minds long after the Master had moved elsewhere. However, the Spirit with which He spoke challenged people to respond, and many of those who heard Him spoke positively of His impact on their lives.

pedagogy
the practice of teaching

In addition to the teaching methods of Jesus that Tenney discusses, there are three other effective methods that He used that should be mentioned. They are:

1. His miracles.

2. His prayers.

3. His discourses.

The discourses of Jesus are too numerous to list at this point, but they were an excellent teaching method. While it is often overlooked, Jesus used His miracles and prayers to teach great truths. These are listed on the charts of "Miracles of Christ," Appendix B; and "Prayers of Christ" located in Appendix C of this Study Guide.

Jesus' teaching includes every subject that is essential to man. While the Gospel accounts are not characteristically doctrinal, they do briefly introduce many doctrines Christ taught that are developed more fully in the Epistles. In Lesson 4, you will study an extended list of the doctrines that Christ taught, but in this lesson you should just carefully read the sections under "Content" and "Doctrine" and not spend any extra time on it.

PLACES SIGNIFICANT TO JESUS

JERUSALEM AND ITS ENVIRONS

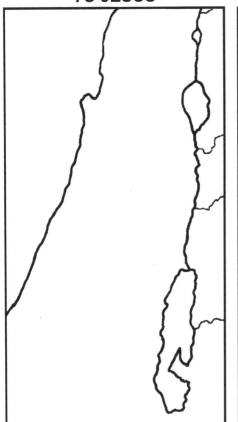

Figure 3.4

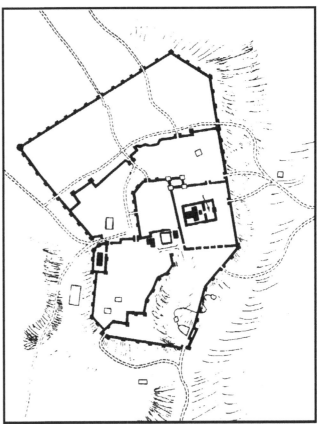

Figure 3.5

11 Match each teaching method (right) with its appropriate description (left).

.... **a** Method in which people posed problems and Jesus answered them

.... **b** Involved debate, usually conducted from the basis of Scripture

.... **c** Device used to make people think, whether direct or rhetorical; generally involved the deepest human problems; called for hearer response

.... **d** Teaching in which a child was used to illustrate humility and a widow putting money in the treasury to illustrate the principle of giving

.... **e** An extended metaphor easy to understand, remember, and apply spiritual truth

.... **f** Healing of man born blind used to teach about spiritual blindness (John 9:14)

.... **g** Terse statement that sticks in hearer's mind, often contains a paradox

.... **h** Every work designed to advance God's glory should be based on communication with Him (See Luke 6:1216)

1) Parable
2) Epigram
3) Argument
4) Question and Answer
5) Object Lessons
6) Miracles
7) Prayers
8) Discussion

Total Time
(Read, answer questions, check answers)

Hr_____ Min_____

Self-Test 3

Start Time

_____

Matching. Match the name or subject (right) with the definitions (left).

.... **1** Where Jesus walked with two disciples after His resurrection

.... **2** The record of the character of God and establishment of a new dealing of God with men through Christ

.... **3** Where Jesus ate with Martha and Mary, between the Mount of Olives and Jerusalem

.... **4** Stands for the German word meaning "source"

.... **5** Where Jesus retired when the hostility became too great; is near the wilderness

.... **6** A valley between Jerusalem and the Mount of Olives

.... **7** Mentions Christ very little, AD 6–60

.... **8** The principal city of Judea in which Jesus ministered

.... **9** As a teacher, was characterized by directness, freshness, and authority

.... **10** The English word which establishes the time relationship of the first and second covenants between God and man

.... **11** Used by Jesus as a teaching method, because they were easily understood, remembered, and applied to spiritual lessons

.... **12** Latin word meaning a "will" or "testament"

.... **13** A combination method of teaching used much by Jesus

.... **14** Comes from two Greek words which mean "to see together"

.... **15** A terse, pungent statement used as a method of teaching

.... **16** Centers around such questions as: Did the writers of Matthew, Mark, and Luke copy from each other, use a common source, or collaborate?

.... **17** Was a method in which people posed problems and Jesus answered them

.... **18** A theory which assumes that Matthew and Luke borrowed material for their books from Mark and a collection of the sayings of Jesus

.... **19** Lessons illustrated with people: Jesus' use of a child to illustrate humility

.... **20** A logical method which Jesus used in teaching from the Scriptures

a) Argument (or reasoning)
b) Bethany
c) Parables
d) Documentary hypothesis
e) Jesus
f) Synoptic
g) The New Testament
h) Question-and-answer method
i) Secular literature
j) Object
k) Ephraim
l) New
m) "Q"
n) Synoptic problem
o) Discussion
p) Testamentum
q) Jerusalem
r) Emmaus
s) Epigram
t) Kidron

Multiple Choice. Select the best answer.

21 Which one of the following was NOT one of the historical preparations for the New Testament era?
a) Cultural
b) Religious
c) Geographical
d) Political

22 Which one of the following describes the relationship of the Old Testament and the New Testament?
a) The Old was preparation, the New was realization.
b) The New was the foundation, the Old was the structure.
c) The Old was performance, the New was prediction.
d) The New was commencement, the Old was completion.

23 Which statement correctly states the role of Christ in the Bible?
a) Christ is the central theme in the Old Testament only.
b) Christ is the central theme in the New Testament only.
c) Christ is the central but not the uniting theme for both the Old and New Testaments.
d) Christ is the central and uniting theme for both the Old and New Testaments.

24 Which statement is the correct classification of the New Testament by literary character?
a) Christ is presented historically in the Epistles, doctrinally in the Gospel accounts and Acts, and prophetically in Revelation.
b) Christ is presented historically in the Gospel accounts and Acts, doctrinally in the Epistles, and prophetically in Revelation.
c) Christ is presented historically in the Epistles and Revelation, doctrinally in Acts, and prophetically in the Gospel accounts.
d) Christ is presented doctrinally in Revelation, prophetically in the Epistles, and historically in Acts and the Gospel accounts.

25 Which one gives the correct classification of the New Testament by periods?
a) Inception (6 BC–AD 29); consolidation,(AD 29–60); expansion (AD 60–100)
b) Inception (1 BC–AD 5); expansion (AD 6–15); consolidation (AD 16–26)
c) Inception (33 BC–AD 40); expansion (AD 41–55); consolidation (AD 56–75)
d) Inception (6 BC–AD 29); expansion (AD 29–60); consolidation (AD 60–100)

Fill in the Blank. Print one word in each blank.

26 .... is the author of Acts.

27 .... wrote the Epistle to the Romans.

28 .... wrote 1, 2, and 3 John.

29 .... is the author of 1 and 2 Corinthians.

30 .... wrote the book of Jude.

31 .... wrote the book of James.

32 .... wrote 1 Peter.

33 .... wrote 2 Peter.

34 .... wrote Ephesians, Colossians, Philemon, and Philippians.

35 .... wrote Galatians.

36 .... is the author of 1 Thessalonians.

37 .... wrote 2 Thessalonians.

Self-Test Time

Hr_____ Min_____

Answers to Study Questions

6 a The facts about Jesus were organized, then memorized, and delivered orally in a fairly fixed form before they were finally written down.
b Two of the Gospels borrowed from the third.
c Matthew and Luke wrote their Gospels on the basis of Mark's writings, plus another source called "Q."
d A disorganized collection of fragments, or stories about Jesus, that were passed from one speaker to another before they were written down

1 *Testamentum.*

7 c) honest attempts to arrange and record events in the life of Jesus, under the inspiration of the Holy Spirit, in the framework of each author's purposes.

2 b) A binding agreement, or covenant, between two parties.

8 In any order:
a Christianity was widespread by the second century.
b The historic existence of Christ was acknowledged even by those who were against Him.
c In some secular writings Jesus was considered a fanatic whose cult had grown unexpectedly.

3 The old covenant involved a revelation of the holiness of God in a righteous standard of law which those who received it were enjoined to keep; whereas, the new covenant embodies a revelation of the holiness of God in a totally righteous Son, who empowers those who receive the revelation to become sons of God.

9 Statements **a**, **c**, and **d** are true.

4 Check your answers with the chart "The New Testament Classified" in this lesson.

10 Check your maps with those in chapters 10 and 15 of your textbook.

5 Statements **b** and **c** are true.

11 a 8) Discussion.
b 3) Argument.
c 4) Question and Answer.
d 5) Object Lessons.
e 1) Parable.
f 6) Miracles.
g 2) Epigram.
h 7) Prayers.

Note the time you begin reading this lesson. At the end of the lesson, record in the space provided the time it took to complete each segment.

The Gospel Account of Matthew

Start Time

_____

Now that we have seen the relationship of the four Gospels to each other and to the other New Testament books, we are ready to study more fully the purpose and approach of each Gospel. It is appropriate to begin with the Gospel of Matthew.

In Matthew's Gospel, Jesus is presented as the Messiah, the King. There is much teaching concerning the kingdom of God, and who can be part of His kingdom. This Gospel is the bridge between the Old and New Testaments, rich in references to messianic prophecy found in the Old Testament and pointing to Jesus as the fulfillment of that prophecy.

It is interesting to note that this gospel account emphasizes the relation of the gospel to the Law. Until he had a face-to-face encounter with Jesus, the one who wrote it was a notorious breaker of the Law. Matthew learned, first-hand, that Jesus did not come to do away with the Law, but He came to fulfill the Law. Matthew's Gospel was written to those of Jewish heritage whose foundation was the Law of the one true God, but who had failed miserably in keeping His Law.

Because this Gospel contains more of Jesus' teaching than any of the other Gospels, it is a valuable resource for sharing with others the principles taught by Jesus. Matthew's encounter with the Savior was a life-changing experience. His record of Jesus' life, His miracles, His teaching, and His ministry provides the means for a life-changing experience to all who will read it and believe. May you be challenged through this study to share your own experience in Christ with others who have never met Him!

the activities...

◇ Read the gospel account of Matthew straight through in order to get an overview of its message before you begin to study in the lesson development. Then scan the readings for this lesson. As you do, keep your Bible open and read the Scripture references in the textbook as you come to them. The readings for this lesson are

Reading 1: pages 149–150
Reading 2: pages 150–151
Reading 3: pages 151–152
Reading 4: pages 152–159

◇ Work through the lesson development and answer each study question carefully. Be sure to check your answers with those provided at the end of the lesson. Correct any you answer incorrectly, and review the material to make sure you understand before you proceed.

◇ Take the self-test at the end of the lesson and check your answers.

the objectives...

4.1 *Give reasons why it is believed that Matthew wrote the first Gospel in the New Testament.*

4.2 *Describe the environment in which the Gospel of Matthew was written.*

4.3 *Identify the purpose and theme of the Gospel of Matthew.*

4.4 *Explain major doctrines of the book of Matthew, including the relationship between the Law and the gospel.*

4.5 *Define the three special features of Matthew given by Tenney.*

the outline...

1 Origin of Matthew
2 Date and Place
3 Content
4 Outline
5 Emphasis
6 Characters
7 Special Features
8 Golden Passages

Objective **4.1**

Give reasons why it is believed that Matthew wrote the first Gospel in the New Testament.

Origin of Matthew
📖 Reading 1

We begin our study of Matthew's account of the gospel by noting that this book is ascribed to Matthew Levi, one of the twelve disciples. As Tenney notes, we know very little about Matthew other than his name and occupation. However, early church writers knew him and what he did, and their witness enables us to make certain inferences about the origin of the Gospel of Matthew.

1 Review the section in the textbook on "Origin." Locate, mark, and read several times the three "inferences" Tenney says "may be drawn from these early statements concerning the origin of the first Gospel." Write them in your notebook.

2 Do these inferences adequately attribute authorship of this gospel account to Matthew? Explain your answer in your notebook.

3 From the material in the New Testament and in the textbook, write in your notebook the most complete biographical sketch you can about Matthew.

4 Now get acquainted with Matthew by projecting yourself into his era of time, circumstances, and personality. Suppose you were Matthew and that, as one of Jesus' disciples, you were with the disciples mentioned in the following passages. Write beside each reference how you would have felt in Matthew's place.

a Matthew 9:9–13 ....

....

b Matthew 10:2–7 ....

....

c Matthew 26:1–57 ....

....

d Matthew 28:1–9 ....

....

e Matthew 28:16–20 ....

....

f Acts 1:13 ....

....

Objective **4.2** *Describe the environment in which the Gospel of Matthew was written.*

Date and Place
📖 Reading 2

Under this section in the textbook locate and mark the factors that Tenney uses to establish AD 50–70 as the time of the writing of Matthew. You might want to jot these facts down in your notebook also. Turn to the same section in the textbook on Mark, Luke, and John and compare what Tenney says about the dating of each of the four gospel accounts. Then turn to the "Introduction to New Testament Literature at a Glance" chart, in Appendix D of this Study Guide, and observe the chronological relationship that the four gospel accounts have to each other and to the other New Testament books as well. Memorize the order in which the four gospel accounts traditionally are believed to have been written.

Since Matthew is generally considered to have been written in Antioch, locate the town on your Bible map. Also locate Antioch on the "Map of Distances" in this Study Guide, Appendix E. Learn all you can about Antioch from the map.

5 Now read the information about the establishment of the church at Antioch (chapter 15), in your textbook. This will help you feel the environment in which the book of Matthew was written. In your notebook, write six distinctive features of the church at Antioch.

The word *patristic* * used in the textbook refers to the outstanding church leaders and teachers of the first six centuries after Christ.

patristic
of or relating to the church fathers or their writing (especially in the first six centuries after Christ)

Objective **4.3**

Identify the purpose and theme of the Gospel of Matthew.

Content

📖 Readings 3 and 4

The purpose of the writing of the Gospel of Matthew is clearly announced in the opening verse. Go back now and read the first verses of the first chapter of Matthew again and you will see that even the genealogy* is instructive in this regard.

genealogy
descent of a person, family, or group from an ancestor in the direct line

Luke, with the purpose of writing a gospel account for all men, goes back to Adam, the father of all, in his genealogy.

6 Matthew, writing primarily for a Jewish audience, goes back to
...................., the father of the ...., in his genealogy.

Now turn to Reading 4 in the textbook and read the first paragraph under the section "Emphasis." Underscore the first three lines and learn them well. They give the purpose of the writing of Matthew's account of the gospel. Write them down in your notebook to help you remember them. Matthew is placed first after the Old Testament even though Mark was probably written before Matthew. Matthew is placed first in the New Testament because it is more closely related in purpose and content to the Old Testament than are the other gospel accounts. Matthew was written primarily to the Jews to show the relationship between the old covenant and the new covenant, between the Law and the gospel.

Turn to Appendix A, the chart of "Old Testament Quotations in the Gospel Accounts," located in the back of the Study Guide, and you observe that Matthew quotes the Old Testament more often than do Mark, Luke, and John. This in itself is a reliable key to the purpose of Matthew.

didactic
instructional

There are two words in Reading 4 in the textbook that you will want to understand. The first is *didactic,* * which in Tenney's use here means "designed or intended to teach, instructional." The other word is *denouement,* * which means "the ultimate revelation or event which clarifies the nature and outcome of a plot."

denouement
final revelation of an event which clarifies the nature or outcome of a plot

Having now learned that the purpose of writing, or the main theme of Matthew, is to show the relation of Law and gospel, start reading again under "Content" in Reading 3 and carefully consider Tenney's summary of the content of Matthew.

7   Based on our study to this point, circle the letter preceding the best completion. The theme of the Gospel of Matthew is
   a) Christ the servant of man.
   b) the revelation of the fulfillment of the messianic promise through Jesus Christ, the Messiah, and His relation to the Law.
   c) the genealogy of David.
   d) the refusal of the nation of Israel to accept Jesus Christ as the prophesied Messiah.

8   Circle the letter preceding each TRUE statement.
   a   The two biographical divisions of Matthew are centered around the rise of Jesus' ministry and the decline of His popularity.
   b   In the Gospel of Matthew, Jesus does not claim to be the Messiah.
   c   In speaking of the kingdom of God, Jesus was referring to a spiritual kingdom only.
   d   Jesus' purpose in performing miracles was to teach the people the real meaning of living in the kingdom of God.
   e   Jesus used parables as a teaching method to keep his meaning from those who were not ready to accept it.
   f   The crisis in the revelation of the Messiah was His death on the cross.
   g   The denouement, or final outcome of the messianic revelation in Matthew, is the Great Commission.

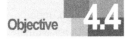

Objective 4.4

Explain major doctrines of the book of Matthew, including the relationship between the Law and the gospel.

Outline
📖 Reading 4

You will be able to get the message of Matthew in focus more easily if you occasionally consult the outlines in the textbook.

Tenney focuses upon a major key to understanding the relationship between Law and gospel in the last two paragraphs on page 153. The heart of this section is the statement explaining Jesus' sermon in Matthew 5. As Tenney puts it: "He demanded a righteousness that exceeded the standard of Jewish legalism, for it was inward, not outward; spontaneous, not legalistic; gauged by a person, not by a code. Its highest standard was God himself." And of course, the New Testament points to Jesus as the standard of our perfection (Ephesians 4:11–13). Examine these two paragraphs in the textbook as they explain a major key that will be essential to your understanding of Law and gospel. It will help you immensely in interpreting the New Testament for your own life and ministry. If you wish to retain these thoughts better, summarize them yourself in your notebook.

9 Which of these statements best explains the relationship between the Law and the gospel as given by Tenney?
   a) The gospel does not do away with the Law; rather, the gospel adds to the Law the requirement that every person must obey the commands of Jesus as well as to keep every part of the Law in order to be accepted into the kingdom of God.
   b) The gospel does not do away with the Law, but through the power of Jesus Christ makes it *possible* for believers to live holy lives in keeping with the Law and the teaching of Jesus.

I am sure that as you read through Matthew and the textbook, you became aware of several important doctrines. The list that follows this section is not intended to be complete. It does give most of the major doctrines and at least an initial reference for each one in Matthew. Check what the textbook and Matthew have to say about each of these. You will only have time to do this briefly. After you have finished the course, you may want to make a thorough study of these doctrines by researching all the biblical references to them, the occasion, method of teaching the doctrine (parable, sermon, miracle, and so on), and the characters involved; by making an outline of the truths taught by each doctrine in Matthew; and by developing lessons and sermons on them. See the chart (Figure 4.1) in this lesson.

10 Check what the textbook and Matthew have to say about each of these five doctrines. Write down the occasion; method of teaching the doctrine (parable, sermon, miracle, and so on); characters involved; and a brief statement of Jesus' teaching for each of the five truths taught.

a *Christ's mission* (Matthew 9:9–13)

   1) Occasion ....

   2) Teaching method ....

   3) Characters ....

   4) Truth(s) taught ....

b *Forgiveness* (Tenney 158; Matthew 6:12, 14–15)

   1) Occasion ....

   2) Teaching method ....

   3) Characters ....

   4) Truth(s) taught ....

c *Conditions of discipleship* (Matthew 16:21–26)

   1) Occasion ....

   2) Teaching method ....

   3) Characters ....

   4) Truth(s) taught ....

d *Christian perfection* (Matthew 5:43–48)

    1) Occasion ....

    2) Teaching method ....

    3) Characters ....

    4) Truth(s) taught ....

e *Christ's death and resurrection* (Matthew 17:1–3, 9; 22, 23)

    1) Occasion ....

    2) Teaching method ....

    3) Characters ....

    4) Truth(s) taught ....

Emphasis

Turn to the chart "Harmony of the Life of Christ." Carefully note the material that is unique to each and what is repeated in two or more of the gospel accounts. Also, turn to the appendix in this Study Guide and study the charts of *Miracles,* Appendix B; *Prayers,* Appendix C; and *Parables,* Appendix F. A comparison reveals the greater emphasis in Matthew's account over that of the other gospel writers. As you study these charts, be sure to get a picture in mind of the chronological sequence of the major events in Matthew.

Chart of Doctrines in Matthew		
Outstanding Doctrine	*Page in Text*	*Passage in Matthew*
Christ's humanity	152–153	1:1–25
Christ's virgin birth	153	1:18–24
Dependability of God's Word		1:22
Messianic prophecies		1:22–23; 2:5–6, 15
The Incarnation	153	1:23
Divine guidance and preservation		2:12–15, 19–23
Repentance		3:2, 6; 4:17; 10:32
God's wrath		3:7
Baptism in water		3:5–6, 13–17; 28:19
Baptism in the Holy Spirit		3:11, 16
The divine Trinity		3:16–17; 28:19
Temptation to sin		4:1–11
The person and work of Satan		4:1–11
Divine call and discipleship		4:18–22
Roles of the ministry		4:23
Relationship of Law and gospel	153	5:1–48
Social relationships	223	5:21–26

Chart of Doctrines in Matthew		
Christian ethics and attributes		Chapters 5, 6, 7
Sexual morality	223	5:27–32
Oaths in speech	223	5:33–37
Attitude toward evil	223	5:38–42
Hell		5:22, 29–30; 10:28; 11:23; 18:8–9; 23:15, 33
Heaven		5:34; 18: 10; 22:30
Love and justice	224	5:44–45
Divine providence		5:45; 6:25–34; 10:29–31
Christian perfection		5:48
Charity	223	6:1–4
Unpretentious giving and praying		6:1–18
Prayer (the model)	223	6:5–17; 7:7–12; 11:12–13; 13:11
The Kingdom	224–225	6:33; 7:21; 13:24, 31, 44; 19:14; 25:1, 31
Fasting	223	6:16–18
Economic life	223	6:19–34
Hypocrisy and judging		7:1–5; 23:23–39
The Golden Rule		7:12
The broad and narrow ways		7:13–14

Figure 4.1

Characters

Since Tenney points out that "Matthew lays less stress on the individual actors in his narrative than the other Synoptists do," we will reserve our study of outstanding characters until the next lesson.

Perhaps a devotional thought would be appropriate at this point. Reading through Matthew today, I was especially impressed with Matthew's record of the variety of people who came to Jesus with such a wide representation of human needs. Matthew keeps saying, "Behold one came to him" or "and they brought unto him." It is wonderful to know that we can also be among those who came to Jesus with many needs and that He will gladly minister to us. I have also noticed that Matthew pictures each one who comes as respectful and worshipful. For the benefit it will bring to your life and ministry after you finish the course, you might read through Matthew again and make a list of these persons who came to Jesus, noting their needs, their approaches, and Christ's responses.

Objective **4.5**   *Define the three special features of Matthew given by Tenney.*

Special Features

You will find it easy to learn the three special features that Tenney attributes to Matthew.

11 List the three special features of Matthew given in Tenney, and explain in your own words the meaning of each. Use your notebook.

In Lesson 3 you studied a section on "The Geography of Jesus' Life." If you find that any of the outstanding places referred to by Matthew cannot be placed in their approximate geographical location from memory, then go back to chapter 12 in the textbook, and also to your personal study notes, and review your geography of the travels of Christ in the Gospel account of Matthew.

Golden Passages

Several special passages in Matthew will greatly enrich your life and ministry if you have the time to memorize them. You should at least become familiar with their content and be able to locate them by memory or with a concordance. Throughout the course we will periodically write test questions based on special passages in various books of the New Testament. For Matthew, these *golden passages* are as follows:

1. The Beatitudes   5:3–12
2. The Lord's Model Prayer 6:9–13
3. The Golden Rule   7:12
4. The Great Commandment   22:37–40
5. The Great Commission   28:19–20

Total Time
(Read, answer
questions, check
answers)

Hr_____ Min_____

Self-Test 4

Start Time

Matching. Match the Scripture passages (right) with the definitions (left).

. . . . **1** Gives the Beatitudes

. . . . **2** Gives the Lord's Model Prayer

. . . . **3** Gives the Golden Rule

. . . . **4** Preaches repentance in the Gospel of Matthew

. . . . **5** Teaches Christ's doctrine of forgiveness

. . . . **6** Gives the Great Commission

. . . . **7** Teaches Christ's doctrine on marriage and divorce

. . . . **8** Receives Christ's statement about the church

. . . . **9** Teaches the doctrine of last things

. . . . **10** Gives the Great Commandment

a   Matthew 5:3–12
b   Matthew 24–25
c   Matthew 28:19–20
d   Peter
e   Matthew 22:37–40
f   John the Baptist
g   Matthew 6:12, 14–15
h   Matthew 7:12
i   Matthew 19:3–12
j   Matthew 6:9–13

Multiple Choice. Select the best answer.

11 According to our discussion, the Gospel of Matthew was written by
    a)   Matthew, the younger brother of Papias.
    b)   Matthew, the older brother of Eusebius.
    c)   Matthew Levi, a tax collector.
    d)   Matthew, the cousin of Luke.

12 Which statement is NOT true concerning Matthew?
    a)   He was a publican.
    b)   He is shown by the book of Acts to have been active in the church until AD 95.
    c)   Nowhere in the first Gospel is he explicitly called its author.
    d)   He was a tax collector.

13 Matthew was probably written from
    a)   Athens in AD 85.
    b)   Capernaum in AD 50.
    c)   Athens in 85 BC
    d)   Antioch in AD 50–70.

14 Which of the following represents the chronological sequence of the writing of the four Gospel accounts?
    a)   Mark, Matthew, Luke, John
    b)   Matthew, Mark, Luke, John
    c)   Luke, Mark, Matthew, John
    d)   Matthew, Luke, Mark, John

15 Matthew was written primarily to a
   a) Jewish audience.
   b) Greek audience.
   c) pagan audience.
   d) Roman audience.

16 Matthew was written to show the relation between
   a) miracles and parables.
   b) Jew and Greek.
   c) history and prophecy.
   d) Law and gospel.

17 The structure of Matthew is built around a double outline. Which choice represents that dual outline?
   a) Geographical and chronological
   b) Biographical and topical
   c) Topical and chronological
   d) Philosophical and psychological

18 Which statement is NOT a key to knowing the purpose of Matthew?
   a) His genealogy goes back to Abraham, the father of the Jews.
   b) He picks up the theme of "the kingdom" repeatedly.
   c) He quotes the Old Testament more often than do the other gospel accounts.
   d) He concludes his book with a reference to the Mosaic Law.

19 Which of these statements best describes the content of Matthew?
   a) It is didactic, messianic, and biographical.
   b) It is more concerned with action than with teaching.
   c) It is more concerned with individual actors than Mark.
   d) It is almost free of discourses.

20 Which of the following is NOT a special feature of Matthew?
   a) The church
   b) The faithful servant
   c) Discourse
   d) The King

21 Which statement best relates to this quotation from Tenney? "He demanded a righteousness that exceeded the standard of Jewish legalism, for it was inward, not outward; spontaneous, not legalistic; gauged by a person, and not by a code."
   a) A major key to understanding the relation between law and gospel
   b) An attempt to reduce the requirements of grace
   c) An effort to bring a modified legalism into the New Testament
   d) An acceptable way to add works to faith

22 Which one of the following major divisions of the outline of Matthew is NOT in correct chronological sequence with the other three?
   a) The Passion of the Messiah Accomplished.
   b) The Prophecies of the Messiah Realized.
   c) The Power of the Messiah Revealed.
   d) The Purpose of the Messiah Declared.

23 Which sequence of events is in the correct chronological order?
a) Advent, miracles, conflict, parables, cross.
b) Advent, conflict, parables, miracles, cross.
c) Advent, miracles, parables, conflict, cross.
d) Advent, miracles, parables, cross, conflict.

24 Which statement is totally correct with respect to geography in Matthew?
a) Antioch is near the coast and is twenty miles from Jerusalem.
b) Galilee is a small town in the province of Capernaum.
c) Nazareth and Cana are small towns, close together, between the Great Sea and the Sea of Galilee.
d) Bethlehem is closer to Antioch than to Jerusalem.

25 While not all of the parables in Matthew are gathered into one place, most of them are. Which of the following statements is a true completion? Parables are strongly featured in chapters
a) 4, 5, and 6 with chapter 6 having the greatest collection.
b) 4, 5, and 6 with chapter 6 having the smallest collection.
c) 11, 12, and 13 with chapter 13 having the smallest collection.
d) 11, 12, and 13 with chapter 13 having the greatest collection.

Self-Test Time

Hr_____ Min_____

Answers to Study Questions

6 Abraham, Jews.

1 **a** If the account were a forgery, the forger would have chosen a more eminent apostle's name.

    b A tax collector would have been able to read, write, and take notes. He could have compiled the sayings of Jesus in the discourses and arranged the narrative.

    c Matthew could have published a Greek edition, even if he had originally written an Aramaic document which has disappeared.

7 b) the revelation of the fulfillment of the messianic promise through Jesus Christ, the Messiah, and His relation to the Law.

2 Yes. Early church writers credited Matthew with the authorship. In the absence of evidence to the contrary, we can accept the opinion of scholars who have studied early documents and have decided to accept the tradition of the church as the best decision.

8 Statements **a**, **d**, **e**, **f**, and **g** are true.

3 You should have noted that he was a tax collector before he met Jesus; was used to keeping tax records; read; wrote; and calculated sums; worked on the Sabbath, and thus violated rules for keeping the Sabbath; probably was guilty of graft and oppression by collecting more than the minimum tax; did not observe the regulations of the oral law of Judaism as did the scribes, Pharisees, priests, elders, and other members of the Sanhedrin (supreme court of Judaism); was never invited to homes of orthodox Jews; was not socially acceptable to orthodox Jews; invited *publicans* and *sinners* and Jesus to dine at his house after Jesus called him to follow Him; and was transformed in character and behavior after he became Jesus' disciple.

9 b) The gospel does not do away with the Law, but through the power of Jesus Christ makes it *possible* for believers to live holy lives in keeping with the Law and the teaching of Jesus.

4 Your answer.

10 **a** (1) A meal at Matthew's house.
      (2) Question and answer.
      (3) Pharisees and disciples.
      (4) To call sinners to repentance.

    b (1) Sermon on the Mount.
      (2) Discourse.
      (3) The disciples.
      (4) Forgiveness and trespasses.

    c (1) Jesus foretells His death.
      (2) Discussion.
      (3) The disciples.
      (4) Denial of self.

    d (1) Sermon on the Mount.
        (2) Discourse.
        (3) The disciples.
        (4) Strive for perfection, God's love and justice.
    e (1) The Transfiguration.
        (2) Miracle.
        (3) Peter, James, and John.
        (4) The Resurrection.

5 You should note that Antioch:

    a Was the first Gentile church, the mother of the others.

    b Sent the first recognized missionaries to unevangelized areas.

    c Was the site of the first controversy over the acceptance of Gentiles as well as Jews as Christians.

    d Was the center for meetings of outstanding church leaders.

    e Superseded the Jerusalem church as the headquarters of evangelism through missionaries and as the home center of Christian preaching.

    f Was the church where members were first called Christians.

11 **a** Matthew is the Gospel of discourse—it contains more of Jesus' teaching than any of the other Gospels.

    b It is the Gospel of the church—it is the only Gospel in which Christ speaks of the church.

    c It is the Gospel of the King—the royalty of Christ is emphasized.

Note the time you begin reading this lesson. At the end of the lesson, record in the space provided the time it took to complete each segment.

The Gospel Account of Mark

Start Time

_____

In the Gospel of Matthew, we saw Christ as the Messiah, the King. What a contrast we find in the Gospel of Mark, which presents Christ as the ministering servant to those in need. It is significant that Mark, who came from a wealthy family which probably had many servants, saw in his Master a spirit of servanthood. He saw in Christ those qualities of meekness, humility, eagerness to serve, and dependability that are so desirable in a servant.

When two of His disciples came to Him requesting places of honor in His kingdom, Jesus responded in part with these words:

Whosoever will be great among you, shall be your minister: And whosoever of you will be the chiefest, shall be servant of all. For even the Son of man came not to be ministered unto, but to minister, and to give his life a ransom for many (Mark 10:43–45).

Repeatedly, in the Gospel of Mark, we read that Jesus referred to Himself as the Son of Man. Since He identified completely with those He came to redeem, the crowds sought Him out. He could have moved among those who had great wealth and prestige. Instead, He chose to eat with the publicans and the sinners, to heal those who were sick or demon possessed, to lift up the fallen. Wherever He went, He transformed lives. His was a ministry of action, of power, of service.

What a challenge to those of us who have been transformed by His power! Have you caught His servant spirit? Are you busy in service for Him wherever you find a need? Have lives been transformed because of your ministry? As you study this lesson, ask your Master to instill in you the same qualities of servanthood that He manifested as He moved among men.

the activities...   ◇ Read the Gospel account of Mark straight through in order to get an overview of its message. The readings for this lesson are

Reading 1: pages 160–161
Reading 2: pages 161–164
Reading 3: pages 164–171
Reading 4: pages 166–170
Reading 5: pages 170–171
Reading 6: page 171

◊ Work through the lesson development as usual. Refer to the textbook readings as necessary when you answer study questions or seek to clarify any point in the Study Guide.

◊ Review the key words list to see if you understand the meaning of each word. Refer to the glossary for the meaning of any word that is unfamiliar to you.

◊ Take the self-test at the end of the lesson and check your answers.

the objectives...

5.1 *Give reasons why it is believed that Mark wrote the second Gospel.*

5.2 *State what we have learned from early scholars concerning the author of Mark, the date written, and the circumstances of the writing.*

5.3 *Explain the purpose and theme of the Gospel of Mark.*

5.4 *Identify characteristics of the Gospel of Mark that apply more to this Gospel than to others.*

5.5 *Give examples of persons with whom Jesus interacted in the Gospel of Mark.*

the outline...

1 Origin of Mark
2 Date and Place
3 Content
4 Outline
5 Emphasis
6 Characters
7 Special Features
8 Golden Passages

Objective **5.1**

Give reasons why it is believed that Mark wrote the second Gospel.

Origin of Mark
📖 Reading 1

Turn to the section in the textbook on "Origin" and read the biographical material on John Mark. While the book of Mark does not name Mark as its author, we accept the traditional assignment of authorship to John Mark. Tenney gives a great amount of data on Mark. Read this section several times to become acquainted with his personality, circumstances, and the people with whom he was associated.

1   Look up the references below and next to each one write what you think the passage says about Mark and his contribution to the gospel. In your notebook add any other observations you consider important.

a   Mark 14:51–52...

b   Acts 12:25; 13:4...

c   Acts 13:13...

d   2 Timothy 4:11; Philemon 24 ....

Objective   **5.2**

State what we have learned from early scholars concerning the author of Mark, the date written, and the circumstances of the writing.

Date and Place
📖 Reading 2

As you study this section of the textbook, notice the way in which the witnesses of Eusebius, Clement, and Origen agree about the writing of Mark. Also, observe the point of disagreement among Irenaeus, Clement, and Origen concerning the writing of Mark.

2   Work through the eight deductions that relate to the authorship of Mark in Reading 2. In your notebook summarize each of the deductions in a brief sentence. Then study your summaries.

Be sure you follow the explanation given in the textbook concerning the belief of some scholars that Matthew and Luke borrowed from Mark's material for their own books. Also, study carefully the alternative view of simultaneous authorship of all three books by the inspiration of the Holy Spirit. This last view is a reasonable answer not only to this question but also to many other questions of authorship raised by liberal scholars.

Tenney indicates that the Gospel of Mark was written prior to AD 70, but he does not try to give its earliest possible date. I am inclined to favor the 50s. You will want to remember that both internal and external evidence point to Rome as the place of the writing of Mark's Gospel.

3   With reference to a date of writing between AD 50 and 70, what is the significance of the deductions you have summarized above? Use your notebook for your answer.

Objective **5.3** *Explain the purpose and theme of the Gospel of Mark.*

Content

📖 Reading 3

For a summary statement on the purpose of Mark, read in the section titled "Emphasize the two sentences which begin with "The purpose of . . ." and conclude with ". . . of the hearer."

Now read the paragraph that comes after the section titled "Outline," in Reading 3. I suggest that you write the second sentence in your notebook. After getting the purpose well in mind, read slowly through "Content" in the textbook again. As you do so, look for the evidences that fulfill Mark's purpose to write an account of the gospel in common language, punctuated by action, in order to evangelize the Gentiles (religiously unlearned). Also, observe points Tenney makes about

1. The centrality of Christ

2. The stress on the supernatural

3. The servanthood of Jesus

4. The urgency of Christ's mission

4 Circle the letter preceding each TRUE statement.

    a When Tenney says the purpose of Mark is primarily evangelistic, he means it presents the message of the gospel in a way that does not require any previous Jewish religious background on the part of the hearers.

    b The evangelistic message in Mark was basically directed to those with a Jewish background.

    c Matthew's Gospel is more closely related to Jewish theology than is Mark's Gospel.

    d Mark's Gospel emphasizes Jesus as both the Son of God and the Servant of God.

    e Mark simply relates the facts about Jesus' life and ministry without making personal comments or stating personal opinions.

    f Mark's Gospel says very little about Christ's miracles.

    g Mark's Gospel is one of action, showing Jesus as He moves quickly toward some unseen goal.

Outline

📖 Reading 4

The outline of Mark is admittedly difficult to grasp because of the style of Mark's writing and because of the length given to the outline in the textbook. Read Tenney's outline to get a general idea of the structure of Mark as Tenney sees it. Then memorize the following brief outline of this gospel of action that highlights the servanthood of Jesus. You should be able to reproduce the main divisions from memory.

The Preparation for and of the Servant	1:1–13
The Work of the Servant	1:14–13:37
The Death of the Servant	14:1–15:47
The Resurrection of the Servant	16:1–20

5 In reviewing Tenney's outline and the short outline above, what would you say is the unifying theme of the Gospel of Mark?

....

Objective **5.4**

Identify characteristics of the Gospel of Mark that apply more to this Gospel than to others.

Emphasis

📖 Reading 5

evangelistic
pertaining to winning individual commitments to Christ

As you read this section of the textbook again, notice a word in the first sentence of each of the four paragraphs that highlights an emphasis in Mark. These words are *action, reaction, vividness,* and *evangelistic.** Circle them.

Turn to the "Harmony of the Life of Christ" (chapter 12) and carefully note the material that is unique to Mark. Also turn to Appendixes B, F, and C in this Study Guide and review the charts of miracles, parables, and prayers of our Lord. This will help you see the special emphasis of Mark as compared with the other Gospel writers. Study these charts and then make sure you can list the major events of Mark in chronological sequence.

6 In comparing the Gospel of Mark with the other Gospels, circle the letter preceding each description below that is more true of Mark than of the others.
   a Literary approach
   b Filled with action
   c Records many miracles
   d Didactic approach
   e Interprets prophecy
   f Shows reactions to Jesus by the crowds
   g Evangelistic approach
   h Emphasizes parables

Objective **5.5**

Give examples of persons with whom Jesus interacted in the Gospel of Mark.

Characters

📖 Reading 6

In Lesson 4 we talked about getting to know some of the personalities in the Synoptic Gospels. The chart of "Persons Mentioned in the Gospel Accounts" in Appendix G of this guide and the textbook section "Index of Persons," pages 441–442 give us an extended list of many of these persons. Read what the Scripture and the textbook have to say about each person who is unfamiliar to you.

7   Fill in the required information on the following chart. Check your answers only after you have completed the chart.

People Who Reacted to Jesus' Responses to Human Need				
1 Reference and Person(s)	*2* Need Of Person(s)	*3* Jesus' Action	*4* Reaction(s) to Jesus	*5* Reason(s) for Reaction(s)
a Mark 1:21–27			Mark 1:27	
b Mark 2:1–12			Mark 2:7 Mark 2:12	
c Mark 4:37–41			Mark 4:41	
d Mark 7:32–37			Mark 7:37	
e Mark 14:1–9			Mark 14:1–2 Mark 14:3–9	

Special Features

The textbook does not have a "Special Features" section on Mark because these have been considered in previous sections. So, this is a good time to get a better grasp of the geography of Mark. There are several helps for you to use in your study of the places of importance in Mark.

1   Turn to the chart of "Places Mentioned in the Gospel Accounts" in Appendix H of the Study Guide. Locate those mentioned in Mark and read their Scripture references.

2. Locate the places on your Bible map and also on the "Map of Distances" in Appendix E of the Study Guide.

3. Turn to the "Index of Places" in the back of the textbook. Then locate and read the areas in the textbook on each place mentioned by Mark.

Golden Passages

There are several special passages in Mark that will greatly enrich your life and ministry. You should become familiar with their content and be able to locate them by memory or with a concordance. These *golden passages* are as follows:

1. The Value of Life and the Cost of Discipleship   8:34–38
2. The Power of Faith and Forgiveness in Prayer   11:22–26
3. The Institution of the Lord's Supper   14:22–25
4. The Great Commission   16:15–20

Now review the topics in the lesson outline, and make sure you can fulfill the objectives of the lesson. Then, take the self-test and check your answers.

Total Time
(Read, answer questions, check answers)

Hr_____ Min_____

Self-Test 5

Start Time

_____

Multiple Choice. Select the best answer.

1   Tradition identifies John Mark as the author of the Gospel account of Mark and indicates that he was the son of
   a)   a Christian family in Jerusalem.
   b)   a Hebrew family in Syria.
   c)   a Greek family in Turkey.
   d)   Ananias and Sapphira.

2   Which statement is NOT true concerning Mark? He was an assistant to
   a)   Paul.
   b)   Barnabas.
   c)   Peter.
   d)   John the Baptist.

3   Some scholars believe that Matthew and Luke borrowed much material from Mark's book. Which is a reasonable alternative to account for so much similar material in the Synoptics?
   a)   They were all written by Mark.
   b)   They were all edited by Paul after being written by different men.
   c)   They were simultaneously authored under the inspiration of the Holy Spirit.
   d)   They were made alike in the publication process in later centuries.

4   Mark's purpose was to write an account of the gospel in common language, punctuated by action, in order to evangelize the Gentiles. In working out this purpose, which of the following emphases does he NOT make?
   a)   The centrality of Christ
   b)   The supernatural work of Christ
   c)   The servanthood of Christ
   d)   The genealogy of Christ

5   Which one of these sets of words best characterizes Mark?
   a)   Action, reaction, vividness, evangelistic
   b)   Question, answer, problem, solution
   c)   Faith, hope, love, power
   d)   Theology, explanation, discourse, interpretation

6   Which of these did Jesus NOT do at Tyre and Sidon, according to Mark?
   a)   Cast the unclean spirit out of a Greek woman's child
   b)   Tried to hide from the multitudes, in a house, but could not
   c)   Turned water into wine
   d)   Healed many and cast out devils

7   Mark mentions several women in Mark 15:40–41 that ministered to Christ. Which of these was one of those women?
   a)   Mary Magdalene
   b)   Elizabeth
   c)   Herodias
   d)   Anna, the prophetess

8 Mark tells us in Mark 15:21 that a man named Simon was compelled to carry the cross of Jesus. Mark does NOT tell us that Simon
a) was the father of Rufus.
b) was a Cyrenian.
c) had a son named Alexander.
d) had a wife named Joanna.

9 Only Mark (8:22–26) tells us of the healing of a certain blind man. Which one of the following lines does NOT belong to Mark's story?
a) They had come to the town of Bethsaida.
b) Jesus led the blind man out of Bethsaida.
c) Jesus asked the man to dip seven times in the Jordan River.
d) Jesus spat on the man's eyes.

10 Which is true concerning the Gospel of Mark? Mark
a) records little about Jesus' ministry in Jerusalem prior to the Passion.
b) gives a few miracles and uses each for an extensive teaching about the Passion.
c) gives an expansive genealogy of Christ.
d) avoids the use of words that would give the impression that Jesus was ever in a hurry.

11 Mark has Jesus withdrawing to Caesarea Philippi for a season of seclusion. Which statement best locates this town?
a) It was about 115 miles (184 kilometers) west of Jerusalem in the Great Sea.
b) It was about 115 miles (184 kilometers) north of Jerusalem at the foot of Mt. Hermon.
c) It was about 20 miles (32 kilometers) east of Jerusalem near the Jordan River.
d) It was about 100 miles (161 kilometers) south of Jerusalem near the Egyptian border.

Matching. Match each subject (right) with the appropriate Scripture (left).

.... **12** "For whosoever will save his life shall lose it; but whosoever shall lose his life for my sake and the gospel's, the same shall save it."

.... **13** "What things soever you desire, when ye pray, believe that ye receive them, and ye shall have them. And when ye stand praying forgive, if ye have ought against any: that your Father also which is in heaven may forgive you your trespasses."

.... **14** "Go ye into all the world, and preach the gospel to every creature."

.... **15** And he said unto them, "This is my blood of the new testament, which is shed for many."

a) The Institution of the Lord's Supper
b) The Value of Life and the Cost of Discipleship
c) The Great Commission
d) The Power of Faith and Forgiveness in Prayer

16–19 Match each Scripture reference (right) with the correct subject (left).

.... **16** The Preparation for and of the Servant   a) Mark 14:1–15:47

.... **17** The Death of the Servant   b) Mark 16:1–20

                             c) Mark 1:1–13

.... **18** The Resurrection of the Servant   d) Mark 1:14–13:37

.... **19** The Work of the Servant

Self-Test Time

Hr_____ Min_____

Answers to Study Questions

4 Statements **a**, **c**, **d**, **e**, and **g** are true.

1 **a**   Mark himself may have been the "certain young man" who was a witness to this event.

     b   Mark participated as an assistant or understudy of his cousin Barnabas and of Paul.

     c   Mark left Paul and Barnabas and returned from Pamphylia to Jerusalem.

     d   Mark was a most useful servant and fellow laborer of Paul.

5 Jesus Christ, the Son of God, as the Servant of God.

2 (Your own words should summarize Tenney's statements.)

     a   Mark grew up in the pious atmosphere of Judaism when Jesus did.

     b   Mark may have witnessed some of the facts he recorded in his Gospel account.

     c   As an assistant and understudy of the apostles who led the early church, Mark would have been fully acquainted with what they preached about Jesus' life and message.

     d   Mark was an active preacher and witness to the first missions to the Gentiles.

     e   Mark was more concerned with facts than with concepts. What he did not witness, he learned from eyewitnesses.

     f   Mark himself may have been the young man he mentions in Mark 14: 51–52 who followed Jesus and witnessed His arrest in the Garden of Gethsemane.

     g   If Mark and his readers knew Alexander and Rufus, he must have written his Gospel account within a generation after the crucifixion of Jesus (c. AD 30).

     h   Tradition claims that Mark recorded in his Gospel account Peter's oral preaching. In this case it is important to note the correspondence between the outline of the content of Mark, and Peter's sermon recorded in Acts 10:34–43.

6 Statements **b**, **c**, **f**, and **g** are true of Mark's Gospel.

3 Your answer might include the following: Suppose that Mark was twenty years old at the time of the Crucifixion and Resurrection. He would have been forty in AD 50, or sixty in AD 70. He was old enough to be a reliable witness and recorder. If twenty to forty years elapsed between the Resurrection and the writing of the Gospel account, one might think his memory would have been better had he written with the least time between the events and the writing. However, he must have heard the same events recounted over and over during the times he heard Peter preach to different persons.

7 Your chart might include some of the following:
   a Mark 1:21–27
   (1) Man with an unclean spirit. (2) To have the unclean spirit removed. (3) Jesus commanded the unclean spirit to come out. (4) People in the synagogue were amazed. (5) Because Jesus commanded with personal authority (and taught with personal authority, as a positive voice from God).
   b Mark 2:1–12
   (1) Man sick of the palsy. (2) To be healed. (3) Jesus forgave the man's sins, and healed him. (4) Certain scribes were critical. When they accused Jesus of forgiving as only God can do, He told the man to take up his bed and go to his house. Others in the house praised and glorified God. (5) The scribes thought Jesus was a blasphemer. Those who praised God recognized that He did have divine power.
   c Mark 4:37–41
   (1) Disciples in a fishing boat. (2) To be saved from the storm on the Sea of Galilee. (3) Jesus rebuked the wind and calmed the storm. (4) Those in the boat were afraid during the storm. They were puzzled concerning who Jesus was. (5) The disciples were confused, but they must have realized that Jesus was not just a man, for He showed divine authority.
   d Mark 7:32–37
   (1) A deaf person with a speech impediment. (2) To be healed. (3) Jesus touched him, looked up to heaven, and said, "Be opened." (4) People were astonished beyond measure. (5) Jesus appeared to cure the man. But He looked up to heaven to indicate that the healing was from God.
   e Mark 14:1–9
   (1) Scribes and Pharisees, woman who poured precious ointment on Jesus' head. (2) Scribes and Pharisees needed to get rid of Jesus because He taught that the new covenant (testament), which conflicted with their oral Law, completed the old covenant. (3) Jesus knew He would die as a result of the hostility of His opponents, but He allowed the woman to pour the ointment upon Him. (4) Jesus' opponents plotted to put Him to death. The woman who was grateful for the new covenant was faithful to Him. (5) Those who thought the ointment should have been sold for money for the poor were probably not aware, as Jesus was, of His approaching death and burial.

Note the time you begin reading this lesson. At the end of the lesson, record in the space provided the time it took to complete each segment.

The Gospel Account of Luke

Start Time

_____

It is remarkable that although there are four accounts of the life and ministry of Jesus, in which many of the same events are recorded, the approach of each reveals to us a different aspect of God's Son. The emphasis in the Gospel of Luke is on the humanity of Christ.

In Scripture, Christ has been compared and contrasted to Adam, the only other man to enter the world in a state of innocence. According to Oswald Chambers, God placed Adam "in an external setting so that he might transform his innocence into moral character by a series of choices." But Adam failed—he yielded to temptation, and sin entered the world. Since that time, man has been born in sin. Chambers goes on to say this:

> Holiness is the agreement between a man's disposition and the law of God, as expressed in the life of Jesus .... Jesus Christ, the last Adam, did what the first Adam failed to do; He transformed innocence into holy character. The law of God was incarnated in Jesus Christ. He walked this earth in human guise and lived the perfect life which God desired (Chambers 1975, 15).

Jesus walked among men as another human being, subject to the same physical limitations. He was "tempted in every way, just as we are—yet was without sin" (Hebrews 4:15). The Gospel of Luke shows us Christ the Man, the Savior of men, bearing our burdens, feeling our disappointments, suffering pain and loneliness, being tempted as we are tempted—yet through it all, He transformed innocence into holy character! And because of Him, we can find agreement between our naturally sinful disposition and God's holiness!

the activities...

◇ Read the Gospel account of Luke straight through to get an overview of its message. Then scan the textbook readings. While you read the textbook, keep your Bible open and read the Scripture references in the textbook as you come to them. The readings for this lesson are

    Reading 1: pages 173–176
    Reading 2: pages 176–179
    Reading 3: page 179
    Reading 4: pages 179–180
    Reading 5: pages 180–183

Reading 6: pages 183–185
Reading 7: pages 185–186

◇ Study the lesson development material according to the established procedure. Be sure to answer all study questions and check your answers as you proceed. In this way you can learn the content effectively. Then, when you take the self-test, you can review what you have learned and fix it in your mind.

◇ You will find that the appendixes at the back of the Study Guide provides much useful information, especially in harmonizing material that is common to the Gospels.

the objectives...

6.1 *Describe the writer of the Gospel of Luke and give reasons why he wrote this Gospel account.*

6.2 *Explain the purpose of the Gospel of Luke. List the major headings and subheadings in Tenney's outline of the book of Luke.*

6.3 *Analyze several major doctrines of the book of Luke.*

6.4 *Locate on a map the principal places mentioned in Luke.*

the outline...

1 Origin of Luke
2 Author
3 Date and Place
4 Content
5 Outline
6 Emphasis
7 Characters
8 Special Features
9 Golden Passages

Objective **6.1**

Describe the writer of the Gospel of Luke and give reasons why he wrote this Gospel account.

Origin of Luke

📖 Reading 1

As you turn to this section of the textbook, you will find that (unlike the two previous Gospel writers) there is much internal and external evidence on the origin of the Gospel of Luke. Read through the section and keep a sheet of paper near. Outline the most important data about Luke, his circumstances, his associates and his contribution to New Testament literature.

1   Answer these questions based on the textbook in your own words:
   a   In view of the fact there were other accounts of the life of Jesus when the Gospel of Luke was written, why did the author choose to write this account?

   ....

   b   Where did he get the information about Jesus' life and ministry?

   ....

   c   What qualifications did the author have for writing this particular account?

   ....

   d   What can we assume about the person to whom this account was written?

   ....

   e   What can we assume about the person who did the writing?

   ....

Author
📖 Reading 2

As you read this section you will observe that there is strong evidence that the gospel account of Luke and the book of Acts were written by the same author.

2   Circle the letter preceding each TRUE statement.
   a   Since both Luke and Acts are addressed to the same person and the writer of Acts refers to a former treatise, we are led to believe that both books were written by the same author.
   b   The writer of Luke was a close friend of the apostle Paul.
   c   The books of Luke and Acts are different in style and vocabulary.
   d   The writer was one of the original twelve disciples.
   e   Luke accompanied Paul on many of his missionary journeys.
   f   Luke was not a highly educated man.
   g   Luke himself was an active preacher and missionary.
   h   The "we" sections of Acts suggests that the writer was a close associate of the apostle Paul.

Date and Place
📖 Reading 3

As you read this section, you should note that the writing of Luke can be set with reasonable assurance at AD 60. While such assurance is warranted in the dating of Luke, the closest we can come to establishing the location of writing is that it was written somewhere in the Hellenistic world.

Objective

Explain the purpose of the Gospel of Luke. List the major headings and subheadings in Tenney's outline of the book of Luke.

Content

📖 Reading 4

Read the opening sentence under this section and then turn to "Outline." The first sentence under "Outline" clearly states the central theme of Luke. Scan the rest of this section and underscore the statements about Luke's emphasis on the humanity of Christ. Read your underscored lines again and it will become clear to you that Luke wrote to stress the humanity of Jesus: to present Him as the Son of Man. Remember that Matthew stressed His Messiahship, Mark stressed His Servanthood, Luke now stresses His Manhood, and we shall presently see that John stresses His Divinity.

3 Now, from the opening sentence under "Content" and from your underscored lines under "Outline," write a summary statement below on the purpose of Luke.

....

....

....

Outline

📖 Reading 5

Because Luke's account of the gospel is excellent in literary form and content, one can outline it beautifully. Turn to this section in the textbook and go over Tenney's outline of the content of Luke several times to get the structure of the book in focus.

4 Copy the seven main headings in your notebook. Leave space under each heading and from memory list as many subtopics as you can.

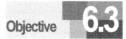
Analyze several major doctrines of the book of Luke.

Emphasis

📖 Reading 6

Read this section of the textbook with a pen in hand and circle the following words. They will help you to organize the emphasis of Luke in your own mind.

1. Songs
2. Historical
3. Cosmopolitan
4. Doctrine
5. Women
6. Children
7. The poor and oppressed

We have noted that Luke introduced several doctrines and gave them a considerable amount of attention. Several doctrines that Luke either introduced or emphasized more than the other Synoptists are these:

1. The humanity of Christ
2. Salvation
3. Justification
4. The Holy Spirit

Take time to read very carefully what the textbook has to say about these doctrines in Reading 6. Use your Bible and read each of the Scripture references to them. Consider the importance of these doctrines in your life and ministry. After you have finished the course, you will want to make a thorough study of these doctrines and develop studies and sermons from them to use in your ministry.

5–8 Analyze the following passages. Fill in the blanks associated with the following subjects.

5 *Humanity of Christ* (Luke 1:26–2:40)

   a Occasion...

   b Teaching method...

   c Characters ....

   d Truth(s) taught (Luke 2:8–20, 52) ....

      ....

      ....

6 *Salvation* (Luke 19:1–10)

   a Occasion ....

   b Teaching method ....

c Characters ....

d Truth(s) taught ....

....

7 *Justification* (Luke 18:9–14)

a Occasion ....

b Teaching method ....

c Characters ....

d Truth(s) taught ....

....

8 *Holy Spirit* (Luke 24:35–49)

a Occasion...

b Teaching method...

c Characters ....

d Truth(s) taught (Luke 24:49) ....

....

Characters

📖 Reading 7

Under the character study in Mark you have already become acquainted with the outstanding personalities mentioned in Luke. However, you will benefit from the section in the textbook where Tenney presents the characters in Luke. Let Luke's portraits of these persons enrich your life.

9 It is clear that Jesus is the central character of the Gospel of Luke. In what manner is He portrayed?

....

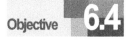

Objective 6.4

Locate on a map the principal places mentioned in Luke.

Special Features

While the textbook does not have a *Special Features* section on Luke, it does present the distinctive aspects of this Gospel in other sections. Turn to "Content" (Reading 4) and read this section to learn about the features that are unique to Luke. Then turn to the "Harmony of the Life of Christ" (chapter 12) and carefully note the material found only in Luke. Also turn to Appendixes B, F, and C in this guide and review the charts of miracles, parables, and prayers of Christ. This will help you to see the special emphasis of Luke as compared with the emphases of the other Gospel writers. As you study these charts, memorize the major events of Luke in chronological order.

10 In order to learn the significant geographical data in Luke, please do the following things:

    a Turn to the chart of "Places Mentioned in the Gospel Accounts" (Appendix H of the Study Guide), locate the places mentioned in Luke, and read the Scripture references associated with each.

    b Locate these places on your Bible map and also on the "Map of Distances" (Appendix E of the Study Guide).

    c Turn to the "Index of Places" in the back of the textbook. Find and read the areas in the textbook for each place mentioned by Luke.

Golden Passages

Several passages in Luke will greatly enrich your life and ministry. If you cannot memorize them, you should at least become familiar with their content and be able to locate them by memory or with a concordance. These *golden passages* are as follows:

1.	The Magnificat (Mary's Song)	1:46–55
2.	Jesus' Criteria for Ministry	4:18–19
3.	Naming of the Twelve Apostles	6:12–16
4.	The Parable of the Good Samaritan	10:30–37
5.	The Father's Desire to Give the Gift of the Holy Spirit	11:11–13
6.	Admonition to Seek Heavenly Treasure	12:22–34
7.	The Parable of the Lost Son	15:11–24
8.	The Return of the Lord in Glory	21:25–28
9.	The Great Commission and Great Enablement	24:46–49

You have now come to the end of Lesson 6. Review the lesson objectives carefully to see whether you can do what they indicate. If you do not understand some material, review the section and its related readings. This should prepare you for the self-test.

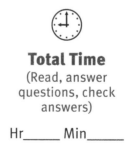

Total Time
(Read, answer
questions, check
answers)

Hr_____ Min_____

Start Time

_____

Self-Test 6

Multiple Choice. Select the best answer.

1   Which is NOT true of Luke the author of Luke-Acts?
   a)   He was a friend and associate of Paul.
   b)   He had some interest in the physician's viewpoint.
   c)   He was a Jew.
   d)   He was the first great church historian and literary apologist
        for Christianity.

2   Luke was probably written after
   a)   John.
   b)   Matthew.
   c)   Mark.
   d)   the Roman persecution (AD 64–68).

3   Which doctrine is NEITHER introduced by Luke NOR emphasized more
    by Luke than by the other Synoptists?
   a)   Salvation
   b)   Justification
   c)   The Holy Spirit
   d)   The Messiahship of Christ

4   Which statement is NOT true concerning Luke?
   a)   Luke's Gospel is predominantly historical.
   b)   Doctrine is emphasized in Luke.
   c)   Luke has many parables that are unique to this Gospel account.
   d)   Luke concentrates on Jesus' fulfillment of messianic prophecies.

5   Which parable is unique in the gospel account according to Luke?
   a)   The Good Samaritan
   b)   The Wicked Husbandman
   c)   The Mustard Seed
   d)   The Bridegroom

6   Luke tells us in chapter 19 that a man named Zacchaeus, chief among
    the publicans, received salvation. Which of these does Luke NOT tell us
    about Zacchaeus?
   a)   He was a short man.
   b)   He agreed to restore fourfold to any man he had cheated.
   c)   He was a Zealot.
   d)   He said, "Here and now I give half of my possession to the poor."

7   In the parable of the Pharisee and the publican in Luke 18:9–14, which one
    of the following is NOT true of the Pharisee?
   a)   He fasted twice a week.
   b)   He was exalted because he humbled himself.
   c)   He gave tithes of all he possessed.
   d)   He thanked God he was not as the publican.

8 Luke records a conversation of Jesus (after His resurrection) with two men on the road to Emmaus. Which statement best locates this town?
a) About 43.8 miles (70 kilometers) north of Jerusalem.
b) About 9.4 miles (15 kilometers) east of Jerusalem.
c) About 8.1 miles (13 kilometers) west of Jerusalem.
d) About 3.1 miles (5 kilometers) south of Jerusalem.

Matching. Match each description (right) with the proper Scripture reference or explanation (left). One item in the right column will not be used. Try to do the exercise without referring to your Bible. Then look up those passages you cannot identify. This exercise will help prepare you to locate key Bible passages from memory, and it will help you to identify some of these passages on your unit progress evaluation.

. . . . **9** Luke 6:12–16

. . . . **10** Luke 12:22–34

. . . . **11** Luke 11:11–14

. . . . **12** Date of writing of Luke

. . . . **13** Luke 1:46–49

. . . . **14** Zacharias

. . . . **15** Luke 24:46–49

. . . . **16** Luke wrote it

. . . . **17** Luke 4:18–19

. . . . **18** Luke 10:30–37

. . . . **19** Apostle John

. . . . **20** Central theme of Luke

a) Jesus the Son of Man
b) The Magnificat
c) The book of Acts
d) The twelve apostles named
e) Is introduced in Luke only
f) Is named in Matthew, Mark, and Luke
g) AD 60
h) The Father's desire to give the Holy Spirit
i) Jesus' criteria for ministry
j) Seek heavenly treasure
k) AD 45
l) The Great Commission and Great Enablement
m) The parable of the Good Samaritan

Self-Test Time

Hr_____ Min_____

Answers to Study Questions

6 a Jesus passing through Jericho.
  b Object lesson.
  c Jesus and Zaccheus.
  d The Son of Man came to seek and to save the lost.

1 You should note in your own words that:
  a He was not satisfied with other accounts available at the time.
  b From eyewitness or from personal observations.
  c He knew the facts, and had a long-time association with other believers.
  d He was probably a person of high position.
  e He had writing ability and knew how to present the message of Christ in a logical, systematic manner.

7 a Two men praying in the temple.
  b A parable.
  c The Pharisee and the publican.
  d A humble man is justified before God.

2 Statements **a**, **b**, **e**, **g**, and **h** are true.

8 a Two men returning from Emmaus.
  b Question and answer.
  c The two men, Jesus, and the eleven disciples.
  d The disciples would complete His work in the power of the Spirit.

3 My statement would be as follows: Luke's purpose was to write an organized, complete, historically accurate account of the gospel. Presenting Jesus in His manhood would appeal to all mankind. (Did your statement or purpose look anything like this? Study this statement thoroughly because it will be a key to help you understand Luke.)

9 As an actual figure in history.

4 Your answer.

10 Your answers.

5 a The birth of Jesus.
  b Question and answer.
  c The angel Gabriel, Mary, Elizabeth, and Zacharias.
  d Christ, the Son of God, is presented both as Deity and humanity. The doctrine of the Holy Spirit is prominent.

Note the time you begin reading this lesson. At the end of the lesson, record in the space provided the time it took to complete each segment.

The Gospel Account of John

Start Time

_____

More than any other Gospel, the Gospel of John reveals to us the magnitude of God's desire for fellowship with His creation. "For God so loved the world, that he gave his . . . son" (John 3:16). Jesus Christ, the Son of God, the Word made flesh, came to earth and dwelt among men. What a revelation of love! The Son was there in the beginning, in creative power, when God made man and breathed into him the breath of life. The Son was there, at the right hand of the Father, throughout the history of man's failure to obey and please God. And the Son was there when God, in compassionate mercy, provided a sacrifice for humanity's sin.

Jesus Christ became that sacrifice. What a beautiful picture of love the Creator allowing Himself to be wounded by His own creation, laying down His own life to save the lives of many! How it must have grieved the heart of the Father to turn his back on His Son as He bore on the cross all the sins of the world! Jesus, through His life and through His death, revealed to us the Father's love. "Anyone who has seen me has seen the Father" (John 14:9).

John's Gospel is the gospel of belief. It is an account of the life and ministry of Christ written with the purpose that men might believe He is the Son of God, and through their belief might find forgiveness for sin, and life everlasting (John 20:30–31). It is such a complete revelation of God's love that, even if there were no other Scriptures, men could read it and believe. May you be encouraged to share its message with those who have not yet experienced God's love, so that they, too, might know Him and experience the creative power of His love in their lives.

the activities...

◊ Read the Gospel of John straight through to get an overview of its message. Scan the textbook readings to develop a proper background for this study. As you do this, keep your Bible open so that you can look up the Scripture references in the textbook as you come to them. The readings for this lesson are
    Reading 1: pages 188–191
    Reading 2: pages 191–192
    Reading 3: pages 192–193
    Reading 4: pages 193–197
    Reading 5: pages 197–198

Reading 6: pages 198–199
Reading 7: pages 199–200

◇ Study the lesson development as usual and take the self-test when you have completed it.

◇ Review the lessons in this unit in preparation for your unit progress evaluation (UPE). Read the instruction page in your Essential Course Materials, then turn to Unit Progress Evaluation 2. When you have completed the UPE, check your answers with the answer key provided in your Essential Course Materials. Review any items you may have answered incorrectly. (Although UPE scores do not count as part of your final course grade, they indicate how well you learned the material and how well you may perform on the final examination.)

the objectives...

7.1 *List important facts about the writer of the Gospel of John.*

7.2 *State when John was written in comparison to the Synoptics.*

7.3 *Explain the significance of the key words and the theme of John, and relate its theme to those of the Synoptics.*

7.4 *Identify basic concepts emphasized in Tenney's outline of the Gospel of John.*

7.5 *Give four characteristics of the Gospel of John and an example of each.*

7.6 *Identify the dual purpose for the writing of the Gospel of John.*

7.7 *Evaluate the manner in which John describes persons in his Gospel account.*

the outline...

1 Origin of John
2 Date and Place
3 Content
4 Outline
5 Emphasis
6 Purpose
7 Characters
8 Special Features
9 Golden Passages

Objective 7.1 *List important facts about the writer of the Gospel of John.*

Origin of John
📖 Reading 1

Since you have just read the Bible and textbook assignments on John, you should have a good general knowledge of them. Now you should go back over some of the material in the Bible and textbook to get the most important features firmly impressed in your mind. We will follow the outline given at the beginning of the lesson. The textbook follows the same outline, except for a "Special Features" section. The outline will help you locate references to the textbook made in the Study Guide. Write down any significant data or thoughts that come to you. Your notes will help you when you review, and they will also provide good material for you to use in your ministry.

1   A brief reading of this section will impress you with the traditional view that the book of John was written by the apostle John. From the large amount of biographical data given under the section "Author," briefly list the most important elements of his biography. Then study them until you feel that you know John well. Would you want to be like him? In your notebook, write what you have discovered on the following subjects pertaining to John.
   a   Family
   b   Length of life
   c   Last place he lived
   d   Nationality and languages
   e   Birthplace
   f   Relationship to Jesus
   g   Earlier occupation and companions
   h   His part in the Resurrection events

Objective 7.2 *State when John was written in comparison to the Synoptics.*

Date and Place
📖 Reading 2

When you begin reading this section, you will note that the writing of John is variously estimated between two dates that are one hundred years apart. Conservative Bible scholars have generally placed the writing of John's account of the gospel just before the end of the first century. You should remember that AD 90 is probably the most acceptable date.

The textbook gives information on where the book of John was written. The most important points for you to know are that it was

   1)   written in Gentile surroundings.

   2)   written in Asia Minor.

3) most likely written in Ephesus.

4) written after the church had achieved a measure of maturity.

2 Notice the accepted dates given for the writing of the Synoptics and John's Gospel. When was John's Gospel written in respect to the Synoptics?

....

Objective   **7.3**   *Explain the significance of the key words and the theme of John, and relate its theme to those of the Synoptics.*

Content
📖 Reading 3

As we study the content of the book of John, we are considering new material for the most part. Scholars have determined that perhaps 92 percent of the content of John does not appear in the other gospel accounts.

Early in this section the textbook shows us the purpose of the writing of John. Tenney indicates that the "key to the content of the Gospel of John" is given by the author himself in John 20:30–31. Learn these verses well; they will open the book of John to your understanding. You should observe that there is a strong emphasis in these verses on the deity of Christ. In fact, this is the main theme that runs through the entire book, because John wants to depict Christ as the Son of God.

3 To review the main themes of the four Gospels, write the one word after each Gospel which best describes the attribute of Jesus it stresses.

a Matthew stresses ....

b Mark stresses..

c Luke stresses ....

d John stresses...

Perhaps this is an appropriate place to develop further the comparison of the four gospel accounts. There are four Old Testament prophecies in which Bible scholars have seen the same four emphases above. Read these four references (in Figure 7.1) and then study the comparisons made by the chart.

Old Testament Prophecies in the Gospel Accounts			
MATTHEW	*MARK*	*LUKE*	*JOHN*
Jeremiah 23:5–6	Zechariah 3:8	Zechariah 6:12	Isaiah 4:2
David's Righteous Branch	My Servant, The Branch	The Man, The Branch	The Lord, The Branch
The Prophesied King	The Obedient Servant	The Perfect Man	The Divine Son
Like a Lion	Like an Ox	Like a Man	Like an Eagle
The Davidic King	The Servant of the Lord	The Son of Man	The Word of God
Prophetic	Practical	Historical	Spiritual
To the Jews	To the Romans	To the Greeks	To the Church

Figure 7.1

As you read through the section "Content," take note of the three key words. The last paragraph in this section is a beautiful summary of what the words *signs, belief,* and *life* do in the book of John.

4 In your own words, briefly explain the significance of each of these three key words in the Gospel of John.

a Signs: ....

b Belief (believe): ....

c Life: ....

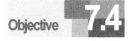

Objective

Identify basic concepts emphasized in Tenney's outline of the Gospel of John.

Outline
📖 Reading 4

The outline of the book of John is structured around the key word *belief.* The structure of the book lends itself to a simple, logical outline. Look at the outline as you study the content of John. It will help you remember the major divisions of the book and follow the sequence of events.

John has selected certain events and miracles, around which he can associate the subjects or doctrines which present the revelation of God in Christ. John's explanations of these *signs* often become expansive. Thus, the book of John is characterized by these explanations or discourses on various subjects. He has twelve discourses that are not in the other three gospel accounts. In the list below, the Scripture reference to each of these discourses is accompanied by a brief description of subject matter. Read the list several times to get an impression of the subjects, because they are the heart of John's account of the gospel. Choose the four discourses that you know the least about, turn to the Scripture references, and read each theme. As you read, keep John's purpose and three key words in mind. This will help you get the full meaning of each discourse, and give you valuable truths to share with others as you minister from the book of John.

1. Spiritual regeneration	3:1–21
2. Eternal life	4:4–26
3. The source and witness of eternal life	5:19–47
4. The true Bread of Life	6:26–59
5. The source of truth	7:14–29
6. The Light of the world	8:12–20
7. The true object of faith	8:21–30
8. Spiritual freedom	8:31–59
9. The Good Shepherd	10:1–21
10. The unity of the Godhead	10:22–38
11. The world's Redeemer	12:20–36
12. The future with Christ and the Holy Spirit	13:31–16:33

5 John carefully selected the events recorded in his Gospel to
    a)   include all of the miracles of Jesus.
    b)   include all of the sermons of Jesus.
    c)   reveal the power and divinity of Christ.
    d)   present the variety of characters who were touched by Jesus' life.

6 The Gospel of John presents Jesus as the
    a)   Son of Man.
    b)   descendant of Abraham.
    c)   Word made flesh.
    d)   Lord to the Gentiles.

7 Jesus' appeal to men to believe in Him was based upon
    a)   their blind faith.
    b)   His claims of divinity.
    c)   His ability to persuade them with His words.
    d)   clear facts and issues.

8 The two opposing principles we see throughout the book of John are
    a)   belief and unbelief.
    b)   forgiveness and unforgiveness.
    c)   selfishness and selflessness.
    d)   action and inaction.

Objective	7.5	*Give four characteristics of the Gospel of John and an example of each.*

Emphasis
📖 Reading 5

9 Read through this section in the textbook with a pen in hand and mark the four main characteristics of John. Then write them below in your own words.

a ....

b ....

c ....

d ....

10 Now refer to the paragraphs dealing with each characteristic. Give an example of each one.

As you have done with the two previous lessons, turn to the "Harmony of the Life of Christ" (chapter 12) and carefully note the material which is peculiar to John. Also turn to Appendixes B, F, and C in this Study Guide. Notice the charts of miracles, parables, and prayers of Jesus. This will help you to see the special emphasis of John as compared with the other Gospel writers. As you study these charts, strive to remember the major events of John in chronological sequence.

Objective	7.6	*Identify the dual purpose for the writing of the Gospel of John.*

Purpose
📖 Reading 6

apologetic
offered in vindication or defense of

Tenney indicates that John had a dual purpose in writing the Gospel of John. One is apologetic.* By this he means that John wrote the book to cause readers to believe the gospel. John's second purpose for writing his account of the gospel is supplementary—that is, John wanted to add to, or fill in other accounts. Perhaps the best way of stating this is to say that John wanted to show the gospel from another point of view to reach a particular audience. You have already learned John 20:31 where John announced his own purpose in writing. In that verse John shows that he wants to induce his readers to believe in the *divinity* of Christ. This is the point of view that he develops in his account of the gospel. This purpose is a supplement to the other gospel accounts. As we have seen earlier in the Study Guide, Matthew stresses Messiahship, Mark stresses Servanthood, Luke stresses Manhood, and John stresses Divinity. Each one emphasizes a necessary viewpoint, and together they furnish a panorama of Christ's life and work.

11 Circle the letter preceding each TRUE statement.

a John's Gospel is called an *apologetic* because it is a systematic discourse in defense of Christian beliefs.

b The Gospel of John contains much information already included in the Synoptics.

c When we say the Gospel of John is supplementary to the Synoptics, we mean that it adds to the other accounts, or fills in details they do not give.

d The details John gives sometimes contradict the other accounts.

e The accounts of events John reports sometimes add to other reports of those same events, but never contradict them.

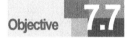

Objective **7.7**

Evaluate the manner in which John describes persons in his Gospel account.

Characters

📖 Reading 7

John uses various persons to represent either belief or unbelief in Christ. None of the other gospel accounts afford such a representative group. John paints strong descriptive portraits of each character with words, actions, and reactions. Turn to the chart of "Persons Mentioned in the Gospel Accounts" in Appendix G of the Study Guide. Select the characters you know the least and those who are of greatest interest to you. Then read the references to them in John. He will really make the characters come alive for you.

12 Which statement is an accurate explanation of John's development of character portraits?

a) Although his accounts of events involving certain persons give us a vivid picture of the characters, his intent is primarily to demonstrate the principles of belief and unbelief.

b) Other than for a few principal characters, John does not give us a clear picture of the individuals involved in the events he records, since this was not his main intent in writing.

Special Features

The places where events occurred during Christ's last fifty days on earth are significant. Turn to the chart of "Places Mentioned in the Gospel Accounts" in Appendix H of this Study Guide. Compare the places mentioned by each of the gospel accounts for the week previous to the Crucifixion, the time of Jesus' trials and crucifixion, and the forty days following His resurrection. Study the map of Jerusalem and its environs, and locate all of the places where Jesus spent His last fifty days on earth.

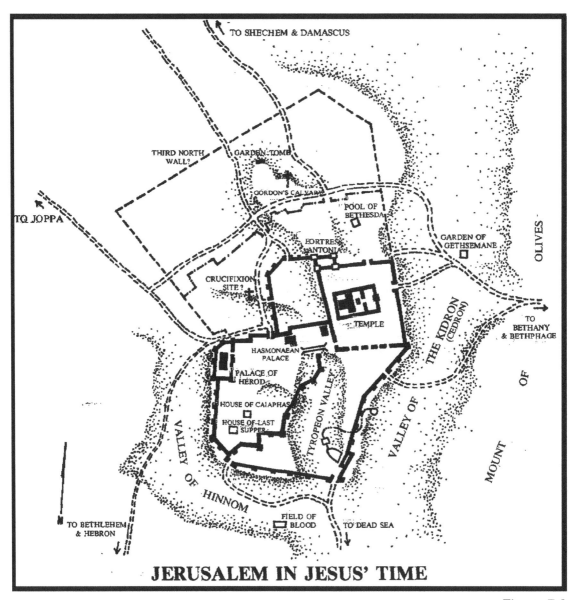

JERUSALEM IN JESUS' TIME

Figure 7.2

Another special feature to consider is the trials of Jesus. They are
outlined below:

TRIALS OF JESUS		
Religious		
TRIAL	JUDGE	REFERENCE
1	Annas	John 18:12–14
2	Caiaphas	Matthew 26:57–68
3	Sanhedrin	Matthew 27:1–2
Civil		
4	Pilate	John 18:28–38
5	Herod	Luke 23:6–12
6	Pilate	John 18:39–19:16

Figure 7.3

Refer to the "Harmony of the Life of Christ" in chapter 12 of the textbook, to understand the time sequence of the events of the last days.

Golden Passages

When we come to the consideration of *golden passages* in John, our options are great. Since there are so many deeply spiritual and beautiful passages in John, we cannot list all of them here, however, the passages we have selected below will enrich your life and ministry. Try to memorize at least half of them in each category. You should become so familiar with the content and location of all of them that you are able to locate them by memory or with a concordance.

The Seven Major "I AMs"

1. I Am the Bread of Life	6:35
2. I Am the Light of the World	8:12; 9:5
3. I Am the Door (of the sheepfold)	10:7
4. I Am the Good Shepherd	10:11,14
5. I Am the Resurrection and the Life	11:25
6. I Am the Way, the Truth, and the Life	14:6
7. I Am the True Vine	15:1

Others

8. John's Prologue (the Deity, reincarnate work, and incarnation of Christ)	1:1–14
9 The Gospel in Brief	3:16–21
10. Jesus' Great Promise of the Holy Spirit	7:37–39
11. Jesus' Promise of Preparing a Place and Returning	14:1–3
12. Jesus' Promise of the Comforter (*Paraclete*)	14:13–16

Total Time
(Read, answer
questions, check
answers)

Hr_____ Min_____

Start Time

_____

Self-Test 7

True-False. Write T in the blank space preceding each TRUE statement. Write F if it is FALSE.

.... **1** The major portion of the content of the Gospel of John does not appear in any other Gospel.

.... **2** The central doctrine of John's Gospel is the deity of Christ.

.... **3** The author of the Gospel of John was the first of the twelve disciples to die.

.... **4** The Gospel of John confirms that Jesus was present with the Father at the time of the Creation.

.... **5** The Gospel of John was addressed mainly to a Roman audience.

.... **6** The Gospel of John was the third Gospel to be written.

.... **7** Jesus was tried in court three times before He was crucified.

.... **8** Three words important to the content of John are *signs, belief,* and *life.*

.... **9** The Period of Conference in Tenney's outline of the Gospel of John refers both to special teaching Jesus gave His disciples and special communication between Jesus and God the Father.

.... **10** The final justification of belief was the resurrection of Christ.

Multiple Choice. Select the best answer.

11 John could be called the apostle of
a) action.
b) humility.
c) patience.
d) love.

12 John recorded the miracles of Christ so that people would
a) be healed.
b) believe.
c) be amazed.
d) seek after miracles.

13 The highest experience that a person can receive is
a) divine life that God gives to one who believes in Christ.
b) the love of his fellowmen.
c) physical or mental healing.
d) a clear understanding of Scripture and mystical and spiritual experiences.

14 In order to present various doctrines that pertain to the revelation of God in Christ, John has
a) borrowed extensively from the other Gospels.
b) avoided the use of specific examples of Christ's ministry.
c) repeatedly referred to Old Testament Scriptures on the same topics.
d) followed descriptions of events or miracles with related discourses.

15 John had two purposes in writing his gospel account. One was to cause readers to believe the gospel. The other was to
   a) gain recognition as one of the disciples closest to Jesus.
   b) train other disciples who were not with Jesus during His earthly ministry.
   c) fill in or add to what was recorded in the other gospel accounts.
   d) condemn those who had rejected Jesus during His earthly ministry.

16 Which of these is found in John's Gospel?
   a) The Magnificat
   b) The seven "I AMs" of Christ
   c) The record of Christ's birth
   d) The parable of the mustard seed

17 Which of these combinations is descriptive of the Gospel of John?
   a) Like an eagle, spiritual, the Lord, the Branch
   b) To the Jews, prophetic, like a lion
   c) The perfect Man, historical, the Son of Man
   d) Practical, like an ox, my Servant, the Branch

18 Which of these is NOT a main characteristic of John?
   a) A special vocabulary
   b) Parables
   c) Emphasis on the humanity of Christ
   d) Emphasis on the deity of Christ

Short Answer. Write in each blank space the answer that best completes each sentence.

19 **a** Matthew presents Christ as ....

   b Mark presents Him as ....

   c Luke presents Him as...

   d John presents Him as ....

20 In the Gospel of John, God reveals Himself through ....
   which produce ....,
   which results in new ....

Self-Test Time

Hr_____ Min_____

Unit Progress Evaluation 2

Now that you have finished Unit 2, review the lessons in preparation for Unit Progress Evaluation 2. You will find it in your Essential Course Materials. Answer all of the questions without referring to your course materials, Bible, or notes. When you have completed the UPE, check your answers with the answer key provided in your Essential Course Materials, and review any items you may have answered incorrectly. Then you may proceed with your study of Unit 3. (Although UPE scores do not count as part of your final course grade, they indicate how well you learned the material and how well you may perform on the final examination.)

Answers to Study Questions

7 d) clear facts and issues.

1 **a** Son of Zebedee and Salome, who was probably a sister of Mary, the mother of Jesus.
  b Last survivor of the Twelve; probably died at end of first century.
  c Spent his declining years in Ephesus.
  d Was a Jew who wrote in Greek but was accustomed to thinking in Aramaic.
  e Was a Palestinian with personal knowledge of the land, Jerusalem and its area, Galilee, and Samaria.
  f Was an eyewitness to the deeds and teachings of Jesus from the beginning of His career and was very near to Jesus during passion week.
  g Was a fishing partner with his brother James and with Andrew and Peter, at least before he followed Jesus.
  h Was one of the first visitors to the empty tomb, saw the empty grave clothes, and believed (John 20:8).

8 a) belief and unbelief.

2 The Gospel of John was the last Gospel to be written, according to Bible scholars.

9 **a** The personal relation of Jesus to man is stressed.
  b A special vocabulary is used.
  c The divinity of Jesus is stressed.
  d The humanity of Christ is stressed.

3 **a** Messiahship.
  b Servanthood.
  c Manhood.
  d Divinity.

10 See Tenney for examples (Reading 5).

4 **a** *Signs* were proofs of Jesus' divine power.
  b *Belief* refers to the total commitment of one's life to Christ.
  c *Life* speaks of the new nature of the believer and what it provides for him in Christ.

11 Statements **a**, **c**, and **e** are true.

5 c) reveal the power and divinity of Christ.

12 a) Although his accounts of events involving certain persons give us a vivid picture of the characters, his intent is primarily to demonstrate the principles of belief and unbelief.

6 c) Word made flesh.

THE RECORDS OF THE EARLY CHURCH— THE PERIOD OF EXPANSION: AD 29–60

Procedures...

1. Read the lesson introduction and study the learning activities to know what to expect.
2. Reflect on the objectives for key concepts and expected outcomes.
3. Study the content, identifying key points by underlining or highlighting, and answer the study questions.
4. Answer the self-test questions to synthesize the lesson.
5. Review the lessons in this unit in preparation for the unit progress evaluation.

Note the time you begin reading this lesson. At the end of the lesson, record in the space provided the time it took to complete each segment.

The Establishment and Transition of the Church

Start Time

_____

The Gospels, which we have just studied, begin with the birth of Christ and end with His death and resurrection. The book of Acts begins with the birth of the church, but in a sense the final chapter has not yet been written for the story of the church continues to this day.

There are three dominant personalities in the book of Acts—Peter, Paul, and more important, the Holy Spirit. When Jesus ascended into heaven His ministry among men was not concluded. He sent "another Comforter" who was not constrained by human limitations. The small, confused band of disciples became a Spirit-controlled body of believers, whose message of salvation turned their world upside down.

Peter's ministry was primarily among the Jews in or near Jerusalem, while Paul was called to a more widespread ministry, which was primarily to Gentiles. The record of Acts is a record of the Holy Spirit's anointing on these two men, and of the outpouring of the Spirit upon the church, the body of Christ. The church has continued to grow over the centuries, and today it reaches to every part of the globe. And the same Holy Spirit is still active in the church today, moving upon the hearts of people in convicting power, and giving power for service to those who have been redeemed.

The record of the early church includes victories and failures, joys and sorrows, growth and persecution. As we study it, our hearts should be inspired to preach the gospel and serve the Lord with the same fervor that was demonstrated by those first Spirit-filled believers whose impact upon the world has reached even into this twentieth century!

the activities...

◇ Read Acts 1 to 11:18 straight through to gain an overview of its message. Scan the material in the textbook. While you read the textbook, keep your Bible open and read the Scripture references in the textbook as you come to them. The readings for this lesson are

    Reading 1: pages 231–242; Acts 1:1–8:3
    Reading 2: pages 245–253; Acts 8:4–11:18

◇ While reading the Bible or other books, have you found words you did not understand? Do you make it a practice to find the definitions for such words in a dictionary? You will have a better understanding of this course if you continually use your dictionary and the glossary of key words at the end of this Study Guide.

◇ Study the lesson according to your established procedure, checking your answers with those provided and referring as necessary to your Bible, the textbook, and your Study Guide.

the objectives...

8.1 *State the three features of the purpose of Acts.*

8.2 *Describe aspects of the church's life emphasized in Acts.*

8.3 *Identify major features and doctrines of the early church.*

8.4 *Describe the result of the dispersion.*

8.5 *Explain the role of the Holy Spirit in the transition period.*

8.6 *Describe characteristics of Paul before and after his conversion.*

8.7 *Summarize the major changes in the church resulting from the period of transition.*

the outline...

1 The Establishment of the Church
   a The Record: Acts
   b The Foundation
   c The First Dispersion

2 The Transition of the Church
   a The Preaching in Samaria
   b The Ethiopian Eunuch
   c The Conversion of Paul
   d The Preaching of Peter

Objective **8.1**

State the three features of the purpose of Acts.

The Establishment of the Church
📖 Reading 1

The textbook indicates that there was "a tremendous gap" between the little group of disciples who had received the commission to preach Christ's name among all nations and the dynamic young church that was soon to take the gospel to the known world. Tenney raises seven complex questions about how the "gap" can be bridged. He asserts that the book of Acts provides the answers to these questions.

The book of Acts is the second volume in Luke's historical series on the acts and teaching of Jesus. In the first volume (Luke's account of the gospel) he reports what Jesus did and taught in person. In the second volume (Acts of the Apostles) he reports what Jesus continued to do and teach through Christians empowered by the Holy Spirit. Whereas, Luke's source for his first volume was reliable firsthand informants; he narrates his second volume from reliable firsthand experience. While the first volume presents the life and ministry of Christ, the second volume presents the birth and growth of the church. Thus, Acts can rightfully be considered as the sequel to the gospel accounts and as the preface to the Epistles, or as the epilogue to the Gospels and as the prologue to the Epistles.

The *purpose* of Acts is beautifully stated in Acts 1:1–8—to continue the acts and teaching of Christ. These verses promise the *power* with which to fulfill the purpose. They also prescribe the *plan* by which the purpose is to be carried out. Acts 1:8 clearly gives these three features of the purpose of Acts, and it seems to provide a key to the outline of the book.

1   Read Acts 1:8, then fill in the chart with that portion of the Scripture text which applies to each of the three features of the purpose of Acts.

   a   The Purpose: ....
       (Acts 2:14–28:31)

   b   The Power: ....
       (Acts 2:1–4)

   c   The Plan: 1)..
       (Acts 1:12–7:60)

                    2)..
       (Acts 8:1–11:18)

                    3)..
       (Acts 12:1–28:31)

We studied the authorship of the book of Acts at length in Lesson 6. There we found that Luke, the Gentile physician, made an immeasurable contribution to Christianity in his two-volume work. Can you imagine what the history of the church would be like without the book of Acts? As we move on in the lesson development, we will consider some of these contributions.

The place and date of the writing of the book are probably Rome about AD 63, just at the end of the career of the apostle Paul and just before Nero's great fire in Rome in AD 64.

Objective 8.2   *Describe aspects of the church's life emphasized in Acts.*

The Record: Acts

Turn now to Acts 1:1–5 and compare it with Luke 1:1–4 and 24:46–53. You should be able to see quite clearly that Acts is the sequel to Luke and that the books share the same overall purpose. Moreover, you should be able to sense the close relationship between Luke's two books.

In this reading, the author considers the entire book of Acts to help you to get a telescopic view of Acts. However, our more detailed study in this lesson will only take us through Acts 11:18.

In the textbook, Tenney says that Acts 1:8 affords a geographical outline of the book. We observed this truth in the paragraph above where we discussed the purpose of the book. In fact, the church did follow the plan prescribed in Acts 1:8—taking the gospel to Jerusalem first, and then to Palestine (". . . all Judea and in Samaria . . ."), and eventually to Rome and the world-at-large (". . . the uttermost parts of the earth").

It is important to notice that the early Christians did not wander aimlessly. Rather, they followed a plan of evangelizing in key cities from which the gospel could flow out in ever-widening circles. Some of these strategic cities were: Antioch, Iconium, Lystra, Derbe, Ephesus, Philippi, Thessalonica, Corinth, and Rome.

It will be instructive at this point in your study to get acquainted with many places that are significant in the book of Acts. Locate, on your Bible map in the textbook, all the places in the following list which you cannot place appropriately from memory. Then, as you read the textbook and the book of Acts, be ready to learn more about each place mentioned.

Amphipolis	Cnidus	Melita	Rhodes
Antioch	Cos	Miletus	Rome
Antipatris	Crete	Mitylene	Salamis
Appolonia	Cyprus	Myra	Samaria
Assos	Damascus	Mysia	Samos
Athens	Derbe	Neapolis	Samothracia
Attalia	Ephesus	Paphos	Seleucia
Azotus	Gaza	Patara	Sidon
Berea	Iconium	Perea	Syracuse
Caesarea	Jerusalem	Philippi	Tarsus
Cenchrea	Joppa	Ptolemais	Thessalonica
Chios	Lydda	Puteoli	Troas
Clauda	Lystra	Rhegium	Tyre

In this reading of the textbook, the author points out another interesting feature of the book of Acts. Various statements about the numerical and spiritual growth of the believers can outline the book. Turn to the references that the textbook makes about such growth and read them in the book of Acts. You may want to mark or number them in some way in your Bible.

The textbook discusses a third way that Acts can be outlined on the basis of its major personalities. They are Peter, Stephen, Barnabas, Philip, and Paul. You will want to know which major personality (or personalities) is dominant in the various chapters. Among these personalities Peter and Paul are the most outstanding in the history of the New Testament Scriptures. Study the parallel descriptions given in the textbook about these two great men.

Acts also introduces many other personalities. Here is a list of personalities whose acquaintance you will want to make in your journey through the book of Acts.

Aeneas	Claudius Caesar	John Mark	Sceva
Agabus	Cornelius	Lucius	Secundus
Agrippa	Crispus	Lydia	Sergius Paulus
Alexander	Damaris	Manean	Silas
Ananias	Demetrius	Mary	Simeon
Andrew	Dionysius	Matthew	Simon
Annas	Dorcas	Matthias	Sopater
Apollos	Drusilla	Mnason	Sosthenes
Aquila	Erastus	Nicanor	Stephen
Aristarchus	Eutychus	Nicolas	Tabitha
Augustus	Felix	Niger	Theophilus
Bar-Jesus	Festus	Parmenas	Theudas
Barnabas	Gaius	Paul	Timon
Barsabas	Gallio	Peter	Timotheus
Bartholomew	Gamaliel	Priscilla	Trophimus
Bernice	Herod	Prochorus	Tychicus
Blastus	Jason	Publius	Tyrannus
Caiaphas	Jesus	Rhoda	
Candace	John	Sapphira	

Luke presents a wide range of men and women in this book: Christian, pagan, Jew, Gentile, learned and unlearned, religious, and civil. Both friend and foe are shown in their encounters with the church.

The textbook offers little help on the chronology of the book of Acts, although Tenney does make an attempt in Reading 1 to correlate some of the events in Acts with some contemporary political events. While Luke apparently does not intend to write a continuous chronological sequence, he does casually give enough references to contemporary secular history to enable the careful scholar to piece together (with help from the Epistles and secular history) a satisfactory time sequence for the book of Acts. From these references, we can construct the following chronology:

Acts 1:9	Ascension of Christ	AD 30
Acts 2:4	The church's first Pentecost	AD 30
Acts 7:54–60	The death of Stephen	AD 34
Acts 9:1–19	The conversion of Saul	AD 34–36
Acts 9:26	Paul's first visit to Jerusalem	AD 37–38
Acts 11:26	Paul at Antioch	AD 44
Acts 11:30	Paul's second visit to Jerusalem	AD 45
Acts 13:4	Paul's first missionary journey	AD 48
Acts 15:1–29	The Council at Jerusalem	AD 51
Acts 18:1	Paul's first visit to Corinth	AD 51
Acts 18:22	Paul's fourth visit to Jerusalem	AD 54
Acts 20:22	Paul leaves Ephesus for Jerusalem	AD 56

Acts 21:33	Paul is arrested in Jerusalem	AD 58
Acts 28:16	Paul arrives in Rome	AD 61
Acts 28:30–31	Acts written and circulated	AD 63

We see then, that the book of Acts covers a little over thirty years, which is about the same length of time as that covered by the gospel accounts. The division of time for the book of Acts is as follows:

Chapters 1:1–9:25	AD 30–37 = 7 years
Chapters 9:26–12:24	AD 37–44 = 7 years
Chapters 12:25–15:35	AD 44–51 = 7 years
Chapters 15:36–21:16	AD 51–58 = 7 years
Chapters 21:17–28:31	AD 58–63 = 5 years

As you study the book of Acts, these time divisions will help you connect the aspect of time with the events. I am amazed when I read what the early church accomplished in each of these seven-year periods. This is especially true when I consider that the whole book spanned only thirty-three years. Oh, how completely this world would have been evangelized if in each thirty-three-year period of its history, the church had been as successful as it was in the book of Acts!

In the textbook, Tenney gives several aspects of the church's life that are shown in the book of Acts. Take these as important points to recognize as you study the book of Acts and notice what the textbook has to say about them.

2 Here are seven aspects of the church's life. Briefly define each of these aspects.

  a The objective: ....

  b The power: ....

  c The method: ....

  d The organization: ....

  ....

  e The means of guidance: ....

  f The discipline:..

  ....

  g The relation to government: ....

  ....

3 Circle the letter preceding each TRUE statement about the emphases in the book of Acts.

a The first half of the book is more concerned with the development of the church as a group, and the last half emphasizes Paul as an individual.

b The growth of the church receives little attention in Luke's account.

c Personalities are emphasized in their relationship to the development of the church.

d Although Peter ministered mainly to the Jews and Paul ministered primarily to the Gentiles, they worked in harmony with one another.

e The book of Acts records all of the events that took place in the growth and development of the early church.

f The pattern of church life in Acts, including its missionary outreach, is still valid for the church today.

g We can say that the book of Acts is apologetic in nature.

 Objective **8.3** *Identify major features and doctrines of the early church.*

The Foundation

In this section the textbook shows that while Christianity was founded on Judaism, it had its own, distinctive features from the very beginning. These included the life, death, and resurrection of Jesus. And within five short years the church had developed a character of its own which included four additional distinguishing features.

4 According to your textbook, the four features that characterized the church were all of the following but one. Which one is NOT one of its characteristics?

a) A distinct body of people

b) Unique organization

c) A set of beliefs

d) A formally recognized hierarchy

e) A distinct purpose

According to Tenney, "The birthday of the church was Pentecost." The event and the experience enabled previously insignificant disciples to "turn the world upside down." Luke very deliberately emphasizes the role of the Holy Spirit in the lives of these early Christians. Notice the references the textbook makes in the second paragraph under "Pentecost." Read these references in Luke and Acts again and you will see the importance that Luke attaches to the Holy Spirit in the church. Also, observe how Luke stresses the doctrine of the Spirit at the end of his Gospel and the beginning of Acts.

Luke 24:49	Luke gives Jesus' promise of the Spirit.
Luke 24:49	Luke gives Jesus' command to tarry in Jerusalem until the coming of the Spirit.
Luke 24:52–53	Luke shows the disciples' obedience in returning to Jerusalem to worship and wait.
Acts 1:4–5, 8	Luke gives both Jesus' promise of the Spirit and His command to the disciples to tarry in Jerusalem until they are baptized with the Spirit.
Acts 1.12–14	Luke shows that the disciples obediently returned to Jerusalem to worship and wait.

It is important to notice that this spiritual baptism, foretold by John the Baptist and promised by Christ, was actually accomplished in Acts 2:4. We also observe that it was repeated on several other occasions (Acts 4:8, 31 and 13:9). In addition, three other groups were filled with the Holy Spirit following the initial outpouring upon the group in Acts 2:4. Turn in your textbook to page 247 and read the paragraph that discusses the Holy Spirit baptism of the following groups. Then read the references to these outpourings of the Holy Spirit in your Bible:

1. Upon the disciples of Jesus at Pentecost   Acts 2:1–4
2. Upon the Samaritans   Acts 8:17
3. Upon the Gentiles at the house of Cornelius   Acts 10:44–46
4. Upon the disciples of John the Baptist   Acts 19:4–6

One cannot help but get the impression in reading of such representative occurrences of the Holy Spirit baptism that this experience was intended to be *normative*** for Christians universally and in all ages. In Peter's sermon on the occasion of the church's first Pentecost, he said concerning the gift of the Holy Spirit, "For the promise is unto you, and to your children, and to all that are afar off, even as many as the Lord our God shall call" (Acts 2:39). Peter had explained the outpouring of the Holy Spirit in Acts 2:4 and the manifestations that followed as the fulfillment of the prophecy of Joel about a universal outpouring of the Spirit in the last days. In our own day we are witnessing the second major wave (Acts 2:4 being the first) of the fulfillment of Joel's prophecy. Today, around the world, God is filling hundreds of thousands of sincere believers with His Holy Spirit, He is doing it for all of the same reasons that He did it in Peter's day. Do not fail to receive the baptism in the Holy Spirit yourself and share the truth about this experience with those to whom you minister.

normative
relating to the standard

One of the great values of the book of Acts is its doctrinal content. Those doctrines, which were mentioned in the gospel accounts, are developed a little further in Acts. However, no doctrine is more prominent in the book of Acts than the doctrine of the Holy Spirit. The book is punctuated throughout with the activities of the Holy Spirit in relation to individual Christians and the church. He is seen as The Spirit of . . .

	Ch		Ch
Promise	1	Wise Counsel	15
Power	2	Providential Protection and Direction	16
Healing	3	Teaching and Preaching	17
Unity and Boldness	4	Revelation	18
Judgment	5	Signs, Wonders, and Miracles	19
Administration	6	Compassionate Ministry	20
Religious Truth	7	Prophecy	21
Evangelism	8	Counsel in Tribunals	22
Conviction, Conversion, and Comfort	9	Wisdom and Deliverance	23
Guidance	10	Defense and Favor	24
Universal Call	11	Victory	25
Miraculous Deliverance	12	Christian Testimony	26
Missions	13	Divine Preservation	27
Protection and Organization	14	Ultimate Triumph	28

In your reading the textbook begins a discussion of "Early Preaching." As you study this section in the textbook, mark the various elements of apostolic preaching that are presented. I have analyzed Peter's sermon on the Day of Pentecost and find that his is typical of all of the apostolic preaching recorded in Acts.

Peter's Sermon

His main theme: Jesus is Lord and Christ (Messiah).

His sermon falls into four main parts:

I. Announcement that the time of fulfillment has come (2:16–21, 33, 38–39)

II. Review of the life, ministry, death, and resurrection of Christ (2:22–24)

III. Quotation of Old Testament Scriptures as proof of the Messiahship of Jesus (2:25–36)

IV. Application to the audience and invitation to repent and believe upon Christ (2:37–40)

Compare the various elements of apostolic preaching which you marked in the textbook with the theme and four main parts of Peter's sermon and see if there is any difference.

5–8 In the section "Organization and Leaders," you can find the answers to the following questions. Answer them in your notebook.

5 Was the church highly organized? Explain.

6 What essentially was the government of the early church?

7 Why were the first deacons chosen?

8 How would you describe the leadership of the following persons?

a Peter

b John

c Stephen

Objective 8.4

Describe the result of the dispersion.

The First Dispersion

In this section you will discover the event that caused Christians to be scattered from Jerusalem. Read Acts 8:1 and you will note that all Christians were scattered "except the apostles."

9 Why do you suppose the leaders stayed in Jerusalem?

....

....

10 What do you think was the major benefit that came as a consequence of this scattering?

....

Objective 8.5

Explain the role of the Holy Spirit in the transition period.

The Transition of the Church
📖 Reading 2

transition
a change from one condition to another

You have already learned much of the material in this section in the earlier part of the lesson. Perhaps it will be sufficient at this point to note that the transition* from law to gospel was neither accidental nor a long evolutionary process; on the contrary it was ordered by the Holy Spirit and it came swiftly and deliberately. Trace this idea of purposeful transition through the pages of this chapter in the textbook, reading the Scripture references as you go along.

The Preaching in Samaria

In this section you will see what happened to the seven men who were elected in Acts 6 to minister to the temporal needs of the congregation of Jerusalem. When the church was scattered, several of them became evangelists.

11 Philip's preaching in Samaria was unusual for a Jew. Explain why it was unusual and what it showed about Philip's understanding of the gospel? Use your notebook.

12 Peter and John also ministered in Samaria. They wanted "to make sure that the Samaritans received the

.... "

At this point in the textbook the author gives references in Acts to four distinct visitations of the Holy Spirit. About these visitations he says, "Each of these instances represents the introduction of the Holy Spirit to a different class of people." Do you think his interpretation is correct?

The Ethiopian Eunuch

Philip's ministry to the Ethiopian court official is an illustration of the universal call and appeal of the gospel. In addition, his ministry to this man shows us something about personal evangelism as compared with mass evangelism.

13 What lesson can we learn from this experience about personal and mass evangelism? Use your notebook.

Objective **8.6** *Describe characteristics of Paul before and after his conversion.*

The Conversion of Paul

It is generally accepted that only the work of Christ Himself is more important to Christianity than the contribution of Paul. As you study the life of Saul of Tarsus, I think you will be convinced that he was providentially prepared for an outstanding role in the church through his upbringing and education in Judaism.

14 See how many features of Paul's life before conversion you can find that prepared him for Christian leadership. Use your notebook.

Paul's second major preparation for assuming a large role in the church was a dramatic, radical, supernatural conversion to Christ. Search out the features of his conversion that you think were important in his preparation for Christian ministry and leadership.

15 Do you think a conversion experience is essential for one to become a Christian today? Explain. Use your notebook.

16 Do those who are to become Christian ministers need to have spiritual experiences similar to Paul's? Explain. Use your notebook.

17 Why is Paul's conversion considered to be a part of the *transition* from the Jewish-centered church of Jerusalem to the Gentile-centered church of the world-at-large? Use your notebook.

Objective **8.7** *Summarize the major changes in the church resulting from the period of transition.*

The Preaching of Peter

The preaching of Peter at the house of Cornelius is important for several reasons. Find these reasons, in your textbook, then underscore them, and keep them in mind. They take the transition from law to gospel a little further than we have seen before.

18 In the final paragraph of Reading 2, you will find a summary of the period
of transition. From the summary list the six "changes" or "new things"
which the transition brought to the church.

a ....

....

b ....

....

c ....

....

d ....

....

e ....

....

f ....

....

Total Time
(Read, answer
questions, check
answers)

Hr_____ Min_____

Start Time

_____

Self-Test 8

Matching. Match each entry (right) with the appropriate description (left).

.... **1** Was one of the key cities in the evangelism plan of the early church

.... **2** Dominates the scene in chapters 6 and 7 of Acts

.... **3** Is the approximate date of the writing of Acts

.... **4** Presents the life and ministry of Christ

.... **5** Can rightfully be considered as the sequel to the gospel accounts and as the preface to the Epistles; presents the birth (Paul) and growth of the church

.... **6** Dominated the scene in chapters 1–5 of Acts

.... **7** Place where believers were first called Christians

.... **8** Dominated the scene from chapter 13 to the end of Acts

.... **9** Is the approximate date of Paul's arrival in Rome

.... **10** Next to the work of Christ, was probably the most important event in the history of Christianity

.... **11** Were baptized in the Holy Spirit (Acts 8:17)

.... **12** Was "the novel element" in Peter's sermon at the house of Cornelius

.... **13** Was the birthday of the church

.... **14** The first place where the church was to take the gospel

.... **15** Were baptized in the Holy Spirit at the house of Cornelius (Acts 10:44–46)

.... **16** Was one of the distinctive features which the church taught from its beginning

a) Luke's first volume
b) The book of Acts
c) Gentiles
d) Antioch
e) Rome
f) Peter
g) Stephen
h) Paul (or Saul)
i) AD 63
j) Pentecost
k) AD 61
l) Conversion of Saul (Paul)
m) Universality
n) Samaritans
o) Jerusalem
p) Resurrection of Jesus

Multiple Choice. Select the best answer.

17 What volume in Luke's historical series on the acts and teaching of Jesus is the book of Acts?
a) First
b) Second
c) Third
d) Fourth

18 The major Christian personalities in Acts were Peter, Barnabas, Philip, Paul, and
   a)   James.
   b)   Mark.
   c)   John.
   d)   Stephen.

19 Acts 1:1–9:25 covers a period of
   a)   ten years.
   b)   one year.
   c)   seven years.
   d)   fifteen years.

20 Within five years, the church had become a distinctive body of men with its own peculiar beliefs, purpose, and
   a)   organization.
   b)   roles.
   c)   membership.
   d)   all of the above.

21 Acts 21:17–28:31 covers a period of
   a)   three years.
   b)   nine years.
   c)   two years.
   d)   five years.

22 Apostolic preaching usually included quotations from the Old Testament as proof of Jesus'
   a)   death.
   b)   resurrection.
   c)   incarnation.
   d)   ascension.

23 The government of the early church was essentially
   a)   monarchal.
   b)   bureaucratic.
   c)   theocratic.
   d)   democratic.

24 The scattering of believers after Stephen's death resulted in
   a)   missionary witness.
   b)   cessation of public witnessing.
   c)   a falling away of believers.
   d)   less Christian martyrdom.

Self-Test Time

Hr_____ Min_____

25 Acts was probably written in
   a)   Jerusalem.
   b)   Rome.
   c)   Antioch.
   d)   Lystra.

Answers to Study Questions

10 The gospel of Christ was spread by the witnessing of those who were scattered.

1 **a** "Ye shall be witnesses unto me."
 b "Ye shall receive power after that the Holy Ghost has come upon you."
 c (1) ". . . in Jerusalem."
   (2) ". . . in all Judea and in Samaria."
   (3) ". . . and to the uttermost parts of the earth."

11 Because of tension between Jews and Samaritans (who were not purely Jewish in religious practice and in descent), Jews did not usually travel in Samaria. However, Philip showed that the Holy Spirit led him to give the Christian message to others, not keeping it just for Jews.

2 **a** To witness and to grow.
 b The Holy Spirit's enablement.
 c Witness at home and to the world.
 d Establishment of churches in key cities, from which the gospel was spread to smaller towns and villages.
 e The Holy Spirit working through church leaders.
 f Sometimes immediate and strict (Acts 5:1–11; 13:6–11).
 g The church was persecuted by the government, but it did not actively oppose the government.

12 Holy Spirit (Acts 8:15).

3 Statements **a**, **c**, **d**, **f**, and **g** are true.

13 Both types of evangelism are empowered by the Holy Spirit. Also, prejudice against race and background were overcome in both types. Both mass and individual ministry are important to God. Preaching from the Old Testament about Jesus is effective in both.

4 d) a formally recognized hierarchy.

14 He had a good Jewish education in the Scriptures and the Hebrew language, knowledge of Aramaic, Greek, and possibly Latin, skill in tent-making, (useful in earning his living as a Christian leader) a superlative education under Gamaliel, and he was a leader in Judaism as a Pharisee and perhaps also as a member of the Sanhedrin.

5 No. Neither persons nor the administrative system was highly organized in the church in Jerusalem at the beginning nor did it own property.

15 Yes. Jesus clearly taught the necessity of conversion. As Tenney says, the Scriptures "still convey the living gospel of the eternal God to the thirsty souls of sinning men" (p. viii).

6 The government of the first church in Jerusalem was essentially democratic.

16 Yes, it is necessary to be converted and to be filled with and directed by the Holy Spirit as Paul was. However, while not everyone will have the same dramatic experience, each one needs the assurance that God has called him into His service as Paul had.

7 They were chosen to distribute food daily.

17 Paul, who was formerly a zealous Pharisee, was well acquainted with Judaism. He could have accepted Christianity as part of Judaism. However, God revealed to him that the gospel should also be preached to the Gentiles.

8 a Peter was a preacher whose sermons were characterized by boldness and spiritual power.

   b John was a less prominent leader than Peter or Stephen in the early period.

   c Stephen was an outstanding apologist in the early church, a peerless debater in foreign synagogues, an evangelist, and a distributor of food to the poor.

18 a The church was no longer confined to Jerusalem. It now included all of Palestine, Samaria, Syria, and Damascus.

   b The constituency was no longer confined to the Jews. It also included Samaritans, Ethiopians, and Gentiles.

   c The preaching method was expanded to emphasize forgiveness of sins.

   d New interpretations of the Law and its place in the gospel were needed as Gentiles came into the church.

   e New leadership promoted the missionary expansion of the church.

   f The church began to experience greater growth.

9 They undoubtedly felt that it was their duty to be faithful in their places of leadership, and Jerusalem was still the headquarters of the church.

The Gentile Church

Start Time

_____

As we continue our study of the growth of the early church, we begin to feel the impact of the predominant theme in the message of the apostles: Jesus Christ. Peter's message emphasized the _Lordship_ of Christ. Paul's theme was the _crucified_ Christ: "For I determined not to know any thing among you, save Jesus Christ, and him crucified" (1 Corinthians 2:2). Their lives were dedicated to leading men and women into a personal relationship with Jesus Christ.

As the young church reached beyond the Jewish community to the Gentiles, problems arose because of differing backgrounds. There was conflict over whether Gentile Christians should obey the Jewish Law. In this lesson we see how the conflict was resolved, and a basic Christian principle emerges: Christ came to fulfill the Law, not to destroy it. We are not bound by Law, but by love.

The apostle Paul not only visited the people in the new churches, but also wrote to them, instructing them in the faith, giving them encouragement, and reminding them of the eternal hope of their new life in Christ. Other apostles also wrote to the churches, and their letters, such as the Epistle of James, balance and complement the writings of Paul in a beautiful way.

These letters were written to deal with specific issues within the early church, but their message is timeless: we are justified by faith in Jesus Christ, not by works, but faithfulness in our daily walk is the natural outcome of our life in Him.

the activities...

◊ The reading assignment for this lesson is a bit longer than usual. Thus, for the first half of the lesson, "The Pauline Mission," read Acts 11:19–15:35, the Epistle of James, and the Epistle to the Galatians straight through to get an overview of each. Then, for the second half of the lesson "The Pauline Program," read Acts 15:36–21:16, and 1 and 2 Thessalonians straight through to get an overview of each. Read the assigned readings in Tenney when instructed. The readings for this lesson are

Reading 1: pages 255–273
Reading 2: pages 277–296

◊ Review the key words to see if there are any with which you are not familiar. Be sure to look up the meaning of any such words in the glossary in the back of this Study Guide.

◊ Work through each part of the lesson according to your established procedure, writing your own answers first and then checking them with those suggested.

the objectives...

9.1 *List the key cities that could be reached from Antioch.*

9.2 *Describe the subject of Paul's message at Antioch and its results.*

9.3 *Explain the purpose of the Council at Jerusalem and its results.*

9.4 *Compare the purpose and content of James with the standard of the gospel.*

9.5 *Explain how the Epistles of Galatians and James complement each other.*

9.6 *Identify the results of Paul's second mission to Asia Minor and his mission to Macedonia.*

9.7 *Identify the purpose and major doctrine of 1 and 2 Thessalonians.*

9.8 *Describe the culture of Corinth at the time of Paul's mission in that city, and state Paul's decision there concerning the synagogue.*

9.9 *Explain how Paul solved two important problems at Ephesus.*

the outline...

1 The Pauline Mission
    a The Church at Antioch
    b Mission to the Gentiles
    c Council at Jerusalem
    d Literature of Protest
    e The Epistle of James
    f The Epistle to the Galatians

2 The Pauline Program
    a Second Mission to Asia Minor
    b Mission to Macedonia
    c Thessalonian Letters
    d Mission to Achaia
    e Mission to Asia

3 Golden Passages

Objective *List the key cities that could be reached from Antioch.*

The Pauline Mission

📖 Reading 1

In this section you will learn that certain Cypriot and Cyrenian believers departed from the general procedure by preaching to Greek Gentiles in Antioch. This opened the gateway for the preaching of the gospel to the Gentiles, and soon it became the standard procedure.

The Church at Antioch

One might be inclined to think of these towns and cities of the New Testament era as small, primitive, insignificant places, but so often, the opposite is true. The key cities in the evangelism program were impressive metropolises for the most part. In fact, Antioch was a prosperous, advanced, cosmopolitan city ranking next to Rome and Alexandria in size.

In Lesson 4 you considered Antioch as the likely place where Matthew wrote his Gospel account and you listed six distinctive features of the church there. Now take time to review these features, for they make Antioch important in the early history of Christianity.

1   For help in understanding the strategic geographic importance of Syrian Antioch, locate it on the map (in chapter 13) on the northeast coast of the Mediterranean Sea. Then find in chapter 2 (section on Transportation and Travel), the list of cities located on the same Roman road as Syrian Antioch.
   a   Write the nine cities in the order that Tenney gives them.

   ....

   ....

   b   As you study the map of Paul's missionary journeys (in chapter 13), underline the name of each of these nine cities he reached by road. Which places did he reach by boat?

   ....

   c   Where else could missionaries go from Antioch of Syria (ch. 2)?

   ....

   ....

Objective  *Describe the subject of Paul's message at Antioch and its results.*

Mission to the Gentiles

The church at Antioch quickly became the headquarters for the evangelistic mission to the Gentile world. Here, the believers were spiritually mature and financially strong. Moreover, their impact on Antioch was such that they were first called Christians in this city.

The itinerary out of Antioch began with Cyprus; however, one important change took place on this island. One of the missionaries moved into prominence as the leader, and he maintained that leadership role until his death.

2 Who was that missionary?

....

3 What do you think of Mark's failure to go to Asia Minor with Paul?

....

4 In his message in the synagogue at Antioch of Pisidia, Paul introduced a new element. In your study of church history you will discover that this *new element* in Paul's theology became *new* again at the time of the Protestant Reformation.

    a What was this new element?..

    ....

    b What were its results?...

    ....

In addition to Cyprus and Antioch of Pisidia, the itinerary of this mission to the Gentiles included Iconium, Lystra, and Derbe. And while opposition was at times fierce and determined, the missionaries planted churches as they went and strengthened and organized them as they retraced their steps on the way back to Pamphylia and then to Syrian Antioch.

5 In your notebook, list the five important benefits given in the last paragraph of Tenney's discussion of the mission to the Gentiles.

Objective **9.3**   *Explain the purpose of the Council at Jerusalem and its results.*

Council at Jerusalem

As your textbook makes clear, the controversy that made the Council at Jerusalem necessary was no momentary quarrel. In order to understand the issues more clearly, we will focus on the cause, the principal speakers, and their decision in the following exercise.

6 Since the information in this section is very important, answer each of the following questions carefully. This will help you to organize the information so you can learn it easily. Use your notebook.
    a Why was it necessary to have the Council?
    b What deep question was involved?
    c Why was the question raised?
    d Who were the principal speakers?

7 Do you think the Council's communication was a series of suggestions or a set of rules?

....

8 Does a group of men or a group of churches have a right to establish policy for other men or churches?

....

9 What do you think of this statement? "It seemed good to the Holy Spirit and to us not to burden you with anything beyond the following requirements: You are to abstain from food sacrificed to idols, from blood, from the meat of strangled animals and from sexual immorality. You will do well to avoid these things" (Acts 15:28–29).

....

....

Literature of Protest

The Council at Jerusalem prayerfully considered this question: What place should the Law have in the lives of Gentile Christian believers? After seeking the guidance of the Holy Spirit, they arrived at a unanimous decision. The Council then sent out a communication through personal representatives to convey their decision to the Gentile churches.

legalistic
condition of observing strict, literal, or excessive conformity to the practices, observances, or principles of a code such as the Law and oral law of Judaism

The problem of law and grace was very deep. In addition, legalistic* teachers persisted in working at this time among the Gentile converts. So, additional measures had to be taken. These additional measures included what the textbook calls "Protest Literature." The Epistle of James and the Epistle to the Galatians are considered here because their contents are closely related to the issues of law and grace that were discussed at the Council of Jerusalem.

Objective **9.4**

Compare the purpose and content of James with the standard of the gospel.

The Epistle of James

James, the brother of Christ, is generally accepted as the author of the Epistle of James, which bears his name. There is strong evidence within the book itself to make this a reasonable conclusion. This evidence includes:

1. His name in the salutation
2. A greeting to the twelve tribes
3. The style
4. The content

The date of AD 45–50 for the writing of the Epistle of James, suggested by the textbook, is acceptable. Remember the date and the fact that this early date is chosen on the basis of the content of the book. You will see this argument in the section, "The Epistle of James" in your textbook. Incidentally, this is not really the kind of proof upon which one can make a dogmatic conclusion.

10 What does Tenney present as the basis for accepting James as the author?

....

....

11 The description of James' personality, beliefs, and ministry depicts him as rather legalistic. Do you think this is a fair portrait of James when you consider his speech in the Jerusalem Council and read his Epistle? Give a reason for your answer.

....

....

12 How does the purpose and content of James compare with the standard of the gospel that you studied in the textbook? Use your notebook.

As I said earlier, if you learn this standard of the gospel, it will help you immensely in interpreting the New Testament for your own life and ministry. Now, turn again to page 153 and review this paragraph in order to compare it with James.

If you are familiar with what Martin Luther thought about the Epistle of James and the Epistle to the Galatians, compare it to the way Tenney explains the relationship of the two Epistles in your readings for this section of the textbook.

Objective *Explain how the Epistles of Galatians and James complement each other.*

The Epistle to the Galatians

The Epistle to the Galatians is a product of the controversy over law and grace, and it was written at approximately the same time as its counterpart, the Epistle of James. Tenney does a fine job of reconciling these two Epistles and the two great men, James and Paul. The textbook sees the principles of these two Epistles as supplementary, not contradictory, and this is an important point of interpretation for you to remember. Read the first paragraph under this section very carefully several times in order to get the viewpoints of James and Paul firmly fixed in your mind.

How we date the writing of Galatians depends on two theories about the territory that actually made up the Galatia to which the Epistle was written. Read through these two theories in the textbook. They are usually referred to as the *North Galatian Theory* and the *South Galatian Theory.* Use the map in chapter 13 of the textbook to get the geographical extent of each theory in focus.

I agree with the textbook in the choice of the South Galatian theory as most likely denoting the group of churches to which Paul wrote the Epistle. If you agree with this choice, you will accept AD 48 or 49 as the date of the writing of the Epistle to the Galatians, and Antioch as the place from which it was most likely written.

justification
acceptance of those who respond in wholehearted faith to God as revealed in Jesus Christ; His regard of them as free from sin, as righteous, and as reconciled with Him

From even a casual reading of the Epistle to the Galatians, it is easy to discover that Paul's purpose in writing was to promote the doctrine of justification* by faith. This doctrine was intended to be a check on the doctrine of justification by works of the Law, which was being taught to the Galatian converts by a group of Judaizers.

As you read the sections on "Content" and "Outline", you will see how skillfully and tenaciously* Paul works this purpose out in his Epistle. Since Tenney's outline of the content of Galatians is so faithful and so beautiful, most preachers or teachers would find it a delight to follow for a series of Bible studies with a congregation. You might prayerfully consider doing this at some time. Every congregation needs to have the persistent trends toward legalism* pushed back and justification by faith emphasized periodically. The Epistle to the Galatians also includes many other related truths, which need to be read, lived, preached, and taught.

Under the heading "Evaluation", the author approaches the correlation of the themes of James and Galatians again. However, this time he does so from a different angle.

13 Write briefly how the two Epistles complement each other, either in the words of the textbook, or in your own words. Use your notebook.

As chapter 15 closes, we can summarize its topic, "The Gentile Church and the Pauline Mission," by saying this:

1. The universality of the gospel was recognized.

2. The doctrine of justification by faith without works was accepted.

3. The expectation that ethical living would be the fruit of faith was advanced.

The Pauline Program
📖 Reading 2

This chapter of the textbook opens with Paul and Barnabas returning to Antioch where they taught and preached for a considerable length of time with many associates.

While in Antioch Paul suggested another mission to Barnabas. The first mission to Asia Minor was evangelistic, but Paul introduces a new missionary policy on this second mission. According to the textbook, Paul felt that "Evangelization should be followed by consolidation . . . of the converts."

14 What were the two means Paul proposed to accomplish this consolidation?

....

Watch for evidence of the activities denoted by these two words as you study the second mission to Asia Minor.

Prior to beginning the second mission to Asia Minor, Paul and Barnabas disagreed over whether or not to take John Mark. You will recall that Mark had refused to go on the first mission to Asia Minor. Are you inclined to agree with Paul, or with Barnabas, in the dispute? Do you think they were both wrong? Do you think they were both right?

15 What position does Tenney take relative to the disagreement between Paul and Barnabas?

....

tenaciously
tending to adhere or cling to; holding fast

legalism
practices, deeds, observances, principles, or characteristics of a code such as the Law or oral law of Judaism

Objective 9.6 *Identify the results of Paul's second mission to Asia Minor and his mission to Macedonia.*

Second Mission to Asia Minor

Barnabas and Mark started their itinerary in Cyprus. Paul, with his new associate, Silas, started through Syria and Cilicia. Locate these places on the map in chapter 13 of the textbook. This is a good point at which to spend some time with the map. I think that if you trace each of Paul's missionary journeys you will be convinced that he traveled a great deal by the standards of his day. His journey to Rome measured approximately 1400 miles (2240 kilometers) in a straight line and 2000 miles (3200 kilometers) by the sea route that he traveled from Jerusalem.

On his second mission to Asia Minor, Paul met and added Timothy to his team. Learn as much as you can from the textbook and Bible about Timothy's background and personality. You will meet him often in the rest of the New Testament.

By adding Timothy to the team, Paul added a new problem. Are you surprised that the Paul who wrote the strong Epistle to the Galatians against the Judaizers, and who reprimanded Peter for his momentary defection into a Judaistic attitude, would concede to having Timothy circumcised?

Mission to Macedonia

Following the second mission to Asia Minor, which included a visit to Galatia, Paul made his way up to Troas. There, he waited for an indication of the direction he should go. The textbook identifies two important events that occurred at Troas:

1. The Holy Spirit called Paul in a vision to go into Macedonia.

2. Luke, the writer of the account, joined Paul's company for the crusade in Macedonian Philippi.

It seems that in every section we discover something new or outstanding in the history of the church. In this section Paul made the momentous decision to go across the Aegean Sea from Troas into Macedonia, and in so doing, he took the gospel into Europe. As a result, the gospel made a tremendous impact upon western civilization. Let us look at the unusual series of events that gave the gospel its start in Europe.

1. The Holy Spirit had closed all doors in Asia and Asia Minor to Paul (for the present), and this was unusual.

2. The Holy Spirit impressed Paul in a vision to go to Macedonia.

3. Paul's first gospel service in Europe was a small prayer meeting on a river bank in Philippi.

4. Paul then moved the gospel services to the house of a woman (Lydia, a convert whose home was Thyatira in Asia).

5. Paul cast a demon out of a young woman (a clairvoyant* who earned money for her masters).

6. Paul and Silas held their next gospel service in the Philippian jail because the young woman's masters brought charges against them.

clairvoyant
person professing to have insight into what is distant, hidden, or beyond moral perception

7. The jailer and his household were converted through the ministry of Paul and Silas and their miraculous deliverance from jail.

8. A strong church developed in Philippi. (You will see this when you study Paul's Epistle to the Philippians.)

It is interesting to note that, according to the textbook, Luke stayed in Philippi while Paul went on to Thessalonica. Thus, Luke is credited with contributing to the growth of the Philippian church by serving as its pastor. It is also possible that he served as an evangelist throughout Macedonia. If this is so, we have Luke as the physician, the historian, the pastor, and the evangelist!

In Thessalonica, Paul preached in the Jewish synagogue for three weeks and managed to create a sharp division of opinion. Out of such a short and stormy presentation of the gospel, a strong Christian church developed in Thessalonica.

16 What did he preach that produced such a great, favorable response among the proselyte Greeks, caused some Jews to believe, and caused other Jews to make him flee from the city by night?

....

....

Thus, Paul and his company fled from Thessalonica to Berea. You will find Berea a few miles inland from Thessalonica. Paul's initial reception in Berea was cordial, and he gained converts until a delegation of Jews intervened.

17 Read the textbook and answer these questions.
a Where was the delegation from?

....

b Why do you think they would want to follow after Paul?

....

c What did they do to Paul?

....

d Where did Paul go from Berea?

....

Thessalonian Letters

Paul's ministry in Macedonia was attended with much violence, but it was highly productive for the cause of Christ. As we have observed, strong congregations of Christians developed both at Philippi and at Thessalonica; consequently, both of these congregations were later to be recipients of Epistles from Paul. We will consider the two Epistles to the Thessalonians at this point because of their relation to our discussion about the church at Thessalonica. Then, we can better understand the Epistles against this background.

Because of Jewish opposition in Thessalonica, Paul had gone to Berea; however, the Jews followed him there. As a result, the believers sent him to Athens to escape them. Some time later, Timothy brought news to Paul in Athens about the persecutions and temptations of the believers in Macedonia. This prompted Paul to send Timothy back to Macedonia to encourage the people and to get the latest news from them. Then Paul went on to Corinth.

18 Circle the letter preceding each TRUE statement concerning Paul's second mission to Asia Minor and his mission to Macedonia.

a Timothy's circumcision indicated that Paul was repudiating the principle that Gentiles need not submit to the Law.

b Two important events occurred at Troas: 1) the call to Europe, and 2) Luke joined the missionary party.

c Paul's first service in Europe took place in the Philippian synagogue.

d We can conclude that the strong church in Philippi was partly the result of effective leadership by Luke.

e Paul ministered in Thessalonica for about three weeks before he was forced to flee by night to Berea.

f The Jews in Berea were characterized by openness and honesty in their response to Paul's gospel message.

g Paul was forced to leave Berea because of opposition; therefore, he took Silas and Timothy with him to Athens.

Objective 9.7 *Identify the purpose and major doctrine of 1 and 2 Thessalonians.*

First Thessalonians

During his stay in Corinth Paul wrote 1 Thessalonians. Many Bible scholars place the writing of 1 Thessalonians first among the Pauline Epistles. Because of the date that we have accepted for Galatians (on the basis of the South Galatian theory), we would place 1 Thessalonians next after the writing of Galatians. Our time sequence would have Paul in Corinth in late AD 51 and early AD 52. Thus, the date of the writing of 1 Thessalonians would be late AD 51 or early AD 52. Let us take AD 51 as the date to remember.

The purpose for writing this letter is pastoral. Paul was unable to visit the church, and the report that Timothy brought indicated that the people needed pastoral encouragement and advice. Therefore, Paul wrote to assure them of his love and to encourage them to trust God as they faced persecutions and temptations. He also wrote to correct some doctrinal errors, to strengthen other doctrines, and to encourage growth in Christian ethics. You will discover that Paul's main doctrinal theme is the return of Christ.

19 Use your textbook and Bible to answer the following questions about apostolic preaching on the second coming of Christ. Write your answers in your notebook.

a Which apostle first mentioned the second coming of Christ?

b Which apostles mentioned the doctrine of the Second Coming?

c In what way are their statements about the Second Coming similar?

d In what ways do their statements differ?

e What does Paul say about the second coming of Christ in 1 and 2 Thessalonians?

Paul has a lot to say in these letters about the second coming of Christ and about related themes. Try to make an outline of Paul's doctrine of the second coming of Christ as it appears in these two Epistles. You will benefit by taking time to do this now.

At your earliest opportunity, after finishing the course, you may want to expand your outline into a full study of the doctrine of the second coming of Christ as it appears in the Bible. This is a major New Testament doctrine, and your ministry should include frequent teaching and preaching on this and related subjects. Just to give you an idea of the extent of the doctrine of the second coming of Christ in the New Testament, consider these facts:

1. Water baptism is mentioned 19 times in 7 Epistles and not at all in the other 14 Epistles.

2. The Lord's Supper is mentioned only 5 times in the whole New Testament. Only one of the 21 Epistles mentions it.

3. The doctrine of the second coming of Christ is mentioned 318 times in the New Testament. It is mentioned in every New Testament book except the small personal letters of Philemon and 3 John. And even the writers of these two letters often mention the doctrine elsewhere in their writings.

We will consider the content of 1 Thessalonians further when we study 2 Thessalonians.

Second Thessalonians

The second Epistle of Paul to the Thessalonian congregation was also written during the apostle's stay in Corinth.

Since we have concluded that 1 Thessalonians was written in late AD 51 and since it is generally held that the second Epistle was written a few months later the best date for the writing of 2 Thessalonians is early AD 52.

The purpose for the writing of 2 Thessalonians is basically the same as that of the first Epistle.

Once again the main doctrinal theme is the Second Coming.

In the section under the heading "Evaluation," the author makes a very important point with respect to the content of apostolic preaching and teaching. The more liberal Bible scholars are generally inclined to accept a long evolutionary growth of doctrine in the New Testament. This is based upon the idea of the theological maturation of the churches and writers. It is also based upon the rise of various problems within the Christian community.

Tenney supports a more conservative point of view. This view maintains that doctrine was given by divine inspiration. In other words, doctrine did not grow out of a deeper spiritual understanding on the part of those in the church or out of needs arising from problems in the church. I believe his point of view is indicated by three elements of evidence in the Thessalonian correspondence:

1. Paul refers to a *tradition,* a body of carefully formulated teaching which was *delivered.* (Underscore in your textbook at least five features of this tradition.)

2. Almost every doctrine of Christianity is introduced in these two brief Epistles.

3. These two Epistles were written at an early date.

Thus, it seems clear that: (1) if there were an identifiable body of teaching, (2) if this teaching included the majority of the Christian doctrines, (3) if these doctrines were introduced early in the history of the church, then it is true that this tradition was *delivered* at a certain point (by divine inspiration), and did not slowly *evolve* to that point.

Tenney's observation that "practically every major doctrine in the catalogue of faith is represented in these two small Epistles" is most significant. I would suggest that, as an exercise for learning the content of these two Epistles, you outline the doctrines that are summarized in this section of the textbook. This outline, when expanded by additional study, will give you some excellent material to use in teaching and preaching.

There is one additional point that you should know relative to the doctrine of the second coming of the Lord as it appears in 1 and 2 Thessalonians. There are actually two aspects of Christ's second coming given in these two Epistles (and in other parts of the New Testament). It is essential to know this and to be able to tell which aspect is being spoken of in a given passage.

These two aspects are commonly referred to as the *Rapture* and the *Revelation.*

The *Rapture* (1 Thessalonians 4:13–18) is the *parousia,* the *coming* of Christ in the *air* to catch away or *rapture* His church.

The *Revelation* (2 Thessalonians 2:2–12) is the *apocalypsis* (2 Thessalonians 1:7), the *revelation,* the *coming* of Christ to the *earth* to execute judgment upon the wicked world.

Second Thessalonians 2:6–7, which concerns the identity of the *hinderer,* is somewhat difficult to understand. These verses refer to "the one who now holds it back . . ." (referring to the secret power of lawlessness). Some have suggested that the influence which prevents the coming of the Antichrist "the man of lawlessness" (2 Thessalonians 2:3), "the lawless one" (2 Thessalonians 2:8) is government (as a principle or a particular government). Others teach that the restraining influence is the Holy Spirit. Still others believe that "the one who now holds back" refers to the Holy Spirit working through the church. In their view, the Holy Spirit hinders the revelation of "the man of lawlessness" until the church is raptured. Then, His restraining influence will be removed, the Antichrist will be revealed and then Christ will come at the *revelation* to execute judgment and consummate his redemptive program.

20 Circle the letter preceding each TRUE statement concerning the purpose and major doctrine of 1 and 2 Thessalonians.

    a The purpose of these two Epistles is primarily the same: it is pastoral and concerns admonitions, comfort, and the reiteration of sound doctrine.

    b The major doctrine Paul addresses in these letters is the second coming of Christ.

    c The discussion on the "hinderer" indicates clearly that the issues surrounding the Second Coming are fairly straightforward and easy to understand.

    d The discussion in the textbook about end-time events suggests that ultimately there will be a confrontation between the forces of Antichrist and Christ in which Christ will triumph.

Objective **9.8**

Describe the culture of Corinth at the time of Paul's mission in that city, and state Paul's decision there concerning the synagogue.

Mission to Achaia

You see in this section that the people of Athens reacted differently to Paul's ministry than they had reacted elsewhere in his career. However, the gospel received much the same response in Athens as it has received in some other learned societies down through history, including some societies in our day.

21 Study the culture of Athens, Paul's sermon on Mars' Hill, and the responses of the people. Then compare them with your knowledge of similar cultures today, the message being preached, and the response being given. Use your notebook for your answer.
   a How are they alike?
   b How are they different?

Paul went from Athens to Corinth and found that the cultural difference was far greater than the miles that separated them.

22 Make a study of the culture of Corinth and, in your notebook, describe the main traits of each aspect of the culture listed below.
   a Commercial character
   b Political character
   c Racial and ethnic character
   d Economic character
   e Moral character

Paul's ministry in Corinth at this time did not seem to gain a wide acceptance for the gospel. Yet we know from the Corinthian correspondence, which we will study in the next lesson, that he established an impressive church there.

23 Get acquainted with the personalities who were associated with Paul in Corinth. Identify them by their names and activities. Use your notebook.

24 Paul announced a new decision concerning the synagogue while he was in Corinth. What was it?

....

....

Trace Paul's route from Corinth to Antioch and then to Ephesus on the map in chapter 13 of your textbook.

Objective **9.9**

Explain how Paul solved two important problems at Ephesus.

Mission to Asia

25 In Ephesus Paul found a city with several assets that made it a key city for the evangelization of Asia. Mark these assets in your textbook and list them in your notebook so you can get an impression of Ephesus.

You will want to be sure to remember that Paul's ministry was very effective in Ephesus and that the church which he established there was for centuries a key Christian center for that part of the world.

26 The textbook indicates that Paul encountered two important problems in Ephesus. In your notebook, assess the problems according to the guidelines provided below.

Paul's Problems in Ephesus
a (1) Problem
    (2) Solution
    (3) Results
    (4) Persons Involved
b (1) Problem
    (2) Solution
    (3) Results
    (4) Persons Involved

Golden Passages

There are several special passages in Acts 11:19–21:16, James, Galatians, and 1 and 2 Thessalonians that will greatly enrich your life and ministry. You should become familiar with their content and be able to locate them by memory or with a concordance. These *golden passages* are:

1. Paul's sermon on Mars' Hill	Acts 17:22–32
2. Baptism of the Ephesians in the Holy Spirit	Acts 19:1–6
3. Paul's testimony to dedication and faithfulness	Acts 20:17–35
4. Being doers of the Word	James 1:22–25
5. The evidence of pure religion	James 1:27
6. The bridled tongue: a sign of perfection	James 3:2–18
7. Effectual prayer for sicknesses	James 5:13–16
8. The Christian life as identity with Christ	Galatians 2:20
9. Justification by faith, not by law	Galatians 3:10–13
10. Christian equity	Galatians 3:28
11. Redemption from servanthood to sonship by Christ	Galatians 4:4–7
12. The Fruit of the Spirit	Galatians 5:22–23
13. The dominion of the cross	Galatians 6:14
14. The promise of the Rapture as comfort	1 Thessalonians 4:13–18
15. Exhortation to be spiritually vigilant	1 Thessalonians 5:1–11

Total Time
(Read, answer questions, check answers)

Hr_____ Min_____

Start Time

_____

Self-Test 9

Matching. Match the subjects (right) with the description of each (left).

.... **1** Written to discourage license in the use of ethical freedom

.... **2** Written in early AD 52

.... **3** Allows for an earlier date for the writing of Galatians

.... **4** Where Paul was when he received the call to Macedonia

.... **5** The second of Paul's writings

.... **6** Written to show that justification could not come by keeping a set of ethical principles

a) Galatians
b) South Galatian Theory
c) 1 Thessalonians
d) 2 Thessalonians
e) Troas
f) James
g) North Galatian Theory

True-False. Write T in the blank preceding each statement that is TRUE. Write F if it is FALSE.

.... **7** Cypriot believers departed from the general procedure by preaching to Greek Gentiles in Antioch.

.... **8** The key cities in early church evangelism were often small and primitive.

.... **9** The church at Antioch was the mother of Gentile churches.

.... **10** The Jerusalem church was the strongest Christian evangelistic center for the first five centuries.

.... **11** John Mark withdrew from Paul's company enroute to the first mission to Asia Minor.

.... **12** John Mark made the second mission to Asia Minor with Paul.

.... **13** Paul's message in the synagogue clearly included justification by faith.

.... **14** The first mission to Asia Minor brought Barnabas to prominence as leader of the missionary team.

.... **15** The church at Antioch brought into effect the Jerusalem Council by sending delegates to discuss some issues with the elders.

.... **16** Peter's speech in the Council showed that God had given the Holy Spirit to the Gentiles without discrimination.

.... **17** James suggested that the Gentile Christians be asked to keep only the first four of the Ten Commandments.

.... **18** The Literature of Protest was written as an effort to deal with the issue of the place of the Law in the lives of Christians.

.... **19** The authorship of the Epistle of James cannot be supported on internal evidence.

. . . . **20** The Epistle to the Galatians was probably written in AD 58 or 59.

. . . . **21** Paul wrote the Epistle to the Galatians to promote the doctrine of justification by works as an antidote to the doctrine of justification by faith.

Short Answer. Write one word in each blank.

22 .... stayed as pastor in Philippi while Paul went on to Thessalonica.

23 .... refers to Christ's coming in the air for His church.

24 .... refers to Christ's coming to the earth in judgment.

25 The .... of the Spirit is named in Galatians 5:22–23.

Self-Test Time

Hr_____ Min_____

Answers to Study Questions

13 Paul and James both emphasize the law of love and ethical living. James is not in disagreement with Paul's insistence that belief in Jesus should permeate every part of life. For belief is more than intellectual assent; it includes practice.

1 **a** Troas, Ephesus, Laodicea, Colosse, Antioch of Pisidia, Iconium, Derbe, Tarsus, Antioch of Syria.
   b Troas and Ephesus.
   c To ports in the Mediterranean world by boat or by caravan toward the Euphrates, and from there to India.

14 Organization and instruction.

2 Paul.

15 The solution was the best one under the circumstances.

3 Your answer. In the absence of more information in Acts, I think Tenney is wise to suggest varied interpretations for Mark's decision.

16 He preached that Jesus was the predicted Messiah, who died and rose from the dead.

4 **a** It was the assurance of salvation by faith without the necessity of works according to Law.
   b Many people responded, the Jews opposed his message, and Paul decided to take the gospel to the Gentiles.

17 **a** Thessalonica.
   b Maybe they were doing what they thought God would want them to do, according to their background.
   c They began to attack him.
   d Athens.

5 (In any order)
   a Paul's leadership established.
   b Paul accepted on the level of the apostles.
   c Preparation of Mark for future service.
   d Paul's contact with Timothy established.
   e Beginning of theology of justification by faith.

18 Statements **b**, **d**, **e**, and **f** are true.

6 **a** The Council was necessary to determine whether Gentile Christians should be required to observe the legalistic ceremonies of Judaism.
   b If Gentiles who became Christians no longer needed to observe ceremonies of their former religions, why should they observe those of the Jews?
   c Judaizers thought that Gentile Christians should conform to the law of Moses.
   d The principal speakers were Peter and Paul.

19 a Peter.

b Paul and James.

c They all emphasize the return of Christ.

d Paul spoke about waiting for the hope. Peter said Christ must remain in heaven until the full restoration. Paul said that Christ would be the Judge of the world.

e First Thessalonians: It should not take us by surprise as a thief; we should keep awake and sober. Second Thessalonians: Three major events will precede the Lord's coming.

7 Your answer. As Tenney notes, these regulations were suggested more as a basis of fellowship than a platform of ethics. There was no attempt to decree that a rigid set of rules had to be followed for one to be saved.

20 Statements **a**, **b**, and **d** are true.

8 This is a difficult question. However, the Council in Jerusalem seems to have set a good example in wisely communicating a broad decision. Yes, a group of men or a group of churches seems to have a right to establish policy for other groups or churches; however, the policy should be biblically based, objective, and fair to those it will affect.

21 a You probably noted that they are alike in their quest for earthly wisdom and their indifference to the gospel.

b In some ways, it seems they are different primarily in point of time.

9 Your answer. The requirements given by the Council would seem reasonable for those who sincerely desired to grow spiritually.

22 a Corinth profited from monopoly of trade and two seaports.

b This city was governed by Rome as a colony.

c Corinth included peoples from every corner of the Mediterranean world.

d Both the wealthy and the very poor lived there.

e Corinth was viewed by others as a city of unusually corrupt moral standards.

10 He points out that his teaching parallels Jesus' teaching and it places heavy emphasis on ethics rather than on the nature of Christ.

23 Priscilla and Aquila were Christian Jews who left Rome when Jews were expelled from the city in the reign of Claudius. Timothy and Silas were leaders in church growth in Macedonia.

11 Rather than regarding the description as fair or unfair, I think it is incomplete. Many people have legalistic tendencies. The important point is that James, as led by the Holy Spirit, was responsive.

24 Paul decided to change his headquarters from the synagogue to the home of Titus Justus, a proselyte (convert).

12 The standard of the gospel identified on page 153 was not that of the Law but of the Heavenly Father who is perfect. Jesus' standard of righteousness is to know Him and to hear and do His sayings (Matthew 7:23–24). James, in writing about the perfect law of freedom, also stresses action. In stressing ethical living, he emphasizes conformity to Jesus' teachings, although he does not identify the precepts as coming from Jesus.

25 You may list them in any order. Ephesus was the:
    a most important city in the Roman province of Asia.
    b connecting point of routes for trade and travel on the Mediterranean Sea, Cayster River, and caravan routes to the East. Thus, geographically, Ephesus was a strategic point for evangelistic outreach.
    c outstanding center for worshipers of the goddess Diana.

26 a (1) Continuation of the teaching of John the Baptist by those without knowledge of the teaching of Jesus.
       (2) To bring believers up-to-date by teaching the baptism of the Holy Spirit.
       (3) Church in Ephesus a missionary center. Ephesian church a stronghold in Asia Minor.
       (4) Apollos, Priscilla, Aquila, disciples of John the Baptist, Paul.
    b (1) The occult.
       (2) Preaching and miracles of Paul.
       (3) Demonstration that the power of Christ is greater than the power of the occult. Christianity not syncretistic.
       (4) Jewish exorcists, Paul.

Lesson 10

Note the time you begin reading this lesson. At the end of the lesson, record in the space provided the time it took to complete each segment.

The Corinthian Correspondence

Start Time

_____

We are greatly indebted to the apostle Paul for his significant contribution to the writing of the New Testament. Three of his letters form a substantial part of New Testament teaching and doctrine. In this lesson we will consider 1 and 2 Corinthians and Romans. While each of these letters was written in response to a certain need, together they contain a rich treasure of truth for every Christian of every age.

The writings of Paul were not based on untested theories, rather they grew out of his own experiences. Because he truly sought to do God's will and keep his life free from sin, he could give wise counsel to Corinthian believers when it was necessary to deal with sin in the church. Because he had experienced the work of the Holy Spirit in his own life, he was able to give instruction to believers concerning manifestations of the Spirit in the body of Christ. Because of his own deep devotion to his Savior and his Christ-like love for his brothers and sisters in the Lord, he could speak with authority on the subject of love. And because he had known great suffering and tribulation as a preacher of the gospel, he could share in the suffering of others and teach them to rejoice in their salvation.

As ministers of the gospel, we can learn much by observing the spirit in which Paul wrote his Epistles to the church. Let us approach our own ministry with the same spirit of love, joy, and holiness that Paul manifested.

the activities...

◇ Read 1 and 2 Corinthians and Romans straight through to get an overview of the message of each. Then read the textbook assignment to help you fix the background facts in your mind. While reading the textbook, keep your Bible open and read the Scripture references in the textbook. The readings for this lesson are

    Reading 1: pages 296–301
    Reading 2: pages 296–297
    Reading 3: pages 297–301
    Reading 4: pages 301–303
    Reading 5: page 303
    Reading 6: pages 303–304

Reading 7: pages 304–307
Reading 8: pages 308–309

◇ Work through the lesson development and complete each assignment. When you have completed the lesson, review the lesson objectives again to be sure that you can fulfill them. Remember that the self-tests, unit evaluations, and final examination are based on these lesson objectives.

◇ Finally, take the self-test at the end of the lesson and check your answers.

the objectives...

10.1 Describe the contributions of Peter and Apollos to the Corinthian church.

10.2 Explain the major problems in the Corinthian church and Paul's instructions concerning these problems.

10.3 Identify six major teachings of Paul in 2 Corinthians.

10.4 Describe the fourfold purpose of Paul's Epistle to the Romans.

10.5 Identify the accomplishments of Paul's career.

the outline...

1 Background
2 The "Lost Letter"
3 1 Corinthians
4 2 Corinthians
5 The Last Visit to Corinth
6 The Projected Mission
7 The Epistle to the Romans
8 The Mission Concluded

Objective **10.1**

Describe the contributions of Peter and Apollos to the Corinthian church.

Background
📖 Reading 1

I have assigned your reading in the Bible and textbook in order to give you a general understanding of the Corinthian correspondence, of Paul's last visit to Corinth, and of his plans to go to Rome. By contrast, the lesson development is intended to help you focus your attention on the most important features of the lesson.

While the amount of material in the textbook for this lesson is smaller than that of previous lessons, the amount of material in the Bible is much larger. Moreover, the Corinthian correspondence is highly significant. For that reason, I have assigned fewer pages in the textbook so that you can give more time to the study of the Epistles themselves.

In your study of this section on the "Background" of the Corinthian correspondence, you will find it helpful to go back to your sketch of the culture of Corinth that you did in Lesson 9. This sketch was drawn from the material in the textbook. If you will review the cultural characteristics of Corinth, you will see why the Corinthian church needed to receive letters from Paul.

Paul could not visit Corinth at the height of their crisis when many of the church's problems occurred. However, it was his nature to correspond extensively with both individuals and churches. These facts reveal the need for pastoral counsel and his disposition to write shed further light on the reason for the letters.

We should keep in mind that while the New Testament Epistles were written with immediate needs in view, they were ordained and called forth by the Holy Spirit to guide believers and churches in later centuries of Christendom.

1   Write a brief description of the contributions of Apollos and Peter to the church in Corinth. We have not seen much of Apollos in our New Testament study; however, when he does appear, his contribution seems to be substantial.

   a   Peter: ....

   ....

   b   Apollos:...

   ....

   c   What kind of character sketch does the book of Acts give of Apollos? See the following Scriptures: Acts 18:24, 28; 19:1; 1 Corinthians 1:12; 3:4–6, 22; and 4:6.

   ....

   ....

The "Lost Letter"

📖 Reading 2

We have no doubt that Paul and other early Christian leaders wrote many letters that are not available to us today. This raises an important question about some of the letters of contributors to New Testament Scriptures. Some were lost; others were preserved. Some persons are inclined to wonder if some letters were lost that should have been added to the New Testament, and if some letters were added to the New Testament that should have been lost!

2   Do you think that the situation described in the last sentence is a real possibility? Give a reason for your answer.

....

....

Objective **10.2** *Explain the major problems in the Corinthian church and Paul's instructions concerning these problems.*

1 Corinthians

📖 Reading 3

The writing of 1 Corinthians occurred between the events recorded in verses 20 and 21 of Acts 19. The textbook shows that it was most likely from internal evidence written during the fall or winter near the end of Paul's stay in Ephesus. The date of AD 55 given by the textbook is an acceptable date for you to remember for the writing of 1 Corinthians.

soteriological
pertaining to the theological doctrine of salvation by divine activity

The Epistles of 1 and 2 Thessalonians are classified as *eschatological* books because they are heavily concerned with the doctrine of last things. Galatians, 1 and 2 Corinthians, and Romans are classified as *soteriological** books, because they are primarily concerned with various aspects of the doctrine of salvation through the cross of Jesus Christ. This last group includes three volumes from the Corinthian correspondence. It was written at a time in Paul's life, and in the experience of the recipients, which called forth a solid, clear statement of the place of grace in the life of the believer. Paul's encounter with Judaistic teachers, his confrontation with Peter, his own experience of grace, and the urgings of the Holy Spirit helped him to pen in these Epistles the standard that has guided Christians through the intervening centuries: liberty from law and justification by grace through faith.

The purpose for writing 1 Corinthians should have become obvious to you as you studied the culture of Corinth. The church there was surrounded by such pagan immorality that the phrase "to Corinthianize" was coined. It referred to the state people reached when they became as immoral as they could be and then seemed to degenerate a little more—to sink into the depths of immorality. Obviously, a group of converts to Christianity from this background would need much pastoral instruction in order to mature morally and spiritually. Paul wrote, therefore, for the express purpose of helping them.

In the section on "Content" you will learn that the central theme can be called "the doctrine of the cross in its social application." The paragraph ends with an observation about the relevance of the content of 1 Corinthians today. As you study the content, watch for those truths that you feel are especially relevant in your community today.

3 Tenney points out that this Epistle is more varied in two ways than all the other Epistles of Paul. What are these two ways? Use your notebook.

The variety of literary styles that are identified by the textbook certainly makes the book sound interesting.

The outline of the content of 1 Corinthians, as focused on these two items mentioned by Paul in the book, is quite natural and makes the study of this Epistle easy.

Look at Divisions II and III of Tenney's outline on page 298 and you will see what I mean. Notice, also, that Paul furnishes a natural and easy division of the topic *Reply to Questions in Letter* by the repetition of a certain word at the beginning of each subdivision.

4 Under the heading "Evaluation," Tenney notes that Paul's spirituality is observable in the fact that he proposes spiritual solutions rather than psychological manipulations. Take a few moments to fill in the chart below as you refer to the first paragraph under "Evaluation." Enter in Column 2 the solutions proposed by Paul to the problems listed in Column 1. Then enter in Column 3 the manipulations or responses that an unspiritual person might propose.

Coping with Problems of the Corinthian Church		
Church Problems	*Solutions Proposed by Paul*	*Unspiritual Responses*
a Schism		
b Fornication		
c Litigation		
d Marriage of an unbeliever and a believer		
e Unmarried virgins		
f Eating food that was offered to idols		
g Spiritual gifts		

Which type of solution are you most inclined to propose for similar problems when you encounter them in your ministry? Give this serious thought.

We observed earlier that 1 Corinthians contains a greater variety of subjects than any of Paul's other Epistles. Each chapter teaches one or more vital truths as the following list of subjects will show.

1. The conflict of the cross with human wisdom	1:17–31
2. Spiritual truths spiritually revealed	2:1–16
3. Two kinds of ministry and their results	3:10–23
4. Judgment of Christians: not by men but by Christ	4:1–5
5. The necessity of discipline of sinful members	5:1–13
6. Relationship of Christians to civil courts of law	6:1–8
7. Instructions concerning marriage and domestic relations	7:1–40
8. Christian liberty	8:1–13
9. Ministerial support	9:7–18
10. The divine/human relationship and the husband/wife relationship	11:1–15
11. The conscience in relation to law and liberty	10:23–33

12. Instructions concerning the Lord's Supper	10:16–22; 11:17–34
13. Spiritual gifts in the body of Christ	12:1–31
14. Spiritual gifts to be exercised through the motive of love	13:1–13
15. Spiritual gifts: their use and regulation	14:1–40
16. Christ's resurrection attested, explained; ours promised	15:1–58

As you read these passages of Scripture, think about the truths they teach. In view of our understanding of human need and the ministry, you can really appreciate 1 Corinthians. Study these truths as much as you can now. At your earliest convenience, after you have finished the course, come back to them for extensive study. They are vital to your own spiritual experience and to your ministry. Let me just make a few applications to show you what I mean.

In view of the current worldwide increase in divorce, should we not consider what Paul has to say about marriage and domestic relationships?

In view of the historic rebellion of humanity against the headship of Christ and the current questions concerning husband/wife relationships, should we not consider what Paul has to say about the divine/human relationship and the husband/wife relationship in chapter 10?

In view of the importance of the Lord's Supper to Christian worship, should we not consider what Paul has to say about this ordinance of the church as much as possible? Paul's instructions on the Lord's Supper in chapters 10 and 11 are more complete than any others in the New Testament.

In view of the historical importance of spiritual gifts in the church and the current worldwide outpouring of the Holy Spirit, should we not be prepared to give instructions about the proper exercise of spiritual gifts? Paul's trio of chapters (12, 13, and 14) is the most elaborate treatment of this subject in the New Testament.

Such applications could be made extensively, but those given should be sufficient to impress you with the richness and relevance of the subjects in 1 Corinthians. They should encourage you to come back to this book again and again for your own edification and for the benefit of those to whom you minister.

Before leaving the study of 1 Corinthians, you will want to read about Paul's efforts to quiet the turmoil in Corinth. He attempted first to send Apollos, but he declined to go; therefore, Paul sent Timothy, but he failed to accomplish the desired results. Finally, Paul went to Corinth himself (at least the textbook builds a good case that he did) and was badly insulted. In spite of this, the apostle did not give up. Instead, he determined to write another letter.

5 Now to summarize this section, read the statements below and circle the letter preceding each TRUE statement based on the textbook.

   a The Epistle of 1 Corinthians is really the second letter Paul wrote to the church at Corinth.

   b The Epistle was probably written about AD 55, while Paul was in Ephesus.

   c There is not really a major theme in 1 Corinthians, because it covers such a wide variety of subjects.

   d Paul's letter to the Corinthians was in response to questions they asked him.

   e Paul used spiritual principles to solve problems in the church.

   f When Timothy took Paul's letter to the Corinthian church, there was an immediate revival and the problems were solved.

   g Later Titus reported to Paul that the Corinthian church had experienced revival and a changed attitude.

 *Identify six major teachings of Paul in 2 Corinthians.*

2 Corinthians

📖 Reading 4

Titus brought Paul the news that revival had broken in the Corinthian church. He also indicated that the Corinthian believers had the penitent and humble attitude which Paul had called for in his first letter and had sought on his visit with them. So, when he received this good news, Paul wrote 2 Corinthians.

You will discover by reading the last paragraph just prior to the section, "2 Corinthians," that Paul's purpose in writing 2 Corinthians was to prepare Corinthian believers for his next visit by

   1. defending himself against attacks on his person, character, and teaching.

   2. asking them to prepare an offering for him to take to the Jerusalem assembly.

6 Who was involved in these attacks against Paul?

....

....

Second Corinthians was written a few months after 1 Corinthians. If 1 Corinthians was written in the fall or winter of AD 55, 2 Corinthians was probably written early in AD 56 in Macedonia. Both 1 and 2 Corinthians were written on the third missionary journey during the itinerary described in Acts 20:1–5.

As you read the short paragraph in the textbook under the heading "Content," you will learn that the style and content of this Epistle is much different from the first. In 2 Corinthians Paul reveals deeply personal things about himself that he does not mention anywhere else in his writings.

You can readily see from the outline of 2 Corinthians that Paul's defense of the ministry dominates the book. In fact, this is the longest discourse on the ministry in the New Testament. It abounds with vital instructions for all Christian ministers.

What parts of these instructions on the ministry have been the most instructive and inspiring to you? It is a great encouragement to me to know that even though Paul encountered much opposition and endured much suffering, he did not let anything defeat him. He always triumphed through Christ. Read 2 Corinthians 2:14 and 2 Corinthians 4:7–18 for examples of Paul's victorious attitude.

In the section under the heading "Evaluation," we can consider several values of 2 Corinthians. One of the greatest values of the book is that it gives an insight into the life of Paul. And while the textbook does not do so, I would point out that the Epistle affords an insight into the sufficiency of God's grace as well. No matter how great the demands were upon the apostle's life, he shows us that God's grace is sufficient. It is wonderful to know that we cannot exhaust God's supply of grace.

A second value of this Epistle is that it informs us "that the church of the apostolic age had its struggles and its sins." Tenney shows God's provision for the church as he says, "Only a divine dynamic could have given enduring vitality to so weak and sensual a group as the Corinthian church."

7 A third value of 2 Corinthians is its positive teaching. Identify three valuable subjects that, according to the textbook, are taught by this Epistle.

....

8 Now turn to the Epistle itself and choose three other teachings that you consider to be very important. Give one reference for each teaching. Example: In the context of the Epistle's instruction concerning separation *from* sin and *unto* holiness, we read, ". . . let us strive for perfection out of reverence for God" (2 Corinthians 6:147:1).

a ....

b ....

c ....

The Last Visit to Corinth
📖 Reading 5

Upon receiving good news from the assembly at Corinth through Titus, Paul starts on his journey to visit Corinthian believers. Luke mentions this three-month itinerary in Greece in Acts 20:3.

The indication is that Luke joined Paul during the three-month stay in Achaia and was his most faithful companion during the subsequent years of imprisonment. Tenney demonstrates how much a careful reading of the Scriptures can reveal. From the renewed use of *we* and *us* in Acts 20:5–6, Tenney concludes that Luke, the writer, has become a part of the action with Paul again.

The Projected Mission

📖 Reading 6

Never (with the exception of Jesus' determined movement toward Jerusalem and the cross) did a man move more resolutely towards a goal than did Paul on his long journey to Rome (Acts 19:21). You will sense this strongly as you study "The Mission Concluded." In the meantime, we will study Paul's Epistle to the Romans. This Epistle was a major part of his preparation for his mission to Rome.

Objective 10.4 *Describe the fourfold purpose of Paul's Epistle to the Romans.*

The Epistle to the Romans

📖 Reading 7

This Epistle was dispatched to the believers in Rome just before Paul boarded ship for Troas on the first leg of his journey to Rome. Read the evidence from the Epistle that the textbook refers to in support of this idea.

9 As background material to help you understand the purpose of this Epistle and Paul's interest in going to Rome, read this section of the textbook and answer these questions.

   a Who were Paul's friends in Rome?...

   b Where did they come from?...

   c Why were they in Rome?...

Read the various theories about who began the church in Rome, who its leaders were, who was in its membership, and the racial or ethnic makeup of the congregation.

10 The textbook mentions at least five reasons why Paul wanted to go to Rome.

   a What would you say was the major reason?...

   b What were the other reasons? ....

I agree with the traditional view offered by the textbook that the book of Romans was written in Corinth during Paul's three-month stay there. If this is the case, the Epistle was penned in AD 56 very close to the time of the writing of 2 Corinthians.

I believe Paul's purpose for writing Romans was at least fourfold. The first reason is given by the textbook and the second is implied. The four reasons are:

1. To prepare the believers in Rome for his visit.

2. To give the Roman believers sound doctrinal teaching to help them mature spiritually.

3. To write his own statement of belief, his own system of theology, his own credo.*

credo
strongly held belief, system
of tenets to guide action

— In each of his previous writings he had been pressed to deal with problems, issues, and personal things in such a way that he could not give a full, well-rounded statement of his theology.
— Now he stands at the peak of his career.
— He has fought and won many theological battles.
— He has led the pristine* church through many crises and has seen victory.
— He has been involved in many severe struggles against his character, apostleship, and ministry; he has come out the victor.
— At last the time is ripe for him to write a comprehensive statement of his (and the church's) theology.

4. To write a statement of Christian tenets that could be used to gain official recognition for Christianity by the Roman government.
— No doubt Paul felt that he would have the opportunity to present Christianity to the Roman officials, and if he could gain recognition for Christianity among the other religions that were officially recognized, the persecution of Christians would then become illegal.
— I believe also that Paul had a witness of the Holy Spirit that he would eventually be hailed before Roman tribunals.
— This Epistle would then serve him as an attorney's *brief* in court; it would become the outline or summary of his defense.

Under the heading "Content," Tenney identifies the central theme of Romans as "the revelation of the righteousness of God to man, and its application to his spiritual need." This is a good statement of the main theme of Romans, and you should keep it in mind as you study the content of this great Epistle.

The textbook gives a fine outline of the book of Romans. It is faithful to the contents of Romans, and it is precise and clear. The book of Romans is so full of positive and vital theological truths that I will not take the space in this study to list them separately. For this course, it will be sufficient to study them by following Tenney's outline of the book. Read the ones that are of greatest interest to you, and the ones that are most unfamiliar to you in the book of Romans. Make a few notations on each of the subjects that you study in this manner.

For every New Testament book we have studied thus far, I have recommended that you come back, later, for deeper study at your earliest opportunity. And this is as it should be, for you are only being *introduced* to the New Testament in this course. You may spend a lifetime studying the Bible and never learn it all. But no matter how much you study it, the book of Romans will ever be edifying and inspiring to you and to those to whom you minister.

In this section under the heading "Evaluation" of the book of Romans, Tenney mentions a value that is rarely noticed by Bible scholars. He indicates the vast contribution that Romans makes to the vocabulary of Christian theology through *technical terms* such as *justification, imputation,* * *adoption,* * and *sanctification.* *

Other values of Romans can be gleaned from the textbook. What do you think of the last value of Romans mentioned in the reading? Tenney says, "Romans is a superb example of the integration of doctrine with missionary purpose." Many ministers have to guard against the tendency to become "ivory

---

pristine
extremely pure, unspoiled, relating to the earliest condition

imputation
act by which God ascribes Christ's righteousness to those who believe He paid the penalty for their sin, so that they are justified

adoption
action of God in taking a person into a new relationship with Him as His child and heir with Christ, when the person is saved

sanctification
experience of the Christian believer by which he is freed from sin and enabled by the Holy Spirit to realize the will of God in his life, and to share God's love as a redeemed person who is entirely acceptable to God

tower" theologians, isolating themselves from the problems of everyday life. Paul shows us how to relate the theoretical and the practical aspects of Christianity effectively by applying them in Christian service.

11 When Paul says in Romans that there is no distinction between Jew and Greek, he is saying that salvation is
a) universal, or available for all.
b) limited to Jews and Greeks.
c) available for all who are willing to obey the Law.
d) difficult for any man to find.

12 Paul is saying that righteousness must be accepted by faith because
a) God has chosen those He wants to be saved.
b) the redeemed man cannot live a righteous life.
c) the sinner cannot earn his salvation.
d) only the Jews could earn their salvation.

13 The redeemed person wants to live a righteous life because he
a) does not want other Christians to judge him.
b) feels a sense of debt to Christ who made his salvation possible.
c) is never tempted to do anything else.
d) will offend Jews if he does not.

Objective **10.5**   *Identify the accomplishments of Paul's career.*

The Mission Concluded
📖 Reading 8

Read this section to learn Paul's itinerary enroute to Jerusalem. The statements in the last paragraph make a good summary of the accomplishments of Paul's career. I am listing these statements briefly so that you can learn them more easily.

1. In a little less than a decade he had gained freedom for believers from the bondage of legalism.

2. He had established a chain of churches in key cities from Antioch of Syria to Illyricum.

3. He had chosen and trained ministers such as Luke, Timothy, Titus, Silas, and Aristarchus who were capable of maintaining and extending the work of Christ.

4. He had gotten far along in the writing of a body of literature that was already regarded as a standard for faith and practice—and would continue to be the standard of the church through the following centuries.

5. In his preaching he had laid the groundwork for future Christian theology and apologetics.

6. By his plans, he established a pattern of evangelism and missionary policy, Which would enable the church to fulfill the commission of Christ to take the gospel to all nations.

14 Match the accomplishment of Paul (left) to the time, place, persons, or events (right).

.... **a** Trained these capable ministers to maintain the work

.... **b** Gained freedom from legalism for believers

.... **c** Laid groundwork for future Christian theology

.... **d** Established a pattern of evangelism and missionary policy

.... **e** A body of literature that was already regarded as a standard for faith and practice

.... **f** Established a chain of churches

1) Key cities from Antioch of Syria to Illyricum
2) Little less than a decade
3) Luke, Timothy, Titus, Silas and Aristarchus
4) Barnabas, Mark, Secundus, Demas, and Onesimus
5) Paul's plans
6) Paul's preaching
7) Paul's writings

Golden Passages

The Epistles of 1 and 2 Corinthians and Romans are so rich in devotional theological passages that it is difficult to reduce the list to a few of the most important. The following "golden passages," however, will enrich your life and ministry. You should become familiar with their content and be able to locate them by memory or with a concordance.

1. The order and meaning of the Lord's Supper — 1 Corinthians 11:23–33
2. The bequeathal and exercise of nine gifts of the Holy Spirit — 1 Corinthians 12:4–11
3. Love: the greatest motive — 1 Corinthians 13:1–13
4. Glorification of deceased and living believers at the first resurrection — 1 Corinthians 15:51–57
5. The ministry: With Christ's sufficiency — 2 Corinthians 4:1–11
6. The ministry: Its hardships and ultimate reward — 2 Corinthians 4:8–5:4
7. The ministry: Ambassadors of reconciliation — 2 Corinthians 5:17–21
8. The call to holiness and its benefits — 2 Corinthians 6:14–7:1
9. The sufficiency of God's grace — 2 Corinthians 12:9–10
10. The power of the gospel — Romans 1:14–17
11. Justification by faith — Romans 3:21–28
12. The seven results of justification — Romans 5:1–11
13. Deliverance from the power of sin symbolized by baptism — Romans 6:1–13
14. The law of the Spirit delivers from death unto life — Romans 8:1–13
15. The Spirit's witness to sonship of the believer — Romans 8:14–17
16. The Spirit: Our Advocate in groaning for ultimate redemption and in spiritual praying — Romans 8:18–27
17. God's provision for the believer and the believer's triumph through Christ — Romans 8:28–39
18. The formulas for salvation and for evangelization — Romans 10:8–17
19. The Christian's call to separation and transformation — Romans 12:1–2
20. The body concept of Christian service — Romans 12:3–8
21. Instructions with respect to the nearness of ultimate salvation — Romans 13:11–14

Total Time
(Read, answer questions, check answers)

Hr_____ Min_____

Start Time

_____

Self-Test 10

Short Answer. Briefly answer these questions in your own words.

1 Why are 1 and 2 Corinthians and Romans classified as soteriological books?

....

2 What is the standard for Christian living discussed in these Epistles?

....

3 Summarize what this standard means to you as a Christian.

....

....

4 Why did the Corinthian converts seem to have a greater need for instruction than other converts may have had?

....

5 What kind of solutions did Paul propose for the problems in Corinth?

....

6 Do you believe Paul's solution to these practical problems could be applied to similar problems today?

....

Can you think of examples in your own experience as a Christian which are similar?

....

Were the right solutions applied to these problems?

....

7 What were the two major purposes for Paul's writing of 2 Corinthians?

....

....

8 What does Paul reveal in 2 Corinthians that we do not find in any of his other writings?

....

9 Paul's defense of himself and his teachings is also a defense of the

....

10 Give three values of 2 Corinthians.

a ....

b ....

c ....

True-False. Write T in the blank preceding each statement that is TRUE concerning Paul's main purposes for writing to the Romans. Write F if it is FALSE.

. . . . **11** He wanted to prepare the converts at Rome for his forthcoming visit.

. . . . **12** He wanted to tell them about his own trials and ask for their help.

. . . . **13** He needed to deal with specific problems and issues in the church at Rome.

. . . . **14** He desired to write a complete statement concerning his belief or theology.

. . . . **15** He wanted to make a statement concerning Christian beliefs which could be suitable for presentation to the Roman government.

. . . . **16** He wanted to give the Romans some sound doctrinal teaching.

Self-Test Time

Hr_____ Min_____

Answers to Study Questions

8 Your answer. Paul's defense of the ministry includes much valuable instruction for today's minister.

1 a Peter: He probably preached in Corinth from time to time, since he apparently had converts there.

  b Apollos: Because he was educated, he attracted Jews and educated people. He knew the Old Testament Scriptures, and was convincing.

  c Your answer. It appears that Apollos was a capable and enthusiastic preacher with many converts. He was also a humble servant of Jesus Christ, not seeking glory for himself.

9 a They were Gentile Christians, including Aquila and Priscilla.

  b They came from other parts of the world, possibly from Jerusalem.

  c They probably came because they were citizens of the empire, and Rome was the capital city.

2 I do not think this is a possibility. I believe the Holy Spirit caused the writings to be preserved that He wanted to have included in the Scriptures.

10 a The evidence indicates that it was Paul's desire to make Rome another of his key cities in world evangelization.

  b The Christians in Rome needed instruction; Paul wanted to prevent Judaizers from disrupting the church; he wanted the church to support him in his trip to Spain; and he wanted to see this capital city.

3 a Range of topics (including schism, finance, church decorum, and resurrection).

  b Literary style (including exposition, narration, poetry, scolding, entreaty, sarcasm, and logic.

11 a) universal, or available for all.

4 Column 2
  a Maturity in spiritual life.
  b Church discipline, repentance, and restoration.
  c Arbitration within the Christian community.
  d Concern of the believer to save the unbeliever.
  e Self-control or marriage.
  f Decision based on relation of the believer to God.
  g God's administration.
Column 3
  a You cannot expect all to think alike.
  b Everybody is doing it.
  c There is no other way out.
  d The Bible does not mean me.
  e Let us not offend others.
  f To refuse would hurt my income.
  g It is not my place to ask for them.

12 c) the sinner cannot earn his salvation.

5 Statements **a**, **b**, **d**, **e**, and **g** are true.

13 b) feels a sense of debt to Christ who made his salvation possible.

6 These attacks were initiated by Judaizing teachers who had been following Paul for several years. The attacks were taken up by a minority of professing Christians within the Corinthian assembly.

14 **a**   3) Luke, Timothy, Titus, Silas, and Aristarchus
   b   2) Little less than a decade
   c   6) Paul's preaching
   d   5) Paul's plans
   e   7) Paul's writings
   f   1) Key cities from Antioch of Syria to Illyricum

7 The ministry, life after death, and giving.

Note the time you begin reading this lesson. At the end of the lesson, record in the space provided the time it took to complete each segment.

The Pauline Imprisonment

Start Time

_____

We have now followed the apostle Paul through the early part of his missionary activity of establishing churches and ministering to believers throughout the empire. He preached the Word fearlessly, knowing that persecution would come. So when he decided to return to Jerusalem against the wishes of his fellow-laborers, he was able to say to them, "Why are you weeping and breaking my heart? I am ready not only to be bound, but also to die in Jerusalem for the name of the Lord Jesus" (Acts 21:13).

Paul's first imprisonment was not an unproductive time. Even though chains bound him, he continued his ministry to the churches through his letters. The four Prison Epistles, which we shall study in this lesson, do not reflect a dispirited attitude of hopelessness. Instead, they are declarations of Christ's power and glory. For Paul's joy and peace were not based on outward circumstances, but on an inner relationship with Jesus Christ that transcended his earthly situation.

This attitude is reflected in the four letters Paul wrote while he was in prison. Christ is glorified through all of Paul's suffering, and the principles of forgiveness, joy, and love that are the marks of a Christian are clearly expressed.

As you continue in this study of the New Testament, I trust that its message will penetrate more and more deeply into your heart. Then, like the apostle Paul, you can experience victory through Christ in every circumstance of your life, good or bad. We can always find comfort and strength within the pages of God's Word.

the activities...

◊ Read Acts 21:17–28:31, Philemon, Ephesians, Colossians, and Philippians straight through to get an overview of the message of each. Then, read the textbook to establish a good basis for your study in the lesson development. The readings for this lesson are
> Reading 1: pages 312–329
> Reading 2: pages 313–316
> Reading 3: pages 316–318
> Reading 4: pages 318–319
> Reading 5: pages 319–321
> Reading 6: pages 321–324

Reading 7: pages 324–328
Reading 8: page 329

◇ Work through the lesson development according to your usual procedure. When you complete this lesson, review the lesson objectives carefully and then take the self-test.

◇ Review the lessons in this unit in preparation for your unit progress evaluation (UPE). Read the instruction page in your Essential Course Materials, then turn to Unit Progress Evaluation 3. When you have completed the UPE, check your answers with the answer key provided in your Essential Course Materials. Review any items you may have answered incorrectly. (Although UPE scores do not count as part of your final course grade, they indicate how well you learned the material and how well you may perform on the final examination.)

◇ If you have not already done so, make arrangements now with your enrollment office for taking the final examination.

the objectives...

11.1 *Identify the most likely reason for the content Luke chose to include in Acts 21:17–28:31.*

11.2 *Explain the sequence of events that finally led Paul to Rome.*

11.3 *Compare the characteristics of the Prison Epistles with the earlier Epistles.*

11.4 *List the elements of forgiveness found in Philemon.*

11.5 *Explain the meaning of ekklesia as used in Ephesians.*

11.6 *Identify basic differences between Ephesians and Colossians, emphasizing the purpose for which each was written.*

11.7 *Explain why Philippians is called the gospel of joy.*

11.8 *Explain the two major benefits of Paul's imprisonment.*

the outline...

1 Events in the Life of Paul and in the Church
2 Jerusalem
3 The Prison Epistles
  a Philemon
  b Ephesians
  c Colossians
  d Philippians
4 Results of the Pauline Imprisonment
5 Golden Passages

Objective **11.1**

Identify the most likely reason for the content Luke chose to include in Acts 21:17–28:31.

Events in the Life of Paul and in the Church
📖 Reading 1

Tenney says the part of Acts that is your reading assignment for this lesson "seems almost like an anticlimax." Review the reasons that cause him to feel this way and see if you agree. I am sure everyone wishes that Luke had told us the results of Paul's trial before Caesar and when and how Paul died. However, Luke chose to leave these things unanswered and concerned himself, in the last one-fourth of Acts, with "events that seemingly had no bearing upon the doctrinal or missionary advance of the church." Admittedly, Luke does slow the pace considerably between Acts 21:17–28:31. Acts had moved at such a rapid pace that the change of pace in these chapters is accentuated. Even so, Luke is faithful to his purpose of giving an accurate historical account.

Paul is moving out of the period of hectic missionary itinerary and spontaneous letter writing into a period with a more stationary ministry of conferences, meditation, and more deliberate letter writing.

1   According to Tenney in this section of the textbook, which of the following statements do you think describes Luke's reason for writing Acts 21:17–28:31?
   a) He wrote an up-to-date account about all that he knew, but he did not know the outcome of Paul's trial before Caesar at this time.
   b) He wrote only about what he really knew; consequently, he wrote only about things of which he was an eyewitness.
   c) He wrote only what he wanted Theophilus to know, because he wanted Theophilus to see that Christianity was submissive to the Roman government.
   d) Luke's personal prestige and authority was raised by being in the company of Paul on his travels.

Objective **11.2**

Explain the sequence of events that finally led Paul to Rome.

Jerusalem
📖 Reading 2

The discussion of Jerusalem in the textbook emphasizes the depth and violence of religious and racial hatred. Here the Jews from Asia, who had been harassing Paul from one city to another from Asia to Europe, finally confronted him. These Jews falsely accused Paul and mobbed him, therefore, he was arrested by the Roman guard and taken into custody in the castle (fortress) of Antonia. These soldiers were stationed in the fortress to put down disturbances in the temple.

Paul shows his bravery and determination to expose his enemies to the truth by his request to speak to the mob from the castle steps.

2 Identify and write here what he said in his speech that excited the mob to action again.

....

3 In which city was Paul first kept in protective custody for two years?

....

4 In which city was Paul then kept in protective custody for two more years?

....

5 Why do you think Paul appealed to Caesar?

....

In the last lesson I pointed out Paul's resoluteness in pursuing his mission to Rome. In this reading you will find this noteworthy statement: "In spite of the change in Paul's plans which the imprisonment effected, his sense of destiny and his faith that the purpose of God was sending him to Rome did not alter." Following this statement you will read of two spiritual experiences that, for Paul, reconfirmed that God was sending him to Rome. Can we have such positive confirmation of the will of God for our lives today? I believe that we can, if we will live and walk in the Spirit as Paul did.

Objective 11.3 *Compare the characteristics of the Prison Epistles with the earlier Epistles.*

The Prison Epistles
📖 Reading 3

These four Prison Epistles (Philemon, Ephesians, Colossians, Philippians) are classified as *christological* because they are centered on Christ. If you turn back to Reading 2, you will discover several characteristics of the four Prison Epistles that differentiate them from Paul's six earlier Epistles. In the same paragraph the nature of the assemblies to which these four Epistles were written is given. These assemblies appear to be quite different from the assemblies at Thessalonica and Corinth. From what you have learned about them, which of the following assemblies do you think you would have preferred to pastor if you had been a Christian preacher in AD 60: Jerusalem, Corinth, Thessalonica, Rome, Philippi, Colosse, or Ephesus? I think Paul would have preferred to pastor at Philippi.

Paul, not being free to minister in the assemblies, took up his pen again and wrote the four short but valuable letters that we are now considering. For the reasons given by Tenney, I believe that the Prison Epistles were written in the prison in Rome. The best date for the writing of these four Epistles is around AD 60. While the order of the writing cannot be positively established, it was most likely in this order: Philemon, Ephesians, Colossians, and Philippians.

6 In your notebook, describe four ways in which the Prison Epistles differ from Paul's earlier Epistles.

Objective  *List the elements of forgiveness found in Philemon.*

Philemon

📖 Reading 4

This brief letter, or note, was written to one of Paul's converts who was then living in Colosse. This Christian businessman, named Philemon, was a member of the assembly in Colosse to which Paul wrote the Epistle to the Colossians about the same time. Philemon is the most private of the letters of Paul, which have been preserved, and we are blessed of God to have it.

In the discussion under the heading "Background" you will find, among other information, the purpose of the writing of Philemon. Paul wrote to bring reconciliation between two of his converts. One of these was Onesimus, a slave; the other was Philemon, a slave owner.

7 Do you think Paul and early Christians should have led an active crusade against social wrongs such as slavery?

....

....

8 Should the church be involved in social and political activities today? Use your notebook.

9 Are social wrongs corrected by changing the individual, or the masses, or both?

....

....

10 How do Paul's words in Galatians 3:28 relate to his attempt to reconcile Onesimus and Philemon?

....

In the sections "Content" and "Outline," you will find the theme of Philemon. I would start the theme in this way: Forgiveness and reconciliation through Christian love . . . .

11 Under the heading "Evaluation" Tenney says, "In this letter are found all the elements of forgiveness." Six elements are given. List them here.

    a Philemon 11, 18 ....

    b Philemon 10 ....

    c Philemon 10, 18, 19 ....

    d Philemon 18, 19 ....

    e Philemon 15 ....

    f Philemon 16 ....

I venture to say that if you read Philemon again prayerfully with these six elements before you and with the needs of the people to whom you minister in mind, you will receive a helpful sermon or Bible study on forgiveness or reconciliation. Try it.

This little Epistle was no doubt of great value to Philemon and Onesimus. It must have brought the proposed forgiveness and reconciliation; otherwise, neither of them would have cared to keep the letter or to put it into circulation in the assemblies.

Tradition holds that Philemon freed Onesimus, who became bishop of Ephesus and was later martyred.

12 I will list some of the values I see in Philemon. In your notebook, add others that stand out to you.

(1) It has biographical value because it shows Paul's love and tenderness for young Christians. It also gives us insight into the personalities of Philemon and Onesimus.

(2) It has theological value since it teaches the doctrines of love and forgiveness.

(3) It has evangelistic value because it shows that God will save whosoever will come to Him through Jesus—master or slave, rich or poor, learned or unlearned, black or white, male or female.

(4) It has social value because it shows that Christianity does not attack social institutions as some religions and ideologies do. It reforms society by reforming individuals who comprise society.

Objective  *Explain the meaning of* ekklesia *as used in Ephesians.*

Ephesians

📖 Reading 5

To begin the study of the background of Ephesians, turn back to Reading 3. There you will find that some scholars have doubted the Pauline authorship of Ephesians. However, there is sufficient internal evidence in Ephesians for me to believe confidently that Paul wrote the book.

Ephesians was written from Rome around AD 60. The similarity of theme and content of Ephesians and Colossians suggest that both were written at nearly the same time. Also, the repetition of several names in Philemon, Ephesians, and Colossians indicates that the three Epistles were probably written about the same time. I think Ephesians was written between Philemon and Colossians.

encyclical
a letter intended for general circulation among several churches

I believe the theory that Ephesians was written as an *encyclical** letter is valid. Those who hold this view believe that Paul wanted to convey the same message to several assemblies in Asia. Therefore, he wrote the letter to the chief assembly—the one at Ephesus. The church there was to reproduce the letter and put on each copy the name of the assembly to which it was being sent. It is likely that this circular letter went to each of the assemblies mentioned by John in Revelation 2 and 3.

Paul's purpose in writing Ephesians, unlike that of most of Paul's other Epistles, is not to deal with a particular moral, spiritual, or doctrinal problem in a specific locale. Rather, his purpose in writing Ephesians was to show Christ's relationship to His church universal. Paul was near the end of his career; thus, at this point in his life, he had established local assemblies from Antioch to Illyricum. Moreover, he had been convinced all along that Christ was with him, through the power of the Holy Spirit, helping him in every sermon, every conflict, every conference, every mission, every Epistle, every hardship, and every victory. Now the mature apostle was looking on all of this with a panoramic view. He was seeing the great mystery of the church universal—Christ's church, not Paul's, or Apollos', or Peter's church. He wrote to each of the assemblies to tell them what he had been seeing all along but had not taken the time to tell them previously. He wrote to inform them that Christ was building His church—not a Gentile or a Jewish church, not a Catholic or a Protestant church, not a brown or a white church—but His church, His body.

The word that Paul used in Ephesians to designate the church universal is *ekklesia.* It comes from two Greek words, *ek* which means "out of" and *klesis* which means "a calling." Thus *ekklesia* means "called out ones." It can be used as Christ used it in Matthew 16:18 and as Paul used it in Ephesians 1:22; 5:23, 24 in the plural to refer to the total gathering of Christian believers from Pentecost until the first resurrection. *Ekklesia* can be used in the singular to refer to a local "congregation of called out ones" as in Acts 20:28; 1 Corinthians 1:2; Galatians 1:13; 1 Thessalonians 1:1; and 1 Timothy 3:5. It can also be used in the plural to refer to a group of local congregations in a specific area.

Christ has continued to build His church down through the centuries. In spite of the errors, problems, schisms, and apostasies—in ways mysterious to us—He is building His church. In Ephesians Paul wrote to the church universal and said that Christ is going to "present her to himself as a radiant church, without stain or wrinkle or any other blemish, but holy and blameless" (5:27).

We can sense that Christ is building His church today, can we not? As I write this course, *New Testament Survey,* I am in one of Europe's major cities with colleagues who are assembled from several continents. They are missionaries and educators who, like myself, are grateful to be involved in what Christ is doing in the world today. These friends have come from several European countries, Indonesia, South America, and North America. Each one has reported wonderful testimonies of how Christ is building His church in his part of the world. I hope you are witnessing progress in the work of the Lord through your ministry.

In the section under the heading "Content," you will discover that the main theme of Ephesians is *the church.* Study the content with this theme in mind.

The outline of the Epistle in the textbook is excellent. It should assist you as you study the content and organize it for your teaching and preaching ministry. In fact, either the main divisions or subdivisions of the outline in this book will yield a good and timely sermon or a series of sermons on the church. In these days when the church (along with many other longstanding institutions) is coming under fierce attack, we need to share what Paul says here about the church, which is often termed antiquated, irrelevant, and hypocritical. In spite of these derisive terms, however, the church that Paul describes will never fit such a description.

The value of Ephesians is that it integrates Paul's theology and ethics with the concept of *the church universal as the body of Christ.*

13 Circle the letter preceding each TRUE statement.
  a Ephesians has been called *the Epistle of the church.*
  b The dynamic of the church's life is the body of believers.
  c Ephesians leads the Christian from an understanding of the origin of his salvation to the practical application of his salvation in everyday life.
  d *Ekklesia* means "called-out ones" and refers to the universal church.
  e *Ekklesia* cannot refer both to the universal church and to individual groups of believers.
  f Most of the theology and ethical teaching in Ephesians can also be found in other New Testament Scriptures.

Objective **11.6** *Identify basic differences between Ephesians and Colossians, emphasizing the purpose for which each was written.*

Colossians

📖 Reading 6

Colossians was written from Rome around AD 60.

As you read the paragraph under the heading "Background," you will learn that Colossians is similar enough in content to be called the twin of Ephesians; yet, it still retains a basic difference. Both Epistles have as their theme *Christ and the church,* however, Ephesians focuses its attention on the church and Colossians focuses its attention on Christ. Thus, we could say that in Ephesians it is the church and Christ, and in Colossians it is Christ and the church.

Another difference between Ephesians and Colossians is that the former was written to the church universal without regard to a special problem, and the latter was written to a local assembly to address a specific problem. In reality the problem was twofold. While most members of the Colossian assembly were Gentiles, they were being led by some Jewish Christians into what is called the "Colossian Heresy." As you gathered from reading the textbook, this heresy was a strange combination of Oriental mysticism, Greek philosophy, and Jewish legalism. Out of this mixture a theological problem and a practical problem developed that Paul wrote to correct. The two problems can be charted as follows:

Type of Problem	Influence	Seen in References To	Scripture	Paul's Answer
Theological	Gnosticism	Philosophy	2:8	2:9 "Christ"
		Angel worship	2:18	"Christ"
		"Will" worship	2:23	"Christ"
		Voluntary humility	2:18, 23	"Christ"
		Pride	2:18	"Christ"
Ethical		Circumcision, ordinances	2:11, 13, 14	2:10 "Christ"
		Meats, drinks	2:16	"Christ"
		Sabbaths, new moons	2:16	"Christ"

Figure 11.1

You have been studying Judaism from the beginning of the course. Therefore, you can readily understand the ethical problem that developed when these legalists tried to base their concept of morality on the keeping of rituals and ordinances.

A brief sketch of Gnosticism will help you to understand the theological problem that developed. The Gnostic element in Colosse at the time of Paul's writing was not as fully developed as it came to be in the early part of the second century. In its later expression Gnosticism was anti-Judaistic because it developed the concept of a redeemer.

Gnosticism comes from the Greek word *gnosis*, which means "knowledge" (especially religious knowledge). Gnostics taught a system of salvation based on knowledge which, they believed, was restricted to a select few initiates. Gnosticism was based upon a dualism. Gnostics thus believed that matter was evil, and that God, who is perfect, extended himself through a process of successive emanations called *angels* or *aeons.* With each successive emanation, the divine element was reduced until eventually contact with matter was possible and creation occurred.

Paul's purpose in writing Colossians was to correct these two errors. He refutes the Gnostic problem by showing that instead of a God who reaches out to the material world through emanations of Himself, our God sends His Son into the world of matter. Christ is incarnated—takes on human flesh—but retains His divinity. Thus Paul answers the Gnostic with Colossians 2:9: "For in him dwelleth all the fullness of the Godhead bodily."

Paul answers the Judaistic problem, trying to achieve morality by "doing things," saying, "And ye are complete in him, which is the head of all principality and power" (Colossians 2:10).

Study the content of Colossians with this dual Pauline purpose in mind, and the Epistle will be more meaningful to you. If you will keep Tenney's outline open as you study Colossians, it will help you to get the message of Colossians in focus: the preeminence of Christ.

When you come to the section titled "Evaluation," you should be able to identify both a theological value and an ethical value of the Epistle to the Colossians.

14 Circle the letter preceding each TRUE statement.

a The theme of Ephesians is *Christ and the church,* with attention centered on the church.

b The theme of Colossians is *Christ and the church,* with attention centered on Christ.

c Paul answered the Gnostic problem by saying that God did not reach out to the material world through emanations of Himself, but instead He sent His Son, who took on human flesh, but at the same time kept His divinity.

d To answer the Judaistic problem Paul pointed the Colossians to good works that help one achieve morality.

e Ephesians was written to present new theological and ethical teaching to the people of this church.

f The person for which Colossians was written was twofold: to correct a theological problem and an ethical problem.

Objective  *Explain why Philippians is called the gospel of joy.*

Philippians

📖 Reading 7

Philippians was probably the last of the four prison Epistles to be written from Rome around AD 60.

You should read the "Background" material carefully to learn about the nature of the assembly at Philippi. It will also help you to understand the circumstances out of which Paul wrote to the Philippians.

No doubt Paul was very fond of this first Christian congregation in Europe. Thus, a mutual affection developed between Paul and these believers and is evident throughout the Epistle.

15 What characteristics about this congregation may account for the pleasant association that developed between Paul and the Philippians?

....

....

You have learned from your study of the background of Philippians that this Epistle, like Ephesians, was not written to correct any specific doctrinal error or practice among the believers. Rather, it was written as a note of thanksgiving to the *model* Christian congregation within Paul's circuit of assemblies. Thus, Paul's purpose in writing Philippians is to express thanksgiving for the great Christian fellowship (brotherhood or fraternity) of which the Philippians are models.

From this expression of thanksgiving to the Philippians, Paul soon works back to the basis of thanksgiving—the gospel ("good news"). Tenney ably shows that Paul's use of the term *gospel* in Philippians is one of the two topics that predominate. Study this paragraph carefully to see how Paul uses *gospel*.

The second topic that Paul stresses in Philippians is *joy*. In fact, Philippians can rightly be called the *epistle of joy*. If we join these two topics together, they form Paul's main theme in Philippians—the gospel of joy.

We have now studied about a number of the churches to whom Paul ministered. It would be good for you to make a comparison between the Philippian church and the others. I suggest that you draw a chart in your notebook in which you record this information for each of the churches:

1. Location of the church

2. Type of membership

3. Background

4. Strengths

5. Weaknesses

6. Paul's message to the church (with Scripture references)

Compare the church at Philippi with these churches: Jerusalem, Corinth, Thessalonica, Rome, Colosse, and Ephesus.

As you prepare to study the outline and content of the book, you should consider the circumstances out of which Paul wrote this epistle of joy. Philippians 1:15–16 and 2:20–21 indicate that Paul was in prison, constantly chained to a soldier, aware of a few friends and of many enemies. His circumstances were not conducive to the writing of a letter that is so full of boundless inspiration, illuminating theology, buoyant faith, glorious hope, and radiant joy! And yet, that is what Paul did, for he was not dependent upon circumstances, apparent success or failure, trends, public opinion, or his surroundings. His source of joy was the gospel—the *good news* that Christ brought to mankind at Calvary.

Study the sections "Content" and "Outline" of Philippians with the view that Paul wrote from a source of joy within his own soul and not from outward circumstances. This will help you both to understand and experience the message of Philippians in your life and ministry.

As you study the section titled "Evaluation," think of the value that Philippians has been to you personally, as well as to the church universal.

16 Explain why Philippians is called the gospel of joy. Use your notebook.

Objective  *Explain the two major benefits of Paul's imprisonment.*

Results of the Pauline Imprisonment
📖 Reading 8

Only eternity will reveal the results of the Pauline imprisonment. We are aware of two major results.

17 According to Tenney, what are the two results of the Pauline imprisonment? Write your answer in your notebook.

We have no clear statement about the verdict for Christianity, but it seems apparent that with the execution of Paul the Roman authorities were attempting to suppress Christianity. Tenney indicates that whether the verdict for Christianity was *religio licita* (a permitted cult), or *religio illicita* (a forbidden cult), Christianity would be the winner. Which verdict do you think would have advanced the Christian religion more readily? Is Christianity *religio licita* or *religio illicita* in your area of the world?

Golden Passages

Several special passages in the Prison Epistles will enrich your life and ministry. You should become familiar with their content and be able to locate them by memory or with a concordance. These *golden passages* are:

1.	Seven elements of the believer's position in grace	Ephesians 1:3–14
2.	Prayer for knowledge of Christ's headship of His church	Ephesians 1:15–23
3.	The method and purpose of our salvation	Ephesians 2:1–10
4.	The age-old mystery of the church	Ephesians 3:1–21
5.	The ministry gifts of Christ to His church	Ephesians 4:11–13
6.	The relationship of Spirit-filled husbands and wives	Ephesians 5:22–33
7.	The relationship of Spirit-filled parents and children	Ephesians 6:1–4
8.	The spiritual warfare of believers	Ephesians 6:10–18
9.	Christ the Creator	Colossians 1:15–17
10.	Christ our Reconciler through the cross	Colossians 1:20–23
11.	The believer's new life in Christ	Colossians 3:1–17
12.	Christ our example in humility and in exaltation	Philippians 2:5–11
13.	Giving all of self to gain all of Christ	Philippians 3:7–14
14.	Prayer with thanksgiving brings peace beyond understanding	Philippians 4:5–7
15.	A formula for thoughts and deeds which brings God's peace	Philippians 4:8–9

Total Time
(Read, answer
questions, check
answers)

Hr_____ Min_____

Start Time

_____

Self-Test 11

True-False. Write T in the blank space preceding each statement that is TRUE. Write F if it is FALSE.

.... **1** The final chapters of Acts reveal more of the inner thoughts and teachings of Paul than do the earlier chapters.

.... **2** When Paul spoke from the castle steps and told the crowd of his conversion, they became enraged.

.... **3** Paul was imprisoned for two years in Caesarea. Afterward he was released.

.... **4** Even when Paul was in prison, he had considerable liberty to communicate with the outside world.

.... **5** The Prison Epistles deal more with general teaching than do the earlier Epistles.

.... **6** Paul knew that he would eventually go to Rome because of a vision he had in Jerusalem.

.... **7** The Prison Epistles were directed to a confused, immature group of believers.

.... **8** Paul often referred to the resurrection of Christ in his defense against accusers.

.... **9** In dealing with sinful people, Paul's major effort was to evangelize, because he knew that through salvation their lives would be changed.

.... **10** It is believed that Paul was finally released from prison and that he died a natural death.

Multiple Choice. Select the best answer.

11 When Paul returned to Jerusalem, he made arrangements for some Jewish Christians to take the Nazarite vow. He did this because he
a)   believed the vow was an important part of their Christian experience.
b)   wanted to stop rumors that he was against Jewish customs.
c)   wanted to convince the Roman military authorities of his Jewish beliefs.
d)   thought it would be a sign to Gentile Christians of Jewish dedication to God.

12 The main emphasis in the book of Philemon concerns
a)   the evils of slavery.
b)   the need for forgiveness and reconciliation.
c)   the trials of life in prison.
d)   the relationship between faith and works.

13 What evidence do we have that Paul's letter to Philemon was effective?
a)   The letter was preserved and shared by its owner.
b)   Paul recorded the results in another letter.
c)   Philemon and Onesimus later visited Paul in prison.
d)   Timothy brought to Paul news of the reconciliation.

14 An encyclical Epistle is one which was
 a) returned to Paul by its recipient after it had been read and acknowledged.
 b) carried by hand to its destination.
 c) sent to an undisclosed recipient since the salutation is generally missing.
 d) reproduced and sent to several churches to whom Paul wanted the message given.

15 Which of these is NOT a meaning of *ekklesia*?
 a) The called-out ones
 b) The church universal
 c) A specific call to a specific ministry
 d) A total gathering of Christian believers

16 The purpose of the Epistle to the Ephesians was to
 a) show Christ's relationship to His church universal.
 b) deal with particular doctrinal problems which developed in the church at Ephesus.
 c) warn the church of false prophets that would rise up.
 d) defend the Christian faith.

17 The purpose of the Epistle to the Colossians was to
 a) convince the Jewish converts that they no longer had to observe Jewish customs.
 b) give teaching on the gifts of the Spirit.
 c) prepare the church for persecution.
 d) deal with the problem of heresy.

18 Gnostics believed that salvation came through
 a) faith.
 b) knowledge.
 c) service.
 d) humility.

19 Based on our study of the Prison Epistles, the probable order in which they were written is:
 a) Philemon, Ephesians, Colossians, and Philippians.
 b) Ephesians, Philippians, Colossians, and Philemon.
 c) Philippians, Colossians, Ephesians, and Philemon.
 d) Colossians, Philemon, Philippians, and Ephesians.

20 The two topics Paul emphasized in Philippians are
 a) law and grace.
 b) works and the Law.
 c) thanksgiving and joy.
 d) the church and spiritual gifts.

Self-Test Time

Hr_____ Min_____

Unit Progress Evaluation 3

Now that you have finished Unit 3, review the lessons in preparation for Unit Progress Evaluation 3. You will find it in your Essential Course Materials. Answer all of the questions without referring to your course materials, Bible, or notes. When you have completed the UPE, check your answers with the answer key provided in your Essential Course Materials, and review any items you may have answered incorrectly. Then you may proceed with your study of Unit 4. (Although UPE scores do not count as part of your final course grade, they indicate how well you learned the material and how well you may perform on the final examination.)

Answers to Study Questions

9 Your answer. We believe that it is difficult to legislate most values. Changes that are fundamental to a society require that people be informed and enlightened. Where believers are concerned, the motivation to change ought to be higher because of our Lord's example. As individuals are changed, they can affect the body, and it in turn can act as a powerful force for change in the society. In fact, this change or maturation is working well in many places in our world today.

1 c) He wrote only what he wanted Theophilus to know, because he wanted Theophilus to see that Christianity was submissive to the Roman government.

10 They reveal the oneness of all true believers in Christ.

2 He said God would send him far away to the Gentiles.

11 In this order:
a The offense.
b Compassion.
c Intercession.
d Substitution.
e Restoration to esteem.
f Lifting to a new relationship.

3 Caesarea.

12 Your answers.

4 Rome.

13 Statements **a**, **c**, **d**, and **f** are true.

5 As Tenney points out, Paul may have wanted to get out of the power of Festus rather than stay in prison longer in Caesarea. Personally, I think he still wanted to witness in Rome and establish a missionary center there.

14 Statements **a**, **b**, **c**, and **f** are true.

6 (In any order)
a The Prison Epistles were of a more solid and instructional nature than most of the earlier Epistles.
b The Prison Epistles deal more with general teaching and less with specific questions.
c The Prison Epistles were addressed to a more mature, growing church.
d The Christians were becoming more complacent, and they needed deeper teaching than in the earlier Epistles.

15 Your answer might include their loyalty to Paul, the way they perceived their role as his partners in the gospel, their continuing concern for his ministry and willingness to share in his problems.

7 Your answer. Paul's primary emphasis was on evangelization. When people accept Christ, He can bring about needed changes in their lives. In this way, society can be transformed from the inside out, that is as people's hearts are changed. Paul emphasized a spiritual rather than a political resolution.

16 It is so-called because in spite of outward circumstances the apostle reflects joy, hope, and inspiration, that spring from the brilliant joy of faith deep within his soul. This joy expresses itself in thanksgiving for the people of this church and their response to the gospel.

8 Your answer. We believe that Christians need to think through the practical implications of salvation. For example, we are admonished to act to rectify problems such as poverty and hunger (James 2:14–17) as well as to be involved in the spiritual and physical well-being of the body of Christ (James 5:13–16). To ignore these issues is to present a gospel that ignores the issues of life, the things that are uppermost in people's thinking and feeling. Remember: We are not saved by faith and works, but we are saved by "faith that works."

17 a The enforced retirement provided more time for prayer and contemplation and enabled Paul to produce the priceless revelation of the Prison Epistles.

  b Paul's appeal to Caesar brought Christianity directly to the attention of the Roman government and compelled the civil authorities to pass upon its legality.

THE PROBLEMS OF THE EARLY CHURCH— THE PERIOD OF CONSOLIDATION: AD 60–100

Procedures...   **1** Read the lesson introduction and study the learning activities to know what to expect.

2 Reflect on the objectives for key concepts and expected outcomes.

3 Study the content, identifying key points by underlining or highlighting, and answer the study questions.

4 Answer the self-test questions to synthesize the lesson.

5 Review the lessons in this unit in preparation for the unit progress evaluation.

Note the time you begin reading this lesson. At the end of the lesson, record in the space provided the time it took to complete each segment.

The Church in Crisis

Start Time

_____

As Paul neared the end of his life, the church was experiencing growing pains. There was confusion within the church and persecution without. God was raising up other men in the church to carry on the work that the early apostles had begun. Instruction was needed, prompting the writing of 1 and 2 Timothy, and Titus. These books contain a wealth of teaching for young ministers of the gospel, both in personal conduct, and in doctrine.

From the beginning, the church had struggled over the relationship between the Law and grace. Jewish Christians were torn between their desire to obey the laws and traditions of their people and their equally strong desire to follow the teachings of Christ. It was to help these Jewish converts that the book of Hebrews was written to declare the superiority of Christ over the Law. As you study this Epistle, you should be inspired to greater faith in God, even as those men and women whose faith is so movingly illustrated by the writer. If you study the lives of these godly people, you will see that they, too, were beset by weaknesses and failures. Yet, they were listed among the heroes of the faith because they trusted God in every circumstance.

First Peter is another important Epistle we shall discuss in this lesson. It was written to the suffering church in a time of increasing persecution by the Roman government. Since Peter had been with Jesus and had seen the grace with which He bore suffering and humiliation, he knew through this personal experience that God's grace was more than sufficient for every trial. Thus all of these Epistles teach tremendous lessons, which you will find to be of personal value as you apply them to your own life and ministry.

the activities...

◇ Read 1 Timothy, Titus, 2 Timothy, 1 Peter, and Hebrews as indicated in the lesson development.

◇ Read the textbook pages as background for the lesson development. As you do so, keep your Bible open and read the Scripture references made in the textbook as you come to them. The readings for this lesson are
  Reading 1: pages 333–343
  Reading 2: pages 333–335
  Reading 3: pages 335–337
  Reading 4: pages 337–339

Reading 5: pages 339–343
Reading 6: pages 344–354
Reading 7: pages 355–364

◇ Work through the lesson development and complete each assignment, including the Scripture reading assignments that are coordinated with each section.

◇ Take the self-test at the end of the lesson and check your answers with those provided.

the objectives...

12.1 *Describe Paul's circumstances when he wrote the Pastoral Epistles.*

12.2 *Describe changes Paul found in the church and summarize his advice to Timothy of a minister's responsibilities.*

12.3 *Explain the problems in the Cretan church and how Paul dealt with them by writing to Titus.*

12.4 *Explain how and why 2 Timothy differs in tone from 1 Timothy and Titus.*

12.5 *Discuss the results of changes in the government's attitude toward the Christian church that is evident in 1 Peter.*

12.6 *List six valuable spiritual teachings found in Hebrews.*

the outline...

1 The Institutional Church: The Pastoral Epistles
  a Background
  b 1 Timothy
  c Titus
  d 2 Timothy
  e Evaluation
2 The Suffering Church: 1 Peter
3 The Break From Judaism: Hebrews
4 Golden Passages

 Objective **12.1**

Describe Paul's circumstances when he wrote the Pastoral Epistles.

The Institutional Church: The Pastoral Epistles
📖 Reading 1

During the periods of the mission to the Gentiles and the Pauline imprisonment, the church established itself as an independent movement. It was characterized by dedication to world evangelism, peaceful penetration of society with gospel truth, and boldness to pursue its convictions. Some heresies emerged, causing problems in human relations, moral inadequacies, and spiritual immaturities. In addition, leadership and literature developed and helped advance the church in many areas.

This period brought pronounced changes in the church that enabled it to continue to be dynamic and fulfill its purpose.

First Timothy, Titus, and 2 Timothy are called Pastoral Epistles because they are written to pastors to instruct them regarding their ministry in the assemblies. These "minister's manuals" are the most complete ministerial instructions contained in the New Testament. They include in their content the office, qualifications, and duties of the Christian minister.

Because these Epistles are concerned with the ministry and other aspects of the life of the universal church, they are classified as *ecclesiological*.*

ecclesiological
pertaining to study of the doctrine of the church

Background

📖 Reading 2

The Pastoral Epistles were written during a stage in the career of Paul characterized by observable change in the apostle and in the church. In 2 Timothy, Paul clearly had his own death in view; therefore, his burden was to establish leadership to take up the mission of world evangelism he was about to relinquish. The Pastoral Epistles are major items in the transfer of leadership from Paul to his younger associates, among whom Timothy and Titus are named (while the existence of several others is assumed).

In your study of the "Background" of these Epistles, you will observe that some scholars doubt their Pauline authorship. Locate and mark the reasons for their position in your textbook. Even though the authenticity of these Epistles has been challenged more than any other writings of Paul, I believe the evidence is heavily in favor of Pauline authorship. Tenney lists two arguments in favor of Pauline authorship of the Pastoral Epistles: (1) the Epistles bear Paul's name and (2) their biographical data is similar to that of other Pauline biography. I would add that the witness of the early church to Pauline authorship and canonicity and the close kinship of doctrines in these Epistles to those in his other letters indicate Pauline authorship of the Pastoral Epistles.

The biographical data, movements, and chronological relationships within the Pastoral Epistles seem to indicate that Paul was acquitted at his first trial before Caesar. This evidence also suggests that he was released for an indeterminate period of time, during which he wrote these Epistles and engaged in other ministry.

1   In what way does the biographical data support the statement above?

....

2   In what way does the information on movement within the Pastoral Epistles support the theory of acquittal?

....

....

3 In what way do the chronological relationships in the Pastorals seem to indicate an acquittal?

....

....

From the study of background information on the Pastoral Epistles you should learn the following:

1. There was probably some time lapse between the writing of each of these Epistles.
2. These Epistles are similar in vocabulary and style.
3. The Epistles are from the same hand.
4. These Epistles were written under the same general circumstances.

Objective **12.2**

Describe changes Paul found in the church and summarize his advice to Timothy of a minister's responsibilities.

1 Timothy

📖 **Reading 3**

After being released from the Roman prison, Paul apparently resumed his ministry in the assemblies of Asia. There, he found problems in some of the congregations, including these:

1. Doctrinal confusion
2. Moral declension*
3. Spiritual shipwreck

declension
a sinking into an inferior or lower condition

4 In the section headed "1 Timothy," the textbook discusses four changes that had occurred in the church. I will reduce each of these changes to a brief statement. In your notebook, write the features the textbook associates with each change.

   a There was a spiritual change.
   b There was organizational change.
   c There was change in worship.
   d There was theological change.

Assuming Paul was acquitted in AD 60 or 61, he probably wrote 1 Timothy in AD 62. This first of his Pastoral Epistles was most likely written in Macedonia. Titus was written next and 2 Timothy followed as the last in the series. In fact, if Paul did not write the book of Hebrews, 2 Timothy was the last Epistle Paul wrote.

In this reading and in the title to the outline, you will discover the purpose of the writing of both 1 and 2 Timothy. Since Paul so consistently deals with the ministry of Timothy (and other unnamed young ministers) throughout these two Epistles, it is meaningless to use one verse to establish his purpose. Obviously, he is writing to instruct and challenge Timothy (as an example for all young preachers) for the tremendous task of Christian ministry.

I suggest that you make your own outline of the content of 1 Timothy, using Tenney's outline and explanation of the content along with your Bible and other good commentaries. This will help you learn the material and furnish you with an invaluable source of information on the ministry and related subjects. I dare say that you will be turning to your outline (miniature minister's manual) again and again throughout your ministry.

5 In the last chapter of 1 Timothy Paul identifies the elements of personal ministerial life with the four words *flee, pursue, fight,* and *keep.* Under these topics he outlines some things a young minister should *do,* and some things he should *avoid.* In your own words, write three things under each category that Paul mentioned. Use your notebook for your answer.

   a   *Do*

   b   *Avoid*

Objective   *Explain the problems in the Cretan church and how Paul dealt with them by writing to Titus.*

Titus

📖 Reading 4

Paul wrote Titus after an unknown lapse of time following the writing of 1 Timothy. He probably wrote this Epistle from Macedonia, and he most likely penned it in AD 62 or 63.

As you study the material under the heading "Background," keep in mind the following questions.

6   What was the cultural background of the believers in Crete?

....

....

7   Who was the founding father of the assembly at Crete?

....

8   How did Titus get involved with the assembly at Crete?

....

....

9   What were the two problems in the congregation at Crete that prompted Paul's letter to Titus?

   a   ....

   b   ....

10 Why does Paul, the advocate of salvation by grace through faith, urge the Cretan Christians to produce good works?

....

....

11 Paul's purpose in writing was the same as that for 1 and 2 Timothy. State this in your own words.

....

....

The last paragraph of the section on "Background" in the textbook gives a good character sketch of Titus. If you will get well-acquainted with Titus, you will understand Paul's letter to him more readily. Tenney seems to indicate that Titus may have been a more effective minister than Timothy.

12 What do you think of Tenney's view that Titus "seems to have been a stronger character than Timothy and better able to cope with opposition"? Write your answer in your notebook.

13 Looking at Tenny's list of the content of Titus, write out a simplified statement of belief for followers of Christ. Start out with "We believe…" Use your notebook for your answer.

In your study of the content of Titus you should remember the following points:

1. The Epistle is characterized by much doctrine of a refined type.
2. The doctrines in Titus constitute a fair digest of New Testament theology.
3. The Epistle is a good summary of the doctrine of the church as it emerged into the institutional stage.

I am sure that you are impressed, as I am, with the variety of major doctrines Paul included in this brief letter. I have observed that along with other important doctrines, he deals with four of the five subjects considered "cardinal doctrines" by Bible-believing Christians. Looking at Tenney's list of the doctrines taught in Titus, you should note that Paul taught the following cardinal truths about what Christ makes available to humanity.

1. The vicarious atonement of Christ (2:14) (Tenney No. 8). Through faith (3:7) (Tenney No. 12).
2. The baptism in the Holy Spirit (3:5) (Tenney Nos. 5 and 11).
3. Sanctification (2:12, 14) (Tenney Nos. 13 and 14).
4. The return of Christ (2:13) (Tenney No. 16).

The fifth cardinal truth concerning what Christ makes available to humanity is not represented in Titus. The doctrine of divine healing is taught by Paul in other places.

You should present these cardinal truths frequently in your preaching and teaching, if you and the people to whom you minister are to appropriate the full blessings of Christ.

Explain how and why 2 Timothy differs in tone from 1 Timothy and Titus.

2 Timothy

📖 Reading 5

Under the heading in the section on "Background" trace the proposed last itinerary of Paul up to the time of his sudden arrest and transfer to Rome. (See the map in chapter 13 of the textbook.)

14 What was the probable cause of Paul's final arrest?

....

....

15 What was the situation against which the church was struggling at the time of Paul's final arrest?

....

....

Second Timothy was written, following Titus, after an unknown lapse of time. This Epistle was written from Rome around AD 63 or 64.

We have already discovered that Paul's purpose for writing 2 Timothy, like that of 1 Timothy and Titus, was to instruct and challenge young preachers for the tremendous task of Christian ministry. The main difference among the three Epistles is the note of finality in 2 Timothy. In this Epistle Paul gives his farewell message, which includes his final advice and his final charge to Timothy (and through him to all Christian ministers).

Basically, the content of 2 Timothy gives highly personalized instructions in human relations. Included in the content of 2 Timothy is a warning about the coming of a great apostasy. While this prophetic picture had its primary fulfillment in Timothy's day, it is to have its most complete fulfillment in the "last days" (probably in our day). Paul made this same prophecy in both 1 Timothy 4:1–3 and 2 Timothy 3:1–8.

In his description of the conditions the church could anticipate, Paul lists the sins that will characterize the last days. Paul also catalogues sins in Romans 1:21–32; 1 Corinthians 6:9, 10; and Galatians 5:19–21. Several sins were mentioned in each of these lists. You should study the list that is given in 2 Timothy 3:1–8 to understand what Timothy was facing in his ministry and what you and I are also facing.

When you have finished the course, you will find it instructive to list in separate columns the sins given in each of these Scripture references and who will commit them. You should notice that sins of the kind that John describes as "the cravings of sinful man, the lust of his eyes and the boasting of what he has and does" (1 John 2:16) get in Paul's list of sins most often. This information should give you some guidance about the types of evil you should avoid in your own life and ministry. Tenney indicates that Paul offered one antidote (prevention) for the influx of evil.

16 What was that antidote?

....

Use the Scriptures faithfully in your life and ministry. They will keep you from evil, and they will help you to build your people up so that they, too, can resist and overcome evil.

I feel that Paul's final charge is to me as much as it is to Timothy, and I hope you have taken it personally also. Carefully study this classic challenge to the ministry. Come back to it often, and pray that you may be able to fulfill your purpose in the ministry to the maximum possible. Then you will be able to say what Paul said in 2 Timothy 4:6–8.

I hope you do not feel that I am being too personal in my approach to this course. True Bible study does not concentrate on just receiving historical or factual knowledge alone. Its truths must be experienced in the life of the student if it is to be effective Bible study. Also, a tendency that ministers must guard against is that of always studying for the benefit of others (for ministry) rather than for themselves (for personal benefit).

Evaluation

Under the heading "Evaluation" Tenney indicates that the chief value of the pastoral Epistles is that they help us understand the life of the church in its transition from a pioneer movement to an organized institution.

17 Tenney also discusses two tendencies of the church at the time of the Pastoral Epistles. Locate and state them in your own words. Use your notebook.

18 How do the tendencies of that church compare with those of today's church? Write your answer in your notebook.

19 Can it be said of the church today that spiritual vitality and conduct are more important than ritual and politics—and that the missionary motive is still keen? Use your notebook for your answer.

Objective **12.5**

Discuss the results of changes in the government's attitude toward the Christian church that is evident in 1 Peter.

The Suffering Church: 1 Peter
📖 Reading 6

After a long and interesting study of the assemblies under the leadership of Paul, the scene now shifts to the assemblies under the leadership of Peter. Peter, the original Christian leader, has not been the center of our attention since we studied the first five chapters of Acts in which he was prominent. With the shift to Peter and his first Epistle, we encounter a pronounced change in the situation confronting the church.

In the paragraphs under the heading "Background" you will consider what the original attitude of the church was toward government that was announced in the writings and deportment of the early Christians.

20 What are three reasons for the comparative silence concerning political relations between Christians and the Roman Empire? Use your notebook for your answer.

21 Locate and underline in your textbook four factors that brought about a decided change in the attitude of the Roman government towards Christians. Summarize them in your notebook.

Be sure to get these facts in mind because the change of Roman policy from tolerance to hostility at the time of the death of Paul was a crucial historical moment for the church.

Peter was looked to by the assemblies of Northern Asia Minor for an answer to the persecutions that were evidently becoming widespread. In response Peter wrote his first Epistle.

The purpose for writing is discussed in the textbook. Tenney indicates in these paragraphs that Peter wrote to strengthen believers in a group of assemblies so that they could endure the persecution that seemed inevitable for every Christian. Tenney suggests that there are two themes in 1 Peter: the theme of suffering and the grace of God. I would agree that these two prominent themes are in the book, but I would reverse the priority and put grace first. Thus, the purpose of the main theme of 1 Peter would be to show the sufficiency of God's grace in suffering.

Simon Peter, one of the original twelve apostles, is the generally accepted author of 1 Peter. The section on "Author" in the textbook gives an accurate portrait of the personality of this great man both before and after the crucifixion of Christ. Never was there a more radical change in a personality than that which occurred in Peter.

22 List some words that describe Peter before this great change.

....

23 Describe Peter following this great change.

....

24 What experience or experiences produced this drastic change?

....

....

25 Concerning three possible locations for the writing of 1 Peter, study the textbook discussion of the arguments for each of the theories. Do you prefer to conclude that 1 Peter was written in the historic Babylon in Mesopotamia, a town named Babylon in Egypt, or in Rome?

....

....

While the date and place of the writing of 1 Peter cannot be conclusively established, I believe, on the basis of the evidence available, that 1 Peter was written in Rome around AD 63.

Tenney finds a general likeness between the style, language, and structure of 1 Peter and some of Paul's Epistles. From this and other historical data he assumes that Paul exerted a strong influence on Peter. While this is not an unreasonable assumption, I do not think we have to consider that Peter was heavily dependent on Paul. No doubt Paul did influence Peter as well as James and others, but it is also likely that *they* influenced Paul. I am inclined to believe that Peter stood theologically between Paul and James. With this assumption, Peter's defection to the table of the Jews (for which Paul indicated in Galatians they had a confrontation) probably occurred because Peter was trying to moderate between the positions of Paul and James.

The textbook deals with the doctrine of grace that is presented in 1 Peter. I believe that the grace of God was so central to the Epistle that it afforded the possibility of an alternate outline, and perhaps the best outline, of the book. Working from this paragraph in the textbook and from 1 Peter, make an outline of the book around the sufficiency of God's grace in suffering. This will be a rewarding learning experience, and it will be useful as teaching and preaching material.

The content of 1 Peter is dominated by the themes of grace and suffering and by a most impressive chain of commands that hold the book together. If you will follow these three elements in your study of 1 Peter, you will achieve a better understanding of its message.

Under the heading "Evaluation" you should note a chief value of 1 Peter: it shows Christians how to live out their salvation through grace in a hostile world. Also, you should note a chief problem: how to interpret the passage in 3:18–22. Tenney explains Peter's intention in this passage adequately. Read this explanation until you understand it thoroughly. Then, summarize it briefly in your notebook because you may be called upon to interpret this passage in Peter to others.

Objective 12.6 *List six valuable spiritual teachings found in Hebrews.*

The Break from Judaism: Hebrews
📖 Reading 7

In this chapter you will see how Christianity finally broke away from Judaism. In the first seven lessons you considered the things Judaism contributed to the New Testament and Christianity. From Lesson 8 to this point in Lesson 12 you have studied the transition of the church from its Jewish beginnings in Jerusalem to a chain of predominantly Gentile assemblies that stretched from Antioch to Illyricum. Admittedly, the transition in theology was just as great as was the change in the geographical domain of the church.

In the section under the heading "Background" Tenney gives a masterful treatment of the factors that finally led to the sharp separation between Christianity and Judaism. Find and underline in your textbook the two factors that Tenney indicates contributed to the widening of the breach. His important analysis of the deep problems with which Jewish Christians were confronted adds greatly to our understanding of this important issue.

Study the paragraphs where Tenney discusses the two sides of the problem of the interpretation of the Old Testament. Consider also the problem of *patriotism* to national Judaism versus *loyalty to Christ,* until you know the problems well and can appreciate the tremendous tension under which these sincere Jewish Christians were living. This will keep you from the error of thinking that they were just a group of unsaved legalistic troublemakers who had no appreciation for the Christian revelation. Notice the importance of the decision that they were forced to make and the consequences that would come from their decision. Write in your notebook what you discover.

The book of Hebrews was written out of this background. The purpose of the writing of Hebrews was to show the superiority and finality of Christianity over Judaism.

It has not been clearly determined to whom the book of Hebrews was written, but two theories have been traditionally proposed:

1. It was written to Jewish Christians in Rome.

2. It was written to Jewish Christians in Palestine.

Whether the recipients were Jewish Christians in Rome or in Palestine, we can discern from the content of the book that they had the following characteristics:

1. They knew the Old Testament with its sacrificial systems.

2. They had heard the gospel from preachers who had known Christ and were endowed with the gifts of the Spirit.

3. They had become staunch believers.

Knowing this information about the recipients of the book of Hebrews increases our understanding of, and appreciation for, the hard decision that they faced. The purpose of Hebrews, therefore, was to help them with their decision.

There is not sufficient evidence to be conclusive about the authorship of the book of Hebrews. You should read the various theories and arguments for each in the textbook and decide for yourself about the authorship. On the basis of the use of Habakkuk 2:4 in Romans 1:17, Galatians 3:11, and Hebrews 10:38 there is a remarkably close affinity between the doctrine of Hebrews and that of other Pauline writings. Therefore, in view of the widespread, early testimony of church fathers to Pauline authorship, I prefer to think that Paul was the author of Hebrews. Furthermore, Peter's reference in 2 Peter 3:15 seems to indicate Pauline authorship for Hebrews.

From internal evidence the writing of Hebrews appears to be prior to the destruction of the temple in Jerusalem in AD 70. If it was written by Paul, the date was probably in AD 64 just ahead of 2 Timothy. Notice that this is earlier than the date of the "late sixties" proposed by the textbook.

Tenney accurately notes under the section on "Outline" that the central theme is the word *better.* He uses this word *better* as the key for the main divisions of this outline of the content of the book of Hebrews. Keep this outline open before you as you study the section on "Content" of Hebrews, and it will enhance your learning of the message of this book.

You should be aware of the series of exhortations in Hebrews prefaced with "let us." Consider the list of these exhortations in the textbook. They afford further insight into the style and content of Hebrews. Do you think this list of exhortations would furnish themes for a series of sermons or Bible lessons?

Tenney mentions the three quotations of Habakkuk 2:4 in the New Testament. I want to place them before you graphically because I think they are significant. Notice that the word I have italicized in each quotation is the element of Habakkuk emphasized in the book from which the quotation comes. Habakkuk 2:4 reads, "the righteous will live by his faith."

New Testament Reference	*Quotation*	*Emphasis*
Romans 1:17	". . the *righteous* will live by faith."	being righteous (just)
Galatians 3:11	". . the righteous will *live* by faith."	living
Hebrews 10:38	". . the righteous will live by *faith*."	faith

Figure 12.1

As you turn to the section under the heading "Evaluation," you cannot help but be impressed with the grave problem with which the book of Hebrews dealt and the beautiful way in which it gives the answer. Its purpose was to show the superiority and finality of Christianity over Judaism. The contribution of this book is immeasurable.

26 If you were to see how many values of Hebrews you could list from Tenney's discussion and from your knowledge of the background and content of Hebrews, you would have a long list of great values. I predict most of them would be benefits that would reach beyond the original recipients into the church of our days. In your notebook, list six such valuable spiritual teachings.

Golden Passages

There are several special passages in 1 Timothy, Titus, 2 Timothy, 1 Peter, and Hebrews that will greatly enrich your life and ministry. You should become familiar with their content and be able to locate them by memory or with a concordance. These *golden passages* are:

1. Paul's doxology	1 Timothy 1:17
2. Qualifications for bishops and deacons	1 Timothy 3:1–13
3. Six qualities for Christian youth	1 Timothy 4:12
4. The basis of purity	Titus 1:15
5. The universality and consequences of grace	Titus 2:11–14
6. Gracious justification and Holy Spirit renewing	Titus 3:4–8
7. The prophecy of perilous times	2 Timothy 3:1–8
8. Paul's charge to ministers	2 Timothy 4:1–5
9. Paul's farewell testimony	2 Timothy 4:6–8
10. Suffering, grace, and salvation	1 Peter 1:3–9
11. The brevity of life and the endurance of the Word	1 Peter 1:24–25
12. The necessity of spiritual growth and the consequence of backsliding	Hebrews 6:1–6
13. Christ our superior High Priest	Hebrews 9:11–28
14. Worship under the new covenant	Hebrews 10:19–25
15. The "faith digest" of the Bible	Hebrews 11:1–40

Total Time
(Read, answer
questions, check
answers)

Hr_____ Min_____

Self-Test 12

Start Time

Matching. Match the book, person(s), thing, or place (right) to its appropriate definition or description (left).

.... **1** Presents Paul's farewell testimony

.... **2** Is the mystical name for Rome

.... **3** Was written to show the superiority of Christianity

.... **4** Were torn between national loyalty and Christian loyalty

.... **5** Presents Paul's charge to ministers

.... **6** Is considered by Luther to have written Hebrews

.... **7** Is basically highly personalized instructions on human relations

.... **8** Gives qualifications for bishops and deacons

.... **9** Is a main theme in 1 Peter

.... **10** Was written to help persecuted Christians

a) Hebrews
b) Jewish Christians
c) 1 Peter
d) Grace
e) 1 Timothy 3:1–13
f) 2 Timothy 4:6–8
g) Babylon
h) 2 Timothy
i) Apollos
j) 2 Timothy 4:1–5
k) Egypt

Multiple Choice. Select the best answer.

11 The Pastoral Epistles include:
a) 1 Timothy, Philippians, and 2 Timothy.
b) 1 and 2 Timothy, and 1 and 2 Thessalonians.
c) 1 Thessalonians, Titus, and 2 Thessalonians.
d) 1 Timothy, Titus, and 2 Timothy.

12 The Pastoral Epistles are classified as
a) ecclesiological.
b) eschatological.
c) christological.
d) sociological.

13 Paul was probably released by Caesar for an unknown length of time during which he wrote
a) the book of Hebrews.
b) the Prison Epistles.
c) the Travel Epistles.
d) the Pastoral Epistles.

14 Assuming that Paul was acquitted in AD 60 or 61, he probably wrote 1 Timothy
a) from Jerusalem in AD 63.
b) from Rome in AD 61.
c) from Macedonia in AD 62.
d) from Jerusalem in AD 65.

15 The correct order for the writing of the Pastoral Epistles is
   a) Titus, 1 Timothy, and 2 Timothy.
   b) First Timothy, Titus, and 2 Timothy.
   c) First Timothy, 2 Timothy, and Titus.
   d) Second Timothy, 1 Timothy, and Titus.

16 The founding father of the assembly at Crete was
   a) Paul.
   b) Timothy.
   c) Demas.
   d) Titus.

17 Which statement is NOT true about the letter to Titus?
   a) There is no doctrine in Titus.
   b) It was written to instruct Titus for the task of the ministry.
   c) The book of Titus urges Cretans to produce good works.
   d) The book of Titus was written to address one specific problem.

18 The purpose of the writing of Titus is the same as that of
   a) First and 2 Thessalonians.
   b) First and 2 Timothy.
   c) First Timothy and 1 Thessalonians.
   d) Hebrews and Galatians.

19 The chief value of the Pastoral Epistles is that they help us to understand the life of the church in its transition from
   a) a Gentile to a Jewish organization.
   b) the leadership of Paul to Peter.
   c) a pioneer movement to an organized institution.
   d) the leadership of Peter to Paul.

20 Which of the following is NOT a factor which contributed to the change of Roman policy from tolerance to hostility towards the church?
   a) Nero's spiteful accusations
   b) Christians' talk of coming judgment and overthrow of the world
   c) Belief in an invisible God
   d) Secret Christian meetings in the catacombs to plot Caesar's death

Fill in the Blank. Print one word in each blank.

21 .... Christians living in Rome or Palestine were probably the recipients of Hebrews.

22 The death of .... marked a crucial historical moment in the attitude of the Roman government towards the church.

23 .... change, theological change, spiritual change, and change in worship characterized the church which Paul found upon his acquittal at his first trial before Caesar.

24 The Epistle to .... constitutes a fair digest of New Testament theology.

25 ...., Galatians, and Hebrews each contain the quotation from Habakkuk 2:4, "The righteous shall live by .... "

Self-Test Time

Hr_____ Min_____

Answers to Study Questions

14 Tenney suggests that Jewish metallurgists may have plotted against Paul because of their discontent with his teaching of salvation by faith and because their commerce related to pagan shrines had declined.

1 Paul evidently had freedom to resume his traveling ministry.

15 Jealousy, frustration, and maliciousness in Judaism; indifference, decadence, and corruption of paganism; and the need for soundly instructed pastors to take over Paul's leadership.

2 The lack of correspondence between Paul's travels that are recorded in Acts and in the Pastoral Epistles indicates that Paul continued to travel after his imprisonment.

16 The antidote is knowing the Scriptures, for they "are able to make you wise for salvation through faith in Christ Jesus" (2 Timothy 3:15).

3 The activities and places of work of Paul's companions were different from those mentioned in the prison correspondence.

17 a Younger pastors faced the increasing menace of heresy.
   b There was a growing emphasis on formulation of creed (doctrinal formulas).

4 a Letting go of faith, loss of good conscience.
   b Eminence, instead of usefulness, the objective of church offices. Bishops (probably identical with elders) and deacons mentioned. Widows partly responsible for social service.
   c Characteristic features of services included praying with hands uplifted, laying on of hands, reading, teaching, preaching. Women were modest and took a quiet place.
   d Disagreements over theological differences, increasing threat of heresy, decreasing vitality of theology as people came to take it for granted.

18 Your answer will reflect your environment. Mine is that pastors still need to reply to false doctrine and help their believers to keep the faith, live godly lives, and endure hardship.

5 a *Do:* Follow after righteousness, godliness, faith, love, patience, meekness. Be content with God's provisions. Be faithful in your commitment. Teach men to trust God.
   b *Avoid:* Seeking riches, profane talk, pride, foolish arguments, foolish desires.

19 Your answer. Evidence worldwide indicates that while the church is experiencing tremendous growth, there is an increase in ritual and politics that is alarming.

6 Hellenistic culture was annexed to the Roman Empire by Pompey in 67 BC and was ethically and morally perverse (Titus 1:12–13).

20 a The Kingdom Jesus taught was spiritual rather than political. He and His apostles were not political agitators.

b Christians were casually tolerated as persons within Judaism, a cult protected by the Roman state when claims of Judaism did not conflict with those of the state.

c The spread of Christianity within Roman society was peaceful.

7 Titus.

21 a Christians were recognized as a group apart from Judaism.

b Their belief in the risen Christ and an invisible God was misunderstood.

c Their belief in judgment was also misunderstood.

d Nero's accusations brought about a popular dislike of Christian ideas.

8 When Paul departed from Crete, he left Titus there to correct the errors and to finish the founding of the church.

22 He was a leader, spokesman for the disciples, hasty, vacillating, impulsive, and quick to rebound.

9 a Perversion of morals.

b A Judaizing group of teachers who were mercenary, unruly, divisive, and ungodly (Titus 1:10–16).

23 He was stable, reliable, and faithful to a martyr's death.

10 Perhaps the Cretans had not understood that even though they could not earn salvation by good works, salvation by faith should produce the fruit of ethical living.

24 Regret that he forsook Jesus, joy in seeing the risen Christ, and the infilling of the Holy Spirit produced this drastic change.

11 Your answer: I have noted that it was to instruct and challenge Titus to be an example for all young preachers in the tremendous task of Christian ministry.

25 Your answer.

12 Paul evidently knew that Titus had both the maturity and successful experience to cope with opposition and to follow his advice: "In everything set them an example by doing what is good" (Titus 2:7).

26 Answers from pages 363–364 would include in any order:

(1) Christ, the better priest, ministers to believers under grace (Hebrews 3:17–18; 7:24).

(2) Christ, the better revelation of God, "is the radiance of God's glory and the exact representation of his being . . ." (Hebrews 1:3).

(3) Christ, the Mediator of the better covenant, died to set men free from sin (Hebrews 9:15).

(4) Christ, the better sacrifice, "by one sacrifice . . . has made perfect forever those who are being made holy" (Hebrews 10:14).

(5) Christ, the better key to understanding of the Old Testament, explains the importance of the feast and offerings of Judaism.

(6) The better way to live is by faith, persevering in faith (Hebrews 10:35–36).

13 Your answer might be like this: "We believe in God, the Father, who loves us and gives us salvation by grace through His Son, our Savior. We believe the Father also gives us the Holy Spirit who abides in us and teaches us how to live lives separated from evil. We believe we are justified by faith and sanctified (purified) by the inner working of the Holy Spirit. We believe Jesus Christ will come again to take us to live with Him eternally."

Note the time you begin reading this lesson. At the end of the lesson, record in the space provided the time it took to complete each segment.

The Perils of Heresies

Start Time

_____

When you look back over the New Testament books we have already studied, you can see how complete a guidebook we have for our Christian walk. The Bible is not a collection of abstract intellectual philosophies. Instead, it is God's revelation of Himself to man, a revelation made through people who wrote from their own experiences with God and with His Son. In God's Word we can find direction for every aspect of our lives. The Bible is truly the standard by which we must live.

When people begin to deviate from the standard, or interpret it to suit their own purposes, however, heresies creep in. One of the greatest tricks of the enemy is to bring false teachers into the church to twist the Scriptures and thus lead people away from truth. For example, we have learned that our salvation is by faith in Christ, and not by works. We have also learned that we are no longer under the law of Moses, with its legalism. Rather, we have freedom in Christ. Some would interpret this to say that the Christian is free to do as he pleases, as long as he has accepted Christ as his Savior. This wrong interpretation of Christian freedom often leads to immorality and is a reproach to the kingdom of God.

The New Testament books we will study in this lesson deal with various heresies that crept into the New Testament church. The same heresies, or similar ones, are still being used by the enemy to weaken the church's effectiveness in the world today. We have a responsibility before God to test every doctrine against the standard of His Word and to resist those teachings that would lead us away from a life of holiness, without which no man shall see God. This explains clearly Jude's challenge in verse 3 of his Epistle, "I felt I had to write and urge you to contend for the faith, that was once for all entrusted to the saints." May we accept this challenge and be worthy "contenders" for the faith.

the activities...

◇ Read 2 Peter, Jude, and 1, 2, and 3 John straight through to get an overview of the message of each. Then, read the textbook to get the background fixed in your mind. While reading the textbook, keep your Bible open and read the Scripture references in the textbook as you come to them. The readings for this lesson are

Reading 1: pages 365–380
Reading 2: pages 365–366
Reading 3: pages 366–370
Reading 4: pages 370–374
Reading 5: pages 374–377
Reading 6: pages 377–378
Reading 7: pages 378–379
Reading 8: pages 379–380

◇ Work through the lesson development as usual and complete each assignment. After you complete the lesson development, take the selftest and check your answers.

the objectives...

13.1 *List several major false doctrines that the church has dealt with over the centuries.*

13.2 *State the theme of 2 Peter and how it is developed to deal with errors in the church.*

13.3 *Analyze similarities between Jude and 2 Peter. Then summarize the values of Jude, emphasizing theological values.*

13.4 *Summarize the principal values of 1, 2, and 3 John.*

the outline...

1 The Epistles of Warning
  a The Peril of Heresies
  b Background
  c 2 Peter
  d Jude
2 The Johannine Epistles
  a Background
  b 1 John
  c 2 John
  d 3 John
3 Golden Passages

Objective

List several major false doctrines that the church has dealt with over the centuries.

The Epistles of Warning

We have seen in our reading that the latter years of the first century were characterized as times of distressing heresies* and church schism. These conditions prompted godly men to write powerful, positive letters to bring stability back to the body of Christ. While they reflect concern, they also promote confidence—confidence of the kind Paul referred to when he said that

heresies
beliefs or opinions contrary to the established doctrines of the church or religious system

"he who began a good work in you will carry it on to completion until the day of Jesus Christ" (Philippians 1:6)

The Peril of Heresies

📖 Reading 1

The assignments in the Bible and textbook, should have given you a general understanding of the period when the church was greatly troubled by heresies and factions. This exercise should have helped you gain a general understanding of the literature of the period.

From its very beginning the church was threatened by three basic perils, one of which was the peril of *persecution*. While there were isolated cases of persecution that began with the death of Stephen, persecution became a universal threat to the church following the death of Paul, as we saw in 1 Peter.

The second peril that plagued the church from its beginning was Jewish *legalism*. The legalistic threat, which is evident in much of the New Testament literature, finally reached the critical stage. At this point, the church broke decisively with legalism, which is indicated in Hebrews.

The third peril that threatened the church from its birth was *heresy*. By the time of the Pastoral Epistles heresies had become pronounced. In this lesson you observe that heresies and schisms had become major perils to the church and prompted the writing of 2 Peter, Jude, and 1, 2, and 3 John.

Thus, the battle lines shifted. Now, the major concern was not threats from without (persecution and legalism), but challenges from within (false doctrine and factionalism).

Background

📖 Reading 2

The section on "Background" indicates the widespread and serious nature of the *heresies* and *schisms* that plagued the church from AD 60 onward. The Epistles of 2 Peter, Jude, and 1, 2, and 3 John were written to help believers cope with heresies and schisms.

Answer the following questions in your notebook.

1   According to Tenney, when will false doctrine have its "complete demonstration"?

2   What are the false doctrines against which you have to warn believers in your area?

3   Tenney compares *error* and *human nature*. Do you agree that his comparison is valid? Give the reason for your answer.

4   From your own knowledge identify four major false doctrines that have persisted through the centuries.

Objective **13.2** *State the theme of 2 Peter and how it is developed to deal with errors in the church.*

2 Peter

📖 Reading 3

In the discussion under the heading "Background" of 2 Peter, you will see that there is not as much external evidence for the authorship of 2 Peter, 2 John and 3 John as there is for the other books of the New Testament. In fact, there is less external evidence for the authenticity of 2 Peter than there is for any of the other books. Nevertheless, two very strong points of external evidence the textbook does not note in support of the authenticity of authorship of 2 Peter are:

1. Jude quotes 2 Peter chapter 2 extensively.

2. Jude attributes 2 Peter to "the apostles of our Lord Jesus Christ" (Jude 17–18).

5 Tenney gives several points of internal evidence for Petrine authorship of 2 Peter. Mark them in your textbook and then state four in your own words. Use your notebook.

Tenney concludes that "the internal evidence creates at least a presumption of authenticity" of authorship. I would add other points of internal evidence to those given by Tenney that convince me of the Petrine authorship of 2 Peter. One is that 1 and 2 Peter have basically the same teaching; another is that 2 Peter uses many of the same words that Peter used in his speeches in Acts.

While the date of the writing of 2 Peter cannot be established conclusively, on the basis of current information the best date seems to be around AD 64. This would be some time after 1 Peter and about the time when Hebrews was written. It was most likely written from Rome to the assemblies of Northern Asia Minor, and the recipients were the same as those of 1 Peter.

While 1 Peter was written to encourage believers to trust God's grace under persecution, 2 Peter had as its purpose the correction of doctrinal error. It is especially concerned with errors about the coming of the Lord. As a result, it is classified as *eschatological* (pertaining to the study of last things). In addition to errors about the coming of the Lord, the textbook shows that 2 Peter was concerned about other doctrinal errors and deficiencies that can be summarized as follows:

1. Denial of redemption through Christ, and of His Lordship

2. Spiritual ignorance

3. Selfassertiveness

4. Low moral standards

6 What does 2 Peter suggest as an *antidote* to these doctrinal errors and personal deficiencies produced by false knowledge?

....

Tenney recalls the theme of 1 Peter, which was suffering. Then, he compares it with 2 Peter.

7 What is the central theme of 2 Peter?

....

You will be able to study and comprehend the outline and content of 2 Peter better with the help of this *key* to its message.

The textbook indicates that the chief value of 2 Peter is its teaching concerning the origination of Scripture. You have studied biblical inspiration in Lesson 1, but it is important to remember here that one of the clearest statements on biblical inspiration and interpretation is given in 2 Peter 1:15–21. In this passage Peter plainly declares that Scripture is based upon historical knowledge and divine revelation.

In addition to this chief value, other values of 2 Peter can be listed as follows:

1. It teaches that salvation is assured by true knowledge.

2. It predicts that teachers of error will be more fully revealed in the future.

3. It refutes error about the future with an expansive treatment of the last days and Christ's return.

4. It gives additional biographical data on the apostle Peter.

Objective **13.3**

Analyze similarities between Jude and 2 Peter. Then summarize the values of Jude, emphasizing theological values.

Jude

📖 Reading 4

Tenney's discussion under the heading "Background" takes you immediately into a consideration of the similarities between Jude and 2 Peter (especially 2 Peter 2).

Answer the following questions in your notebook.

8 Identify the three ways presented in the textbook in which the two Epistles are similar.

9 Restate in your own words the four proposed explanations of the relationship between Jude and 2 Peter.

10 Which of the four possible answers to the question concerning these similarities do you think is the most valid?

11 Do any of these answers allow for the Holy Spirit to inspire Jude to utilize information from 2 Peter, from apocryphal literature, from his own knowledge, and from direct inspiration of the Holy Spirit in the writing of this book?

12 Do you accept the possibility of the direct inspiration of the Holy Spirit? Explain.

The book of Jude was written by Jude, the brother of the author of the Epistle of James and half brother of Jesus. Jude was probably written two or three years after the books of 2 Peter and Hebrews. We cannot establish the date when Jude was written with certainty; however, on the basis of available evidence, AD 67 or 68 is an acceptable date. Jude was written to all Christians in general and to Jewish Christians in particular.

In the section on "Content" you find that Jude's purpose in writing was to urge Christians to "strongly defend the faith." By "the faith" Jude meant the body of truth that God *gave* believers once for all to be preserved unchanged through the years. Jude's exhortation to "strongly defend the faith" was needed to counteract false teachers who were teaching a heresy that took Christian liberty to the opposite extreme from the legalism of the Judaistic teachers. Tenney calls this heresy *antinomianism,* * which means "against Law." It is a combination of the Greek word *anti,* meaning "against" or "opposed to," and the Greek word *nomos* meaning "law."

antinomianism
the belief that faith frees the Christian from the obligations of the moral law (you could do as you pleased and it would make no difference); denial of the Lordship of Christ

Jude recognized that this anti-law teaching was a grave error and pronounced God's judgment upon its adherents. Note the graphic language and strong illustrations of judgment that Jude uses.

13 Tenney has clearly summarized the errors of the anti-law libertines and Jude's antidotes for them. For each of the errors listed below, identify Jude's antidote.

a Error: Cain's "way of bloodless sacrifice"

Antidote: ....

....

b Error: Balaam's idea "that God is the minister of man's convenience rather than the Lord of his destinies"

Antidote ....

....

c Error: Korah's "arrogance of a selfdevised faith"

Antidote: ....

....

The little book of Jude has many *values* for Christianity. You should be aware of at least the following:

1. *Historical.* Jude refers to Jewish history more than any other book of its size in the New Testament.

2. *Ethical.* Jude stresses moral values and calls for practice consistent with beliefs.

3. *Spiritual.* Jude presents a program for spiritual edification and security.

4. *Theological.* (Fill in the information requested in the following exercise.)

5. *Religious.* Jude has one of the great benedictions of the Bible.

14 To see the theological values of Jude, complete these exercises:

 a As early as AD 67 or 68 there was a standard by which believers were to live. This was a *given* body of truth that set rigorous doctrinal and behavioral standards. In which verse is it located?

 ....

 b Jude gives a *program for spiritual edification* by which believers can be kept with the standard. Give the reference for the two verses that give this program.

 ....

 c Jude tells believers how to treat those who deviate from the standard. What two verses tell how to treat heretics?

 ....

15 Copy Jude's benediction with its reference.

....

....

....

The Johannine Epistles

The Epistles of John, like 2 Peter and Jude, were written to counteract the heresy and factionalism that were the church's greatest perils during the last forty years of the first century.

Objective **13.4**

Summarize the principal values of 1, 2, and 3 John.

Background

📖 Reading 5

You have already made the acquaintance of the apostle John as the author of the Gospel account that bears his name. He is the generally accepted author of the three short Epistles we are now considering and of the book of Revelation you will study in the next lesson.

Since these Epistles were the last ones written and appeared in the last years of the first century, they came at the time of the greatest threat from heresy the church had known. The purpose of 1 John was to strengthen believers against heresies at two points. One was to give them certainty about their salvation; the other was to insist upon Christ's humanity. At both of these points 1 John is a complement to the Gospel account of John. In his Gospel account, John viewed Christ in His divinity, but, in 1 John the apostle viewed Christ in His humanity. Thus, the picture is complete—Christ is fully God and fully man. In his Gospel account, John stated that his purpose in writing was to enable his readers to have life through their belief that Jesus was the Christ. In 1 John the stated purpose was to enable his readers to "know" they had entered into life.

The purpose of 2 and 3 John is to serve as introductory notes to 1 John. First John, like Ephesians, was a circular letter. It was intended first for the assembly at Ephesus, then for the assemblies of Asia, and finally for the church universal. Second John was attached to one copy of 1 John that was addressed to an assembly in the vicinity of Ephesus. This introductory note conveyed personal greetings and counsel. Third John was attached to another copy of 1 John that was addressed to Gaius, a Christian pastor. This introductory note conveyed personal greetings and counsel about matters of church administration.

It is generally held that the Epistles of John were all written at the same time from the city of Ephesus. Tradition indicates that John moved to this city after the death of Mary, the mother of Jesus, around AD 55. Then, he returned to Ephesus after his Patmos experience and lived there (according to Jerome) until he died at 100 years of age, sixty-eight years after the crucifixion. This would have been about AD 100. While Tenney chose AD 85 as the date of the writing of the Epistles of John, the choices of other Bible scholars, who take a late date, range from AD 85–98. The best date, in my opinion, is AD 90.

Obviously John's Epistles were written in response to the heresy of Gnosticism. You were introduced to Gnosticism in Lesson 2, and again in Lesson 11, which discussed how Paul was counteracting an early form of this heresy. It will be helpful to turn back to Lesson 11 and read the summary on Gnosticism to refresh your mind. Then study the more mature expressions of Gnosticism in the form of *docetism** and *cerinthianism,** as they are discussed in the textbook. Be able to describe each of these forms of Gnosticism, with their beliefs about the nature of Christ, and John's answers to each of them.

1 John

▢ Reading 6

In 1 John we encounter a most unusual style of writing. Tenney says, "1 John is symphonic rather than logical in its plan." This style of writing is beautiful to read but difficult to analyze. In spite of this difficulty, the textbook furnishes an excellent outline of 1 John. Review this outline carefully as you study the content of the Epistle and it will enhance your learning.

2 John

▢ Reading 7

The purpose of 2 John is to serve as an introductory note to 1 John. It then conveys personal greetings and counsel.

While 1 John is keyed to personal experience, 2 John is even more personalized. It seems to be a good example of a personal note from the hand of an apostle. Thus, it is quite different both in style and content from the other Epistles we have been studying. Because of these differences, the canonicity of 2 and 3 John has been seriously disputed. It is interesting to note that the authenticity of authorship of some Epistles, is doubted because of similarities between them (2 Peter and Jude), while that of others is doubted because they are different from other Epistles (2 and 3 John).

Perhaps the main thing for you to remember about the content of 2 John is that it is basically the same as that of 1 John. By stressing the humanity of Christ, both 1 and 2 John complement the Gospel of John, which stresses the divinity of Christ.

docetism
a heresy which held that Christ was not historically real but a phantom that appeared in human guise and then vanished; a form of Gnosticism

cerinthianism
an advanced form of Gnosticism: the belief that the Christ-spirit did not actually inhabit the human Jesus until His baptism and left Him before His death on the cross, making a strange contradiction out of the personality of Jesus; blurred the nature of Jesus so that one would not know if the human Jesus or Divine Christ-spirit were speaking and acting

3 John

📖 Reading 8

The purpose of 3 John is to serve as an introductory note to 1 John. It then conveys personal greetings and counsel to the pastor Gaius, as explained above.

John's concern in 3 John is different from that in 1 and 2 John. Here he addresses the matter of entertaining itinerant missionary workers and the kind of attitude that should characterize those who have been transformed by the truth.

16 What was the subject of John's counsel to the pastor Gaius in 3 John?

....

17 With what concern is 3 John more involved than are 1 and 2 John?

....

Both Paul and John realized that ministers need instructions in practical matters as well as in the content of their message.

Tenney declares, concerning John's Epistles, "Maturity of thought and holiness of life are their objectives . . . ."

18 In keeping with these objectives, the value of these Epistles can be outlined under the theme "A Program for Spiritual Achievement." Values *a*, *b*, and *c* given below are included under this theme. Place brackets around the lines in the textbook that discuss each of these values, and write the identifying letter of the value beside the appropriate bracket in the left margin of your textbook. Then in your notebook, state briefly Tenney's explanation of the value.

a A *clear standard* for spiritual achievement.

b *Clear proofs* of spiritual achievement.

c A *call for a clear decision* of spiritual achievement.

Golden Passages

There are several special passages in 2 Peter, Jude, and 1, 2, and 3 John that will greatly enrich your life and ministry. You should become familiar with their content and be able to locate them by memory or with a concordance. These golden passages are as follows:

1. Growth in Christian virtues	2 Peter 1:2–11
2. The Scripture is based upon historical knowledge and divine revelation	2 Peter 1:15–21
3. The tragedy of backsliding	2 Peter 2:20 22
4. The necessity for readiness for the Lord's return	2 Peter 3:1–14
5. A program for spiritual edification and security	Jude 20–25
6. The conditions of fellowship with God	1 John 1:5–9
7. Christians must not love the world	1 John 2:15–17
8. Divine sonship: Its bestowal, its consequence, its prospects	1 John 3:1–3
9. The witness of our love and His Spirit to our salvation	1 John 3:14–24
10. The circle of love	1 John 4:7–21
11. We can be spiritually prosperous and healthy	3 John 2

Total Time
(Read, answer questions, check answers)

Hr_____ Min_____

Start Time

_____

Self-Test 13

Matching. Match the book, date, doctrine, value or Scripture passage (right) with its appropriate description (left).

. . . . **1** Gives one of the clearest statements on biblical inspiration.

. . . . **2** The value of 1 John is connected with its teaching on maturity of thought and holiness of life.

. . . . **3** Has less external evidence for its authenticity than any other New Testament book.

. . . . **4** A heresy counteracted by Jude.

. . . . **5** Was probably written in AD 67 or 68.

. . . . **6** A heresy counteracted by John.

. . . . **7** Jude offers more of this value for its size than any other New Testament book.

. . . . **8** The date of the writing of 2 Peter.

. . . . **9** Suggested by 2 Peter as the antidote to doctrinal errors and personal deficiencies.

. . . . **10** The date of the writing of John's Epistles.

a) 2 Peter
b) True knowledge
c) Jude
d) Antinomianism
e) Historical value
f) Gnosticism
g) Theological value
h) AD 90
i) AD 64
j) 2 Peter 1:15–21
k) Ecclesiastical value

True-False. Write T in the blank preceding each TRUE statement. Write F if it is FALSE.

. . . . **11** The church was not threatened by persecution, legalism, or heresy until around AD 85–95.

. . . . **12** At the time of the writing of 2 Peter, Jude, and 1, 2, and 3 John, the major threat was from within the church.

. . . . **13** Second Peter and 2 and 3 John do not have much external witness to their authenticity.

. . . . **14** Second Peter was most likely written from Rome to the assemblies of northern Asia Minor.

. . . . **15** Second Peter was written to encourage Christians to trust God's grace while under persecution.

. . . . **16** Jude and 2 Peter chapter 2 are very much alike in content.

. . . . **17** There was a given standard for Christians to live by as early as AD 67–68.

. . . . **18** Jude tells Christians to "burn" heretics "as by fire."

. . . . **19** John the "son of thunder" has little to say about love.

. . . . **20** Jude stresses moral values and calls for a practice that is consistent with belief.

Fill in the Blank.

21 The tragedy of .... is presented in 2 Peter 2:20–22.

22 First John 2:15–17 teaches that Christians must not love the ....

23 The Gospel of John stresses Christ's divinity, while 1 and 2 John stress His

....

24 Third John counsels .... in matters of church administration.

25 John said, "Dear friend, I pray that you may enjoy good health and that all may go well with you, even as your... is getting along well."

Self-Test Time

Hr_____ Min_____

Answers to Study Questions

10 Your answer.

1 Tenney states that "the complete demonstration of this tendency may still await fulfillment in the culmination of this age."

11 Your answer. The Holy Spirit inspired Jude to write the Epistle, whatever resources he used.

2 Your answer might be as follows (without specifically identifying organized groups): The teaching that the Bible does not really mean what it says. For example, the Bible teaches salvation by faith, but false teachers insist that the Bible really means that salvation is by works.

12 Your answer.

3 I think the comparison is valid. In my experiences in observing a succession of churches, I have heard members argue over the same basic errors, calling them by different names from one decade to another.

13 In this order:
  a Remembering Christ's words, as communicated through His apostles.
  b Keeping one's self "in the love of God by prayer and by constructive action" (Jude 2021).
  c Rescuing "others from the errors that surround them, so that their doubt may not lead them ultimately to disaster" (Jude 2223).

4 Your answer may include some like these: Jesus never really lived on earth. The resurrection of Jesus did not really happen. Personal acceptance of Christ as one's Redeemer is not necessary. One just needs to live a good life to be saved. The Bible is not really the revelation of God's will for human life.

14 **a** Jude 3.
  b Jude 2021.
  c Jude 2223.

5 In any order: (1) Allusions to the life of Peter agree with what is known from other sources, (2) author of 2 Peter refers to Paul as to a contemporary (2 Peter 3:15), (3) Peter could have written what it says, and (4) lack of proof that Peter did not write 2 Peter.

15 Jude 2425.

6 Correct knowledge.

16 The practice of truth.

7 Knowledge.

17 Church administration.

8 In any order: (1) Occasion, (2) vocabulary, and (3) thought.

18 In this order:
  a Possession of the eternal life clearly and perfectly revealed in Christ.
  b Living on the appropriate side of the line between four dichotomies: righteousness / unrighteousness, truth / falsehood, light / darkness, love / hatred.
  c Acceptance or rejection of the standard of truth.

 9 In any order: (1) Recipients of the two Epistles faced the same problem. (2) Both Epistles borrowed from a common source. (3) Second Peter borrowed from Jude. (4) Jude was motivated by 2 Peter to write his own Epistle

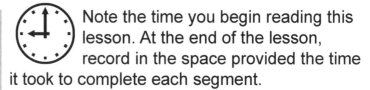

Note the time you begin reading this lesson. At the end of the lesson, record in the space provided the time it took to complete each segment.

The Expectant Church

Start Time

_____

We have already seen how some New Testament books, such as Matthew and Hebrews, are closely linked to Old Testament Scriptures. We see this again in the book of Revelation, as it reveals to us more fully what Ezekiel and Daniel and other Old Testament prophets wrote long before Christ's incarnation.

How fitting it is that the final book in the Bible should give us a glimpse into the new heaven and the new earth that God has prepared for those who are faithful to Him! For those who have rejected God's love, this book presents a fearful, detailed description of final judgment and punishment. But to those of us who have been born into His family, and who are faithful in His service, the book of Revelation is a glorious promise of an eternal life of joy and peace in His presence. No longer will we live in a world made imperfect by sin; no longer will our enemy the devil tempt us; no longer will we suffer pain and sorrow and distress. For God's kingdom will be triumphant over all of these things!

Then I heard a loud voice in heaven say: Now have come the salvation and the power and the kingdom of our God, and the authority of his Christ. For the accuser of our brothers who accuses them before our God day and night, has been hurled down. They overcame him by the blood of the Lamb and by the word of their testimony; and they did not love their lives so much as to shrink from death (Revelation 12:10–11).

As ministers of the gospel, we need to understand this revelation of end-time events for two reasons. First, it is a warning to those who have chosen the way of sin and the world. Second, it is a message of hope and expectancy for the church, the body of Christ, those who have overcome the enemy by the blood of the Lamb. Let us be faithful in sharing this twofold message with others.

the activities...

◇ Read the book of Revelation straight through to get an overview of its message. Then, read the textbook assignment. As you read the textbook, keep your Bible open and read the Scripture references in the textbook as you come to them. The readings for this lesson are

    Reading 1: pages 381–395

    Reading 2: pages 381–385

    Reading 3: pages 385–389

Reading 4: pages 390–393
Reading 5: pages 393–395

◊ Review the key words to see if any are unfamiliar to you. Some of the words in this lesson are especially significant in relation to the study of end-time events. You will understand the lesson better if you know what these terms mean. Take the time to check their meaning in the glossary.

◊ Study the lesson as usual, completing all learning exercises, taking the self-test, and checking your answers

the objectives...

14.1 *Define* apocalyptic *and name the four apocalyptic characteristics of Revelation.*

14.2 *Summarize the major interpretations of the book of Revelation given by Tenney in chart form and identify guidelines of interpretation.*

14.3 *Choose reasons that support the premillennialism view.*

14.4 *Give examples of how different series of seven outline important features of Revelation.*

14.5 *Explain the significance of the messages to the seven churches in Revelation.*

14.6 *Draw a diagram showing the time relation of major events in Revelation.*

the outline...

1 The Expectant Church: Revelation
   a Background
   b Interpretations
   c The Millennial Views
   d Content and Outline
   e Evaluation

2 Golden Passages

The Expectant Church: Revelation

📖 Reading 1

Your reading assignments in the Bible and textbook are designed to give you a general understanding of the book of Revelation. However, because apocalyptic* literature is more difficult to interpret than other types of narrative material in the New Testament, the lesson development is intended to assist you as you consider its most difficult and most important features in greater detail.

In Units 1 and 2 of this course you studied the preparation for the church of Christ. Then in Units 3 and 4 you followed the course of the church from its establishment down through the history of its expansion and consolidation. Now you take up the study of the consummation of the church. In the book of Revelation this grand finale is the expectation and prayer of the true church.

apocalyptic
genre of literature usually produced in times of persecution or oppression as a means of encouraging those who were suffering for their faith; including the judgment of the wicked and the deliverance of the righteous

We begin our study of this book by noting what John wrote in its last two verses. He who testifies to things described in this book says, "Yes, I am coming soon." As John wrote, "Amen. Come, Lord Jesus. The grace of the Lord Jesus be with God's people. Amen." (Revelation 22:20–21).

Objective 14.1 *Define* apocalyptic *and name the four apocalyptic characteristics of Revelation.*

Background

📖 Reading 2

It is very appropriate that Revelation should be the last book in the Bible because it is the great unveiling of God's plan for the age of perfection, for which all the other sixty-five books of the Bible are preparation. Your study of each book of the Bible will therefore contribute to your understanding of this ultimate book. Your understanding of Revelation will furnish the *capstone** for the structure of truth established by the other sixty-five books.

> **capstone**
> final or crowning point, stroke, or culmination

Revelation is classified as *apocalyptic literature* and consequently, it must be studied with an understanding of the style of this type of literature.

1 Reread pages in the textbook concerning apocalyptic literature. Then circle the letter preceding the completion that is NOT one of the five characteristics of apocalyptic literature. It was characterized by
  a) an intense despair of the present and the intense hope that God would intervene in the future.
  b) the use of symbolic language, dreams, and visions.
  c) the introduction of angelic and demonic powers as messengers in the progress of God's purpose.
  d) supernatural deliverance for the righteous.
  e) the use of omens, astrological data, and occultic mediums.
  f) the false ascription of authorship to a prominent character from biblical history.

2 Which one of the five characteristics does not apply to Revelation?

....

Why do you think John gave his name three times in Revelation, while in his Gospel account and in the Epistles he wrote he carefully avoided mentioning his name? I think John gave his name in Revelation to give the book *credence** beyond that of ordinary apocalyptic literature. The book of Daniel in the Old Testament is an apocalyptic book in which we find the same thing. That is, he gave his name to the book he wrote to give it credibility that ordinary apocalyptic literature lacked.

> **credence**
> belief, especially as based on the evidence or reports of others; mental acceptance as real or true

The recipients of the Revelation were the pastors of seven local assemblies in Asia. Turn to the map in chapter 19 of the textbook and locate these seven churches. We will study more about each of these assemblies when we consider the contents of Revelation 2 and 3. Notice the conditions under which the Roman government had placed these assemblies.

You probably gave some thought to the date when the Apocalypse was written as you read the material in your textbook. It should be clear that we can neither assign an exact date nor be dogmatic about the circumstances under which the book was written. So, the scholars who insist on an earlier date believe that Revelation was written during the latter part of Nero's reign (AD 64–68), that is, following the great fire of Rome, when Christians were especially persecuted. Other scholars place the time of writing during the reign of Domitian (AD 81–96), based on external evidence. On the basis of evidence given in the textbook and the almost unanimous testimony of early church leaders, I prefer to believe that Revelation was written in AD 96 at the end of the reign of Domitian, the Roman emperor who imprisoned John on the island of Patmos.

The purpose of Revelation is announced in the name of the book itself. Revelation (Greek *apokalupsis* with its English transliteration *apocalypse*) comes from the Greek verb *apokalupto* which means "to reveal," "to unveil," "to make manifest."

The purpose is announced in Revelation 1:1 also: "The Revelation (*apokalupsis*) of Jesus Christ, which God gave him to show unto his servants what must soon take place . . . ." Thus, the purpose of Revelation was to reveal Christ in His relationship to His church, His triumph over anti-Christian forces and Satan, and His ushering in the kingdom of God. More briefly stated, the purpose was to show Christ in relation to events of the last days. This revelation was intended to give guidance and encouragement to the seven assemblies at the time of writing as well as to believers in the future.

The apostle John, author of the Gospel of John and 1, 2, and 3 John, is taken to be the author of Revelation also. John's authorship received early and widespread acceptance by the church, but later it was vigorously disputed. Tenney presents three good explanations of the language differences between Revelation and the other writings of John. These are important for you to know because the language difference is the source of greatest doubt of John's authorship of Revelation.

Objective **14.2**

Summarize the major interpretations of the book of Revelation given by Tenney in chart form and identify guidelines of interpretation.

Interpretations

📖 Reading 3

The book of Revelation has probably received a greater variety of interpretations than any other book in existence. Most interpretations come under one of four main schools or methods of interpretation. Your textbook discusses these briefly but adequately.

3 Copy the following chart in your notebook. As you study the four methods mentioned in the textbook, fill in the information called for.

Schools of Interpretation of the Book of Revelation				
1 *School of Interpretation*	*2* *Traits Describing This School*	*3* *Strengths*	*4* *Weaknesses*	*5* *Views of Millennium*
a Preterist				
b Idealist				
c Historicist				
d Futurist				

Figure 14.1

Since the book of Revelation is mostly prophetic and apocalyptic in style, several guidelines for interpretation follow. These can be drawn from the first few verses of the book itself.

1. It is *revelational*. As already noted, the very first word in the Greek text is *apokalupsis* (English transliteration *apocalypse*), meaning "a revelation." From this we understand that the book is an unveiling, a manifestation, an uncovering—neither a mystery nor an enigma. Thus we are to approach the book in the belief that God wants us to understand its message.

2. It is *christological*. The very first sentence of the book reads, "The Revelation of Jesus Christ . . . ." (Revelation 1:1). Tenney indicates that the grammatical construction allows one of two interpretations: a revelation *of* Jesus Christ or a revelation *by* or *from* Jesus Christ. I favor the first interpretation but either interpretation calls for a christological interpretation of the book. Even without this opening line, the remaining content of the book is heavily Christ-centered and thus requires a christological approach to interpretation.

In Lesson 4 we observed the centrality of Christ in both the Old and the New Testaments. Turn back to that lesson now and review statements on that subject. Then, review the chart of Old Testament prophecies about Christ that were fulfilled in the New Testament. If Christ is the *key* to interpretation of the Bible in general and the New Testament in particular, He is more emphatically the *key* to unlock the prophetic portions of the Scripture. The book of Revelation is, of course, heavily prophetic, and we must keep the centrality of Christ in mind in its interpretation.

3. It is *symbolical*. Revelation 1:1 (KJV) indicates that the Revelation was *signified*. This means that the message was conveyed through signs, symbols, types, figures, emblems, and metaphors. These methods convey the message through pictures or imagery. The symbols of Revelation are sometimes explained within the context (see Figure 14.2), sometimes taken from the Old Testament, and sometimes drawn from secular sources that were known to the recipients.

Once defined, a symbol generally retains the same meaning in subsequent use.

Among the symbols of Revelation that are drawn from the Old Testament and get their meaning from Old Testament usage are:

1. The tree of life: Revelation 2:7; 22:2
2. The hidden manna: Revelation 2:17
3. The scepter (rod) of iron: Revelation 2:27
4. The morning star: Revelation 2:28
5. The key of David.   Revelation 3:7
6. The living creatures: Revelation 4:7
7. The four horsemen: Revelation 6:1–8
8. The great (mighty) angel: Revelation 10:1
9. The first beast: Revelation 13:1–8
10. The second beast: Revelation 13:11–18

It is essential to have a thorough knowledge of the Old Testament in order to understand the Revelation. While there is not a single direct citation from the Old Testament, 348 passages in Revelation have a verbal likeness to Old Testament passages.

Among the symbols of Revelation explained within the context are:

Symbol	Explanation	Reference
1. The seven stars	The pastors of the assemblies	Revelation 1:20
2. The seven lampstands	The seven assemblies of Asia	Revelation 1:20
3. The seven lamps of fire	The seven spirits of God	Revelation 4:5
4. The bowls of incense	The prayers of the saints	Revelation 5:8
5. The great multitude	Those who came out of The Great Tribulation	Revelation 7:9–14
6. The great dragon	The devil	Revelation 12:9
7. The seven heads of the beast	Seven mountains (hills)	Revelation 17:9
8. The ten horns of the beast	Ten kings	Revelation 17:12
9. The waters	Multitudes of people, nations	Revelation 17:15
10. The woman	The great city	Revelation 17:18

Figure 14.2

4. It is *eschatological*. Revelation 1:19 indicates that the purpose of Revelation is to show "what you have seen [past], what is now [present] and what will take place later [future]". This term refers, then, to all that was prophetically future when it was written. The eschatological view concerns the grand culmination of the entire program of God.

4   Revelation 4:1 is the beginning of which part of the purpose of Revelation?

....

rapture
refers to the doctrine that
members of the true church
will be caught up suddenly
by Christ at His return in
the air

From Revelation 4:1 to the end of the book, Revelation deals with events which are to follow the church dispensation described in Revelation 2 and 3— and the rapture* of the saints in Revelation 4:1.

These *end-time events* are usually classified under *eschatology*, the doctrine of last things.

5. It is *chronological*. Revelation 1:19 divides the book into three broad time categories, and other verses give clues relative to time sequence.

We have observed that prophecy is generally given in broad outlines rather than in minutely outlined sequence. Therefore, the interpreter must follow the order of events as they are given by the author, unless the results will not fit into a meaningful time scheme he has derived from the study of prophetic Scriptures as a whole.

parenthetical
pertaining to a digression or
added passage

The book of Revelation *does* seem to establish its own chronology in Revelation 1:19. Thus, its major events seem to follow a consecutive order that is broken occasionally by a series of parenthetical* passages. Some overlaps, parallels, and interludes do occur and they can only be placed in proper sequence by a prayerful study of God's plan of the last things in the whole of Scripture.

6. It is *prophetical*. In Revelation 1:1 we read, ". . . what must soon take place . . . .". Because of the prophetic nature of Revelation, human language is strained in an effort to convey ideas that have not been experienced. Also, it is difficult for the human mind to understand the prophecy. This has caused some to *spiritualize* or *allegorize* their interpretation.

In order to avoid either extreme of spiritualizing on the one hand or allegorizing our interpretation of prophecy on the other, we should follow these six rules for interpreting prophecy:

1. Take the words of the prophecy as literal rather than figurative, unless the context and related prophecies indicate otherwise.

2. Take the events of a prophecy as viewed in perspective, rather than in a systematic or rigidly outlined sequence in the modern sense. Prophecy usually has a telescopic rather than a microscopic view. It is usually given in broad general outline, and the time sequence and details have to be worked out through careful study of all related Scripture. Prophecy is generally progressive in its revelation and sometimes in its fulfillment. In much of biblical prophecy only the main events are given at first. Then, through progressive revelation (other prophecy) the details are filled in. Also, some prophecy is fulfilled progressively in installments.

3. Consider the occasion of writing, background, and circumstances of the writer carefully to ascertain the meaning of prophecy.

4. Study the language of the prophecy carefully to determine if it is symbolic, figurative, or poetic. The level of language usage needs to be considered. The Scriptures usually indicate the use of symbols.

5. Interpret the meaning of the prophecy in coordination with all other Scriptures. Keep in mind 2 Peter 1:20–21: "Above all, you must understand that no prophecy of Scripture came about by the prophet's own interpretation. For prophecy never had its origin in the will of man, but men spoke from God as they were carried along by the Holy Spirit".

6. Interpret a passage literally unless there are elements within the passage that cannot possibly apply to the actual person or event mentioned. If a double meaning (the law of double reference) is required—one applying to the actual person or event and one applying to a figurative or future person or event—the context or other Scripture will give some clue to such interpretation. In general, there is only one meaning of the prophecy, and unless otherwise indicated it is the *literal meaning.*

5 Match each of the guidelines for interpretation (right) with its description (left).

.... **a** Concerns the broad categories of Revelation in terms of time sequences

.... **b** Refers to all that was prophetically future when it was written; concerns the culmination of God's program

.... **c** Requires the interpreter to be aware that the focus of the book is on our Lord

.... **d** Concerns what has not been experienced

.... **e** Speaks of the nature of Revelation as the revealing or unveiling of God's message

.... **f** Refers to the communication of the message through symbols, signs, types, figures, emblems, metaphors

(1) Revelational
(2) Christological
(3) Symbolical
(4) Eschatological
(5) Chronological
(6) Prophetical

6 Match each of the six rules for interpreting prophecy (right) with its correct completion (left).

.... **a** because the Scriptures usually indicate when symbols are used.

.... **b** unless the context and related prophecies suggest that figurative use is intended.

.... **c** because the unity of Scripture requires that prophecy be interpreted in coordination with all other Scripture.

.... **d** Divine prophecy has a telescopic rather than a microscopic view, giving not an outlined sequence but a broad outline of events.

.... **e** Since these elements can help ascertain the meaning of prophecy.

.... **f** Unless there are elements within the passages that cannot possibly apply to the actual event or person mentioned.

(1) Take prophetic words as literal
(2) Take events of prophecy in perspective
(3) Take the occasion, background, and circumstances into account
(4) Study the language of the prophecy
(5) Interpret prophecy in the light of all other Scriptures
(6) Interpret a passage literally

Objective  *Choose reasons that support the premillennialism view.*

The Millennial Views

In addition to the four methods or schools of interpretation and guidelines for interpreting prophecy, there are three major views of the Millennium.*

Millennium
the thousand years of peace, prosperity, and prevailing holiness during Christ's reign on earth following His second coming after the Tribulation Period and while Satan is in the bottomless pit (Revelation 20)

The view taken on what constitutes the Millennium and when it occurs greatly influences the interpretation of much of the rest of Revelation.

Millennium is a combination of the Latin words *mille* (translated "thousand") and *annus* (translated "year"). Millennium means "thousand years."

As you read the descriptions of the three views of the Millennium given in the textbook, observe carefully how the guidelines for interpreting Revelation contribute to our belief in premillennialism.

As noted above, the first of the six rules for interpreting prophecy states that one should "take the words of the prophecy as literal, rather than figurative, unless the context and related prophecies indicate otherwise." This view contributes especially to belief in a literal thousand-year period for Revelation 20:1–7.

Study the chart in the textbook to see which views of the Millennium are held by the various schools of interpretation. Also, study the chart on "Time Sequence of the Major Events of Revelation" (Figure 14.6 at the end of this lesson). It will help you locate the Millennium in relation to other major events. Notice that the Millennium is bounded on one side by the second coming (revelation) of Christ, and on the other side it is bounded by Satan's last revolt.

7   Based on the brief discussion in the textbook and study question 3, circle the letter preceding each statement that is TRUE in supporting the premillennial view.

    a   The premillennial view takes the Scripture in Revelation 20 literally, and there is no convincing reason to argue for a figurative interpretation.

    b   The consistent progression of events given in Revelation agrees with the rest of Scripture regarding Christ's coming, the judgment of the wicked, and new heavens and a new earth that are required in the culmination of God's program.

    c   Since these prophesied events of the end-time have not been fulfilled heretofore, the future expectation of premillennialists is supported by the entire weight of Scripture that speaks of this time of consummation.

    d   Those who hold the premillennialist view do so because they hold a superior view of the sequence of end-time events.

Objective Give examples of how different series of seven outline important features of Revelation.

Content and Outline

📖 Reading 4

Outline of the Book of Revelation Based on the Series of Sevens

A. *The sevenfold description of Christ 1:13–18*
1. His head 1:14
2. His eyes 1:14
3. His feet 1:15
4. His voice 1:15
5. His hand 1:16
6. His mouth 1:16
7. His face (countenance) 1:16

B. *The seven churches 2:1–3:22*
1. Ephesus 2:1–7
2. Smyrna 2:8–11
3. Pergamos 2:12–17
4. Thyatira 2:18–29
5. Sardis 3:1–6
6. Philadelphia 3:7–13
7. Laodicea 3:14–22

C. *The seven wonders of the heavenly throne 4:1–5:14*
1. The occupant 4:2–3, 9–11; 5:1,7, 13–14
2. The rainbow 4:3
3. The elders 4:4, 10–11
4. The living creatures 4:6–9
5. The Book 5:1–10
6. The Lamb 5:5–14
7. The adoration 5:8–14

D. *The book with seven seals 6:1–17; 8:1*
1. First seal—the white horse 6:1–2
2. Second seal—the red horse 6:3–4
3. Third seal—the black horse 6:5–6
4. Fourth seal—the pale horse 6:7–8
5. Fifth seal—the martyrs 6:9–11
6. Sixth seal—the Lamb's wrath 6:12–17
7. Seventh seal—the period of silence 8:1

E. *The seven trumpets 8:2–9:11; 11:15–19*
1. First trumpet—hail, fire, blood 8:7
2. Second trumpet—burning mountain 8:8–9
3. Third trumpet—wormwood 8:10–11
4. Fourth trumpet—sun, moon, stars smitten 8:12–13
5. Fifth trumpet—super locusts 9:1–12
6. Sixth trumpet—army of 200,000,000 horsemen 9:13–21
7. Seventh trumpet—two great proclamations 11:15–19

F. *The seven personifications 12:1–13:18*
  1. The sun-clothed woman 12:1–2
  2. The dragon 12:3–4
  3. The man child 12:5
  4. The archangel (Michael) 12:7
  5. The rest (remnant) of her offspring 12:17
  6. The beast out of the sea 13:1–8
  7. The beast out of the earth 13:11–18

G. *The seven bowls of plagues 15:1–16:21*
  1. First bowl—ugly and painful sores upon men 16:2
  2. Second bowl—sea becomes blood 16:3
  3. Third bowl—rivers and springs (fountains) become as blood 16:4–7
  4. Fourth bowl—men scorched with great solar heat 16:8–9
  5. Fifth bowl—darkness and pain 16:10–11
  6. Sixth bowl—Euphrates River dried up 16:12
  7. Seventh bowl—loud voice, severe earthquake, huge hail 16:17–21

H. *The seven dooms 17:1–20:15*
  1. The doom of ecclesiastical Babylon 17:1–18
  2. The doom of commercial Babylon 18:1–24
  3. The doom of the Antichrist and false prophet 19:20
  4. The doom of "anti-Christian" nations 19:21
  5. The doom of Gog and Magog 20:8–9
  6. The doom of Satan 20:10
  7. The doom of the wicked dead 20:11–15

I. *The seven new things 21:1–22:5*
  1. The new heavens 21:1
  2. The new earth 21:1
  3. The new city 21:9–23
  4. The new nations 21:24–27
  5. The new river 22:1
  6. The new tree 22:2
  7. The new throne 22:3–5

8 Many writers refer to the *seven sevens* of Revelation. While one could pick out seven major series of sevens, there are still others. Our outline above, for instance, shows nine sevens that are outstanding. As an example of an additional series of sevens, the book of Revelation includes *seven blessings*. Read the reference to each of the seven to identify the blessing. Then state it in your own words. Use your notebook.

  a Revelation 1:3
  b Revelation 14:13
  c Revelation 16:15
  d Revelation 19:9
  e Revelation 20:6
  f Revelation 22:7
  g Revelation 22:14

Objective 14.5 — *Explain the significance of the messages to the seven churches in Revelation.*

Evaluation

📖 **Reading 5**

Ultimate End of Church History

Under his heading "Evaluation" Tenney says concerning John, "His chief purpose is not to predict in advance all the details of church history, but to show the general trends of the present age and their consummation in the personal return of Christ."

We have included two charts in the Study Guide at the end of this lesson, to help you understand the churches mentioned in Revelation:

- "Periods of Church History Illustrated by the Seven Churches" (Figure 14.3)
- "Messages to the Seven Assemblies" (Figure 14.4)

In the book of Revelation the messages to the seven assemblies are descriptive of the actual conditions that existed at the time when John wrote the Revelation.

Now turn to the chart, "Messages to the Seven Assemblies," and study how it depicts the following for each church:

1. Location of the assembly
2. Characteristics of Christ in the assembly
3. Strengths of the assembly
4. Weakness(es) of the assembly
5. Advice to the assembly
6. Warning(s) to the assembly
7. Promise to the assembly

Carefully study the distinctive features of each assembly. Notice also the uniformity of the letters to the assemblies.

9 Which of the assemblies is the only one for which no strengths are mentioned?

....

10 Identify the two assemblies for which no definite weaknesses are mentioned although troublesome elements are noted.

....

With respect to the messages to the seven assemblies there is the *law of double reference*: the seven assemblies were chosen to illustrate types of assemblies that have existed throughout the Church Age.

Christocentric Nature of Revelation

In the second paragraph under the heading "Evaluation" Tenney points up the *centrality of the person of Christ in Revelation*. Since we have dealt with this earlier in the lesson, a brief outline will serve to emphasize the

Christocentric nature of the book. Revelation 1:19 outlines the major divisions of the book. This passage is our *key to the chronology of the divisions,* as you will note in the following outline.

Christ in Revelation

Revelation 1:19 (NIV)

1. Christ in glorification
   "what you have seen"   Scope: Revelation 1:1–20

2. *Christ in the church*
   "what is now"   Scope: Revelation 2:1–3:22

3. *Christ in consolation*
   "and what will take place later"   Scope: Revelation 4:1–5:14

4. *Christ in conquest*
   "and what will take place later"   Scope: Revelation 6:1–20:15

5. *Christ in continuation*
   "and what will be forever"   Scope: Revelation 21:1–22:21

The book of Revelation is of great value:

- *Doctrinally* it presents many vital doctrines.

- *Prophetically* it shows the great end-time events.

- *Ethically* it promotes sanctified living in readiness for the rapture of the church.

- *Devotionally* it presents Christ as our glorified and triumphant Lord.

Objective 14.6 *Draw a diagram showing the time relation of major events in Revelation.*

Chronology of Events

Two more charts are included in the Study Guide at the end of this lesson. I hope they will help you get the time sequence of the major events in mind:

- "Time Sequence of the Parenthetical Passages of Revelation" (Daniel's Seventieth Week) (Figure 14.5)

- "Time Sequence of the Major Events of Revelation" (Figure 14.6)

I have omitted much of the data that is usually given in charts of Revelation. Instead, I have chosen a simple graphic presentation of the major events.

Tenney observes, "The chronological arrangement of Revelation is disputable" (p. 393). The most disputed section is that of Revelation 6:1–20:15.

While it is impossible for one to be dogmatic about the sequence of events in Revelation, these two charts represent my understanding of the chronology.

Notice that I have shown the seventh seal as overlapping or including the seven trumpets and the seven bowls.

I have also shown that the seventh trumpet (coming in the middle of the Tribulation)* overlaps or includes the seven bowls.

You should also know that some interludes occur between some of the seals, trumpets, and bowls. These are required by the parenthetical passages. While

Tribulation
coming period of suffering and terrible affliction never before known, many believe it will occur between the Rapture and the second coming of Christ to earth; also known as the "time of Jacob's trouble" (Jeremiah 30:7)

the first six seals, trumpets, and bowls are indicated by the same length of space on the charts, they are not necessarily identical with each other in length of time.

11 Before going on in this lesson, practice doing the following exercise until you are able to do it correctly. Draw a simple diagram showing the time relation of the following major events of Revelation:

a The rapture of the church

b The revelation of Christ

c The resurrections

d The Great Tribulation

e The Millennium

f The judgments

g The perfect age

Golden Passages

There are many passages in Revelation that will greatly enrich your life and ministry. You should become familiar with their content and be able to locate them by memory or with a concordance. These *golden passages* are:

1. John's vision of the glorified Christ	Revelation 1:11–18
2. The true church to be caught away from the great end-time troubles	Revelation 3:10–13
3. The throne of God	Revelation 4:1–11
4. The opening of the book of our redemption	Revelation 5:1–14
5. Victory over Satan through Christ	Revelation 10:10–12
6. The new heaven and new earth	Revelation 21:1–21
7. The new temple	Revelation 21:22–27
8. The river of life	Revelation 22:1–7
9. The final invitation, warning, prayer, and promise of the Bible	Revelation 22:17–21

As a closing word on this lesson, I would like to ask you to read the last verse of your Bible again (Revelation 22:21).

It is wonderful to know that *grace* is the last promise of the Bible.

Total Time
(Read, answer
questions, check
answers)

Hr_____ Min_____

Periods of Church History Illustrated by the Seven Churches

	Ephesus Period	Smyrna Period	Pergamos Period	Thyatira Period	Sardis Period	Philadelphia Period	Laodicea Period
ASSEMBLY AND PERIOD	Ephesus Period	Smyrna Period	Pergamos Period	Thyatira Period	Sardis Period	Philadelphia Period	Laodicea Period
CHARACTERISTIC	Backslidden Church	Persecuted Church	Paganized Church	Corrupt Church	Lifeless Church	Faithful Church	Compromising Church
DATES	AD 30 to AD 100	AD 100 to AD 313	AD 313 to AD 590	AD 590 to AD 1517	AD 1517 to AD 1648	AD 1648 to Present Time	
CHURCH HISTORY	Apostolic Era	Apostolic Era to Constantine (Union of Church and State)	Constantine to Gregory I (First Pope)	Gregory I to Reformation	Reformation to Peace of Westphalia	From Peace of Westphalia to Present Time	
SECULAR HISTORY	Ancient History		Medieval History (Dark Ages)		Modern History		
	Apostolic Church		Papal Church			Protestant Church Catholic Church	

Figure 14.3

Messages to the Seven Assemblies

Assembly	Character of Christ	Strengths	Weaknesses	Advice	Warnings	Promises
Ephesus 2:1–7	Sovereign Lord, 2:1	Workers, orthodox, patient, 2:2, 3, 6	Left first love, 2:4	Remember, repent, do first works, 2:5	Removal, 2:5	Eat of Tree of Life, 2:7
Smyrna 2:8–11	Resurrected Lord, 2:8	Works, endurance under trial 2:9, 10	Members of Satan's synagogue (blasphemers) present, 2:9	Fear not, be watchful, 2:10	Imprisonment, trial, tribulation, 2:10	Not hurt by second death, 2:11
Pergamos 2:12–17	War Lord 2:12, 16	Faithful in works, belief in persecution, 2:13	Balaamism, 2:14 Nicolaitanism, 2:15	Repent, 2:16	Attack, 2:16	Eat hidden manna, new name, 2:17
Thyatira 2:18–29	Judicial Lord, 2:18	Works, charity, faith, patience, 2:19	Jezebelism (spiritual fornication, adultery), 2:20–22	Repent, hold fast, 2:22, 25	Death, judgment or works, 2:23	Rulership, morning star, 2:26–28
Sardis 3:1–6	Omniscient Lord, 3:1	A few not defiled 3:4	Reputedly alive, but dead, 3:1 Works imperfect, 3:2	Remember, hold fast, repent, watch, 3:3	Surprise appearance, 3:3	White clothes, name in Book of Life, confessed before Father, 3:5
Philadelphia 3:7–13	Authoritative Lord, 3:7	Works, some strength, kept word, name, 3:8, 10	Members of Satan's synagogue (blasphemers) present, 3:9	Hold fast, 3:11	Sudden appearance of Christ, 3:11	Make pseudo-Jews worship you, keep from hour of temptation (Rapture prior to Great Tribulation, 3:10 New position, new name, 3:12
Laodicea 3:14–22	Eternal Lord 3:14	None	Lukewarm, 3:16 Proud but deficient, 3:19	Buy gold, white clothes, anoint eyes, 3:18 Be zealous, repent, 3:19	Separation, 3:16	Share Christ's throne, 3:21

Figure 14.4

TIME SEQUENCE

of the

PARENTHETICAL PASSAGES OF REVELATION

(Daniel's Seventieth Week)

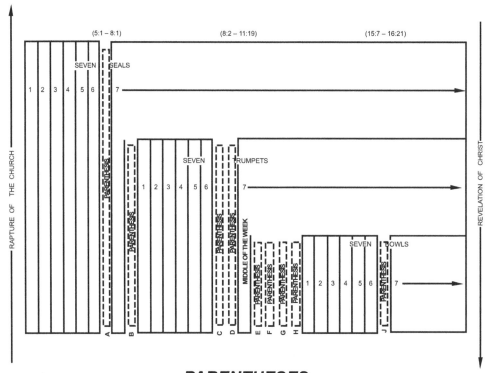

PARENTHESES

A   Remnant of Israel and Gentiles saved out of tribulation, 7:1–17

B   Silence in heaven one-half hour, 8:1

C   The little book, 10:1–11

D   The two witnesses, 11:1–13

E   The woman and the male child, 12:1–13

F   Israel in tribulation, 12:13–17

G   False prophet and antichrist, 13:1–18

H   Vision of the Lamb, 144,000, Babylon's fall, doom of false worshippers, and Armageddon, 14:1–20

J   Gathering for Armageddon, 16:13–16

Figure 14.5

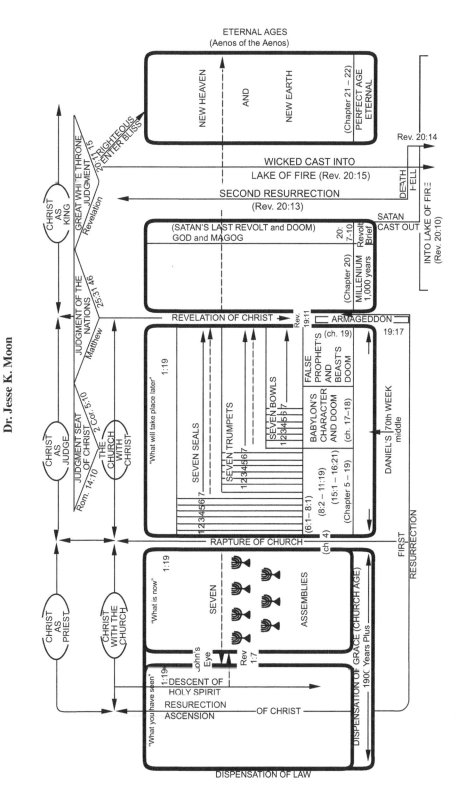

REVISED CHART:
TIME SEQUENCE
of the
MAJOR EVENTS OF REVELATION
Dr. Jesse K. Moon

Figure 14.6

Start Time

_____

Self-Test 14

Matching. In the circles on the "Time Sequence of the Major Events of Revelation" chart that follows, print the correct number of the phrase from the list below.

1 Chapter 1

2 Rapture of the church

3 Chapters 2 and 3

4 Revelation of Christ

5 Chapters 5–19

6 Seven years of tribulation

7 Chapter 20

8 First resurrection

9 Chapters 21–22

10 Great White Throne Judgment

11 Seven bowls

12 Judgment of the nations

13 Seven seals

14 Seven churches (assemblies)

15 Perfect age

16 Millennium

17 Seven trumpets

18 Dispensation of grace

19 Judgment seat of Christ

20 Second resurrection

Self-Test Time

Hr_____ Min_____

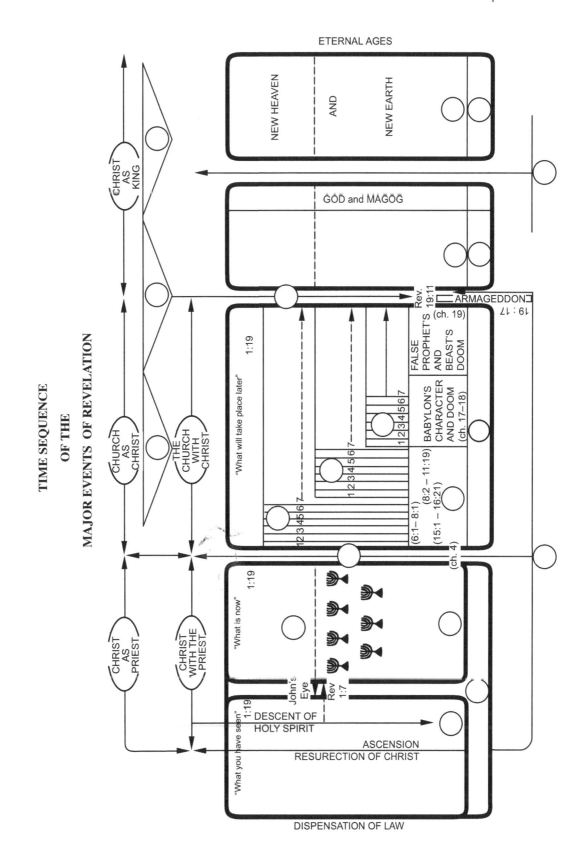

TIME SEQUENCE
OF THE
MAJOR EVENTS OF REVELATION

ETERNAL AGES

NEW HEAVEN AND NEW EARTH

GOD and MAGOG

CHRIST AS KING

CHURCH AS CHRIST

THE CHURCH WITH CHRIST

CHRIST AS PRIEST

CHRIST WITH THE PRIEST

Rev. 19:11

ARMAGEDDON

19:17

FALSE PROPHET'S AND BEAST'S DOOM

BABYLON'S CHARACTER AND DOOM (ch. 17–18)

1 2 3 4 5 6 7

1 2 3 4 5 6 7

(15:1 – 16:21)

1 2 3 4 5 6 7

(8:2 – 11:19)

1 2 3 4 5 6 7

(6:1 – 8:1)

"What will take place later" 1:19

(ch. 4)

"What is now" 1:19

John's Eye

Rev 1:7

DESCENT OF HOLY SPIRIT

ASCENSION

RESURECTION OF CHRIST

"What you have seen" 1:19

DISPENSATION OF LAW

Answers to Study Questions

6 a (4) Study the language.
  b (1) Take prophetic words.
  c (5) Interpret prophecy.
  d (2) Take events of prophecy.
  e (3) Take the occasion.
  f (6) Interpret a passage.

1 e) the use of omens, astrological data, and occultic mediums.

7 Statements **a**, **b**, and **c** are true.

2 Pseudonymous authorship by a prominent person from biblical history.

8 In this order: (Compare your words to these quotes)
  a "The one who reads the words of this prophecy, and . . . those who hear it and take to heart what is written in it."
  b "The dead who die in the Lord from now on." (Persons in whom Christ has lived.)
  c "He who stays awake and keeps his clothes with him."
  d "Those who are invited to the wedding supper of the Lamb!" (See Matthew 26:29.)
  e "Those who have part in the first resurrection."
  f "He who keeps the words of the prophecy in this book."
  g "Those who wash their robes, that they may have the right to the tree of life and may go through the gates into the city." (Those who have accepted for themselves Christ's sacrifice and redemption.)

3 See the following chart.

9 Laodicea.

4 What will take place later (future).

10 Smyrna and Philadelphia.

5 a 5) Chronological.
  b 4) Eschatological.
  c 2) Christological.
  d 6) Prophetical.
  e 1) Revelational.
  f 3) Symbolical.

11 Check your answer by comparing it with the chart at the end of the lesson.

Schools of Interpretation of the Book of Revelation

1 School of Interpretation	2 Traits Describing This School	3 Strengths	4 Weaknesses	5 Views of Millennium
a Preterist	Asserts that symbolist describes only events of the time in which Revelation was written. Holds that mention of future judgment expresses only moral anger about the time when the author wrote.	Relates Revelation to the context in which it was written.	Makes no prophecy for the future.	
b Idealist	Holds that symbolism depicts ideals or trends but not past or future events. (Ideals or trends refer to the conflict of evil and good or to the conflict between paganism and Christianity.)	Focuses on spiritual and ethical meaning rather than any debatable aspects of the symbolism. (Spiritual and ethical meaning of revelation refers to revealing of God.)	Tends to strip symbolism of prediction of the future.	Disassociates from revelation the ultimate climax of Christ ascending a throne one can see—and from the Day of Judgment.
c Historicist	Affirms that symbolism portrays church history between Pentecost and the coming of Christ.	Foreshadows future events.	Lacks unanimity among interpreters about the meanings of the symbols.	Generally postmillennial or amillennial.
d Futurist	Affirms that chapters 1 through 3 refer to the time when the book was written—or that the seven assemblies symbolize seven periods in church history between the time of the apostles and Christ's return. Asserts that 4:1–22:21 relate to the years of the Great Tribulation.			Generally premillennial.

3

Note the time you begin reading this lesson. At the end of the lesson, record in the space provided the time it took to complete each segment.

The Canon and Text of the New Testament

Start Time

_____

There are many volumes of books nowadays that are the collaboration of two or more authors. The need for such volumes is usually established by a primary source, and the work is assigned to experts in the field, who write according to specific requirements. Thus, a unified collection of works by different authors can be presented to the world for any subject.

The primary source for the writing of the New Testament Scriptures was the Holy Spirit (2 Timothy 3:16). The writing did not take place simultaneously; it occurred over a period of about seventy years following Christ's resurrection. The one thing the authors held in common was that they had all been transformed by Jesus Christ through the power of the Holy Spirit. They had a common goal: to preach the redemptive power of Christ to a lost and dying world, that the world might be saved.

It is interesting to review the process by which each of the New Testament books was admitted to the canon. By the end of the first century all the books that make up our New Testament were written and had reached their original destination. In fact, many of the books had circulated fairly widely among the churches. However, there was no recognized _body_ of sacred Scripture that was known and used by all believers. To complicate matters, a considerable body of "so-called secret writings" of heretics was also circulating among churches. To distinguish truly inspired writing from the spurious ones certain criteria were applied to each book. In this lesson we will examine this process and consider how the present canon developed and has stood the test of time. We will also consider the role of the Holy Spirit in preserving it as a fully trustworthy document, our supreme guide in faith and practice.

Let us proclaim its glorious message that all the world may know Christ and His transforming power!

the activities...   ◊ The readings for this lesson are
　　　　　　　Reading 1: pages 401–411
　　　　　　　Reading 2: pages 401–402
　　　　　　　Reading 3: pages 403–405
　　　　　　　Reading 4: pages 405–409
　　　　　　　Reading 5: pages 409–411
　　　　　　　Reading 6: pages 413–423

Reading 7: pages 415–416
Reading 8: pages 416–420
Reading 9: pages 420–423

◊ Scan the key words to see if you understand the meaning of these words. Check the meaning of any that are new to you in the glossary at the back of the Study Guide.

◊ Work through the lesson development as usual. Then take the self-test and check your answers carefully.

◊ Review the lessons in this unit in preparation for your unit progress evaluation (UPE). Read the instruction page in your Essential Course Materials, then turn to Unit Progress Evaluation 4. When you have completed the UPE, check your answers with the answer key provided in your Essential Course Materials. Review any items you may have answered incorrectly. (Although UPE scores do not count as part of your final course grade, they indicate how well you learned the material and how well you may perform on the final examination.)

◊ If you have not already done so, make arrangements now with your enrollment office for taking the final examination.

the objectives...

15.1 *State three principles of canonicity.*

15.2 *Identify three tests of divine inspiration.*

15.3 *Analyze the sources of informal witnesses and formal lists or canons of the New Testament.*

15.4 *Explain the stages of development of the canon and why some books were disputed.*

15.5 *List sources of texts that were transmitted in the early centuries of the church.*

the outline...

1 The Canon of the New Testament
 a Definition and Internal Testimony
 b External Testimony
 c Conclusions

2 The Text and Transmission of the New Testament
 a The Transmission of the Text
 b The Sources of the Text
 c Modern Translations

The Canon of the New Testament

📖 Reading 1

Your textbook treats the canon and text of the New Testament in a separate section designated Part Five. However, we have chosen to include it in Unit 4 of this course.

Since we are so accustomed to having the twenty-seven books of the New Testament in one volume, we may forget that it is the product of nine or ten authors who wrote from a variety of geographical locations during half a century.

1 What was the problem of determining the canon of the New Testament? Write your answer in your notebook.

In this lesson you will learn more about how these twenty-seven books were chosen and brought together as a unit in the canon.

 Objective **15.1** *State three principles of canonicity.*

Definition and Internal Testimony

📖 Readings 2 and 3

Tenney begins with a definition of the word *canon* and then considers the process of the canonization of the New Testament.

2 Which of the following reflects most accurately Tenney's definition of *canon*?
   a) *Canon* refers to the process of declaring something to be officially correct on the basis of enlightened opinion.
   b) *Canon* refers to the practice of making laws or rules on the basis of people's needs.
   c) *Canon* comes from a word that meant a rod or bar used as a measuring instrument, but it has come to mean *a standard.*

Associate *canon* with something in your realm of knowledge or experience that will help you to remember its meaning. I relate the term *canon* to a *straight edge* that carpenters use in many places of the world. A straight edge is a piece of wood that has been tested for perfect straightness (for its straight edge). Having met the standard, it is then used to measure the straightness of other pieces of wood. Hence, a *straight edge* becomes the *standard*. The canon therefore refers to the books that were accepted as divinely inspired and thus became our *standard* or *rule for faith and practice.*

The textbook discusses three principles that influenced the formation of the New Testament canon. The first two principles were helpful but not conclusive.

Fill in the blanks from the discussion of each principle in the textbook.

3 "The canon of the New Testament cannot be settled solely on the question of .... "

4 "The canon cannot be determined wholly by the .... of the books."

5 "The true criterion of canonicity is .... "

6 Now state in your words three principles or criteria of canonicity. Use your notebook.

Objective **15.2**

Identify three tests of divine inspiration.

I strongly recommend that you memorize 2 Timothy 3:16–17 because it is one of the clearest biblical statements about divine inspiration. This is a good point at which to study the "Internal Testimony" of the Scriptures given in the textbook.

7 The textbook presents three ways the inspiration of the New Testament may be supported. I call these "tests of divine inspiration." I have listed them below (right). I have also drawn a summary from the author's discussion of each one (left). Read the material carefully and then match the text of inspiration with its summary statement. Write the number for each term (right) in the blank space preceding its definition.

.... **a** All literature may record human thought, some may influence it profoundly, but the books of the New Testament transform it. Their power is good proof of their inspiration. . . . Wherever its message was proclaimed and received the church expanded and brought with it a cleansing of society.

.... **b** Testimony to inspiration shows the value placed on the books both informally and formally by the Christian church.

.... **c** They all have for their central subject the person and work of Jesus Christ. . . . In precision of narrative, in depth of teaching, and in concentration on the person of Christ, there is a discernible difference between the canonical and the non-canonical books.

1) Intrinsic content
2) Moral effect
3) Historic effects

Objective **15.3**

Analyze the sources of informal witnesses and formal lists or canons of the New Testament.

External Testimony

📖 Reading 4

As you study this topic, you discover there are two types of external witness to divine inspiration of the books of the New Testament.

The informal witnesses. Informal testimony consists of the casual use made of the books of the New Testament by the early church fathers. Their quotations attest both to the existence and the authority of the books.

8 The textbook presents an impressive array of informal witnesses who quoted the various New Testament books in the earliest documents. To get these witnesses clearly in view, select the data from the textbook to fill in Columns 3 and 4 of the following chart.

Informal Witnesses to Canonicity				
(1) *Person*	*(2)* *Document*	*(3)* *Date*	*(4)* *Location of Origination*	*(5)* *Books Known, Quoted, or Inferred*
a —	1 Clement			Hebrews, 1 Corinthians, Romans, Matthew
b Ignatius	—			All Pauline Epistles, Matthew, John
c Polycarp	—			Matthew, John, all Pauline Epistles
d —	Didache			Matthew, Luke, many New Testament books
e —	Epistle of Barnabas			Matthew
f Justin Martyr	—			Matthew, Mark, Luke, John, Acts, many Pauline Epistles
g Irenaeus	Against Heresies III			Matthew, Mark, Luke, John, Acts, Epistles of Paul, general Epistles, Revelation
h Tertullian	—			All books of New Testament except Philemon, James, 2 and 3 John
i Origen				All books of New Testament as then accepted by all the churches, except the following that were not yet accepted by all the churches: Hebrews, 2 Peter, 2 and 3 John, James, Jude.

Figure 15.1

9 According to Tenney, when had public opinion "agreed quite thoroughly on the reliability and authenticity" of the writings now included in the New Testament?

....

10 What was the role of the church councils concerning canonicity of writings now in the New Testament?

....

....

11 What was the decision of the Third Council of Carthage (AD 397) and the Council of Hippo (AD 419) concerning the canon of the New Testament?

....

....

canonical
accepted as belonging to the authoritative list of Scriptures composing the Bible and known as the canon

The formal lists or canons. The formal witness is found in *lists* or *canons* that had been purposely compiled as authoritative, or in the records of the *councils* that dealt with the questions of canonical* authority of writings.

12 Fill in Columns 3 and 4 of the following chart.

Formal Lists or Canons				
(1) Person	*(2)* Document	*(3)* Date	*(4)* Location	*(5)* Books Included
a Marcion	Canon of Marcion			Luke 3–24, Romans, 1 and 2 Corinthians, 1 and 2 Thessalonians, Galatians, Ephesians, Philippians, Colossians, Philemon
b Muratori	Muratorian Canon			All books of New Testament except Hebrews, James, 1 and 2 Peter (beginning of manuscript missing but probably mentioned Matthew and Mark)
c —	African List			Matthew, Mark, Luke, John, 13 Epistles of Paul, 3 Epistles of John, 2 Epistles of Peter
d Athanasius	*Festal Letter*			All 27 books of the New Testament

Figure 15.2

13 What difference do you notice in the span of time covered by the formal lists or canons, compared to that of the informal witnesses? Use your notebook for your answer.

Objective

Explain the stages of development of the canon and why some books were disputed.

Conclusions

📖 Reading 5

14 In your textbook mark the three stages of the early development of the canon. Then list them in your notebook.

15 Seven of the books now included in the New Testament were most generally disputed or omitted before the canon was clearly established. The problems and values involved in the debates will become clear as you fill in Columns 2 and 3 of the following chart. In Column 2 enter the reasons why each of these books was disputed. In Column 3 tell why you feel we need each of the six books in our New Testament. If you cannot think of a reason for keeping each one in your own canon, turn back to the lesson on each and review the values of each of these books.

Books Whose Canonicity Was Debated		
(1) *Book*	*(2)* *Reasons for Dispute*	*(3)* *Value of Book*
a Hebrews		
b James		
c Jude		
d 2 Peter		
e 2 John		
f 3 John		
g Philemon		

Figure 15.3

Contrary to the attitude of modern historical criticism, I hold the New Testament to be so distinctly unique from other literature as to be accounted for only by divine, verbal, plenary inspiration. I hope you feel the same way.

Objective

List sources of texts that were transmitted in the early centuries of the church.

The Text and Transmission of the New Testament
📖 Reading 6

In the introductory paragraph of chapter 24, the author indicates that it is not possible to date positively the first collections of the New Testament writings.

16 In what century did the New Testament as the officially recognized collection of twenty-seven books that now exist emerge?

17 When were the four Gospel accounts combined as a collection apart from the other twenty-three books?

....

18 When was the first harmony of the Gospel accounts prepared and used for public reading?

....

The Transmission of the Text

📖 Reading 7

19 Tenney states that New Testament books were first reproduced by two groups of persons. Identify them and their use of the New Testament.

a ....

b ....

20 Identify the period that dates the major divergencies in the text of the New Testament.

....

21 Which conditions of the Christian world of that period may be reflected in these divergencies?

....

22 How did errors get into the New Testament manuscripts? Write your answer in your notebook.

23 How was the New Testament transmitted from the fourth through the twelfth centuries? Use your notebook for your answer.

The Sources of the Text

📖 Reading 8

24 Praise God for the trustworthiness of the New Testament! Carefully read the first paragraph under this heading. Then, in your notebook, state two reasons why Tenney believes the New Testament is probably the most trustworthy document to come down from antiquity.

25 There are five types of sources presently available for use in reconstructing the text of the New Testament. List them in the following chart and include the information requested in each column.

(1) *Source*	*(2)* *Language*	*(3)* *Type of Letters*	*(4)* *Date*	*(5)* *Part of New Testament Included*
a				
b				
c				
d				
e				

Figure 15.4

In concluding this section I want to quote a sentence from the textbook, "Today there are more than one thousand versions of the New Testament or parts of it, but they do not affect the essential character of the text, which has already been well settled." It is reassuring to know that the text of the New Testament is trustworthy.

Modern Translations

📖 Reading 9

Your introduction to the New Testament would not be complete without a knowledge of the modern versions in your language. The New Testament has been published in many versions since Wycliffe translated the complete Bible into English for the first time: the New Testament in AD 1380 and the Old Testament in AD 1382.

Turn to the Appendix in your textbook and review the chart on "English Versions of the New Testament." You will be able to use it for future reference when you read about various English versions.

It has given me deep spiritual satisfaction to prepare these studies for you. I am praying that your introduction to the New Testament will serve as a foundation for many pleasant hours of advanced study through Global University as well as on your own. I am also praying that you may enjoy a full and rewarding life and ministry for Christ. May He say, "Well done, good and faithful servant! You have been faithful with a few things; I will put you in charge of many things. Come and share your master's happiness" (Matthew 25:21).

Total Time
(Read, answer questions, check answers)

Hr_____ Min_____

Start Time

_____

Self-Test 15

Multiple Choice. Select the best answer.

1   Three principles of canonicity are
   a) style, language, audience.
   b) authorship, date of writing, message.
   c) authorship, general acceptance, inspiration.
   d) inspiration, content, results.

2   Which of these Scriptures gives the clearest statement of divine inspiration?
   a) 2 Peter 3:1–14
   b) 2 Timothy 3:16–17
   c) 1 John 2:15–17
   d) Romans 1:17

3   Which of the following is NOT one of the ways given in the textbook to support inspiration of the New Testament?
   a) Historic effect
   b) Theological effect
   c) Moral effect
   d) Intrinsic content

4   Marcion, Muratori, and Athanasius are names connected with
   a) informal witnesses to canonicity.
   b) translations of the New Testament from Aramaic to Greek.
   c) outstanding Greek classics.
   d) formal lists or canons.

5   Ignatius, Polycarp, and Origen are names connected with
   a) informal witnesses to canonicity.
   b) translations of the New Testament from Aramaic to Greek.
   c) outstanding Greek classics.
   d) formal lists or canons.

6   The twenty-seven books of the New Testament finally become officially recognized as a completed work in the
   a) middle of the second century.
   b) fourth century.
   c) start of the fifth century.
   d) end of the fifth century.

7   Who reproduced the first New Testament books?
   a) Officials of the Roman Empire
   b) Temple priests
   c) The Essenes
   d) Private individuals and professional scribes

Matching. Match each book (left) with the reason why its canonicity was debated (right). Some have two answers each.

. . . . **8** 3 John

. . . . **9** 2 Peter

. . . . **10** James

. . . . **11** 2 John

. . . . **12** Jude

. . . . **13** Philemon

a) Content of a private nature

b) Different in style from another book by the same author

c) Brief and without enough general interest

d) Content of more interest to Jews than to Greeks

Short Answer. Briefly answer each of the following questions.

14 Give an example of internal witness to the authenticity of the New Testament books.

....

....

....

15 Give an example of external witness to the authenticity of the New Testament books.

....

....

....

16 Since the New Testament has been passed through the hands of many copyists and translators over the centuries, what proofs do we have of its trustworthiness?

....

....

....

Self-Test Time

Hr_____ Min_____

Unit Progress Evaluation 4 and Final Examination

You have now concluded all of the work in this Study Guide. Review the lessons in this unit carefully, and then answer the questions in the last unit progress evaluation (UPE). When you have completed the UPE, check your answers with the answer key provided in your Essential Course Materials, and review any items you may have answered incorrectly. Make sure you have sent to your enrollment office the materials indicated on the cover of your Essential Course Materials in the section *Checklist of Materials to Be Submitted to the Enrollment Office*. If you have not already done so, make arrangements as soon as possible with your enrollment office to take the final examination. Review for the final examination by studying the course objectives, lesson objectives, self-tests, and UPEs. Review any lesson content necessary to refresh your memory. If you review carefully and are able to fulfill the objectives, you should have no difficulty passing the final examination.

Answers to Study Questions

13 According to these two charts, informal witnesses were writing fifty years earlier than the date of Marcion's canon. About 117 years after Origen informally witnessed that all the churches had accepted as canonical all but five books, Athanasius' "Festal Letter" formally included all twenty-seven books now in the New Testament (c. AD 367).

1 It involved establishing the principles or criteria as the basis of acceptance or rejection of the books in the collection known as the New Testament.

14 In this order:
   a Quotation of writings by individual authors without argument about the strength of the witness.
   b Engagement of church fathers in argument and definition of authorities without appeal for church decision.
   c Distinction by church councils between apocryphal and canonical writings.

2 c) *Canon* comes from a word that meant "rod" or "bar" used as a measuring instrument, but it has come to mean "a standard."

15 In this order: (See Tenney and the Study Guide for alternative answers for Column 3.)
   a (2) Uncertain authorship.
       (3) Teaching on the present ministry and priesthood of Christ.
   b (2) Content of interest to Jews of the Dispersion more than to Greek Christians.
       (3) How the principles of salvation by faith and works are supplementary (not contradictory) in fostering practical ethical life.
   c (2) Brief, without adequate general interest.
       (3) Presents Christian doctrine already accepted as standard.
   d (2) Disparity between style of 1 and 2 Peter.
       (3) Teaching about origination of Scriptures.
   e (2) Content comparatively private, brief, and without enough general interest.
       (3) Complements stress on divinity of Christ in Gospel of John by stress on His humanity.
   f (2) Content comparatively private, brief, and without enough general interest.
       (3) Instruction in practical matters of church administration.
   g (2) Content's private, brief, and without enough general interest.
       (3) Teaching about what forgiveness means.

3 authorship.

16 It emerged in the early third century but was not officially recognized until the fourth century.

4 church's acceptance.

17 The middle of the second century.

5 inspiration.

18 It was prepared c. AD 170 and used until the start of the fifth century.

6 a Authorship: Evidence that a book was written by the reputed author strengthens the case for its inclusion in the canon.

b Acceptance of a book in the canon corroborates its other evidence for inclusion, but it is not necessarily decisive evidence by itself.

c The true criterion is that the Scripture was given by God's inspiration.

19 a Individual persons for their own private use.

b Scribes working professionally for use by monasteries and churches.

7 a (2) Moral effect.

b (3) Historic effects.

c (1) Intrinsic content.

20 Before Constantine, who reigned from AD 306–337.

8 (3)   (4)

a c. AD 95   Rome

b c. AD 116   Syrian Antioch

c c. AD 150   Smyrna in Asia

d first half of second century   --------------------

e c. AD 130   --------------------

f c. AD 100–165   Born in Samaria, went to Rome

g c. AD 170   Lyons in Gaul

h c. AD 200   Carthage

i c. AD 185–250   Alexandria

21 The confusion, stress, and devastation of the persecutions.

9 By the end of the fourth century AD

22 Tenney states that "it is likely that trained slaves transcribed a number of copies simultaneously from dictation" and that errors "were perpetuated by later copyists. . . ." He adds that scribes may occasionally have tried to correct what they thought was defect in the manuscript from which they copied. Carelessness was a factor.

10 To recognize and give an opinion concerning books that were canonical or noncanonical.

23 It was published as a collection of the Epistles of Paul or of the four Gospel accounts—or occasionally in pandects (completed documents).

11 These councils included the twenty-seven books now in the New Testament in the canon.

24 a Resources for the reconstruction of the text of the New Testament are greater than for other documents of the Classic Age.

b Whereas the Rylands Fragment of John may date from half a century of the life—time of the author—and the Chester Beatty papyri of a large part of the New Testament date from c. AD 250—copies of outstanding Greek classics may date 1,400 years after the life of the authors.

12 (3)   (4)
   a c. AD 140   Pontus
   b Content: last third of second century Milan, Italy
   c c. AD 360   --------------------
   d c. AD 367   --------------------

25 a (1) Manuscripts of ancient Greek texts.
      (2) Greek.
      (3) Uncials.
      (4) Third and fourth centuries.
      (5) Entire New Testament.
  b (1) Cursives.
      (2) Greek.
      (3) Cursive.
      (4) Tenth to fifteenth century.
      (5) Not indicated.
  c (1) Latin and Syriac versions.
      (2) Latin and Syriac.
      (3) Not indicated.
      (4) As early as end of second century.
      (5) Entire New Testament.
  d (1) Writings of early church fathers.
      (2) Latin and Greek.
      (3) Not indicated.
      (4) First six centuries.
      (5) Much of the New Testament.
  e (1) Lectionaries, or collections of readings used in liturgical worship in the church.
      (2) Not indicated.
      (3) Not indicated.
      (4) Ninth century or later.
      (5) Some passages from the Gospels and Epistles.

Appendix A

OLD TESTAMENT QUOTATIONS IN THE GOSPEL ACCOUNTS			
NEW TESTAMENT	*OLD TESTAMENT*	*NEW TESTAMENT*	*OLD TESTAMENT*
Matthew 1:1–17	1 Chronicles 1:34; 2:1–15; 3:1–19	Matthew 16:4	Jonah 1:17
Matthew 1:23	Isaiah 7:14	Matthew 16:18	Psalm 89:4, 26
Matthew 2:2	Numbers 24:17	Matthew 16:27	Psalm 62:12, Proverbs 24:12
Matthew 2:6	Micah 5:2ff.	Matthew 17:5	Deuteronomy 18:15; Psalm 2:7; Isaiah 42:1
Matthew 2:15	Hosea 11:1	Matthew 17:11–12	1 Kings 19:2, 10; Malachi 4:5–6
Matthew 2:18	Jeremiah 31:15	Matthew 18:16	Deuteronomy 19:15
Matthew 3:3	Isaiah 40:3	Matthew 19:4	Genesis 1:27; 5:2
Matthew 3:17	Psalm 2:7; Isaiah 42:1	Matthew 19:5	Genesis 2:24
Matthew 4:4	Deuteronomy 8:3	Matthew 19:7	Deuteronomy 24:1
Matthew 4:6	Psalm 91:11ff.	Matthew 19:18	Exodus 20:13–16
Matthew 4:7	Deuteronomy 6:16		Deuteronomy 5:17–20
Matthew 4:10	Deuteronomy 6:13	Matthew 19:19	Exodus 20:12; 21:17; Deuteronomy 5:16
Matthew 4:15ff.	Isaiah 9:1ff.	Matthew 19:26	Genesis 18:14; Jeremiah 32:17
Matthew 5:4	Isaiah 61:2	Matthew 21:5	Isaiah 62:11; Zechariah 9:9
Matthew 5:5	Psalm 37:11	Matthew 21:9	Psalm 118:26
Matthew 5:6	Psalm 36:8	Matthew 21:13	Isaiah 56:7; Jeremiah 7:11
Matthew 5:7	Psalm 18:25; Proverbs 11:17	Matthew 21:16	Psalm 8:2
Matthew 5:8	Psalm 24:3–5	Matthew 21:33	Isaiah 5:1ff.
Matthew 5:21ff.	Exodus 20:13; Deuteronomy 5:17	Matthew 21:42	Psalm 118:22
Matthew 5:27	Exodus 20:14; Deuteronomy 5:18	Matthew 21:44	Isaiah 8:14
Matthew 5:31	Deuteronomy 24:1	Matthew 22:24	Deuteronomy 25:5–6
Matthew 5:33	Exodus 20:7; Numbers 30:2; Leviticus	Matthew 22:32	Exodus 3:6, 15
	19:12; Deuteronomy 5:11; 23:21	Matthew 22:37	Deuteronomy 6:5
Matthew 5:43	Leviticus 19:18; Deuteronomy 23:6–7	Matthew 22:39	Leviticus 19:18
Matthew 8:11	Isaiah 49:12	Matthew 22:44	Psalm 110:1
Matthew 8:17	Isaiah 53:4	Matthew 23:5–6	Exodus 13:9; Numbers 15:38–39;
Matthew 9:13	Hosea 6:6		Deuteronomy 6:8; 11:18
Matthew 9:36	Numbers 27:17; Ezekiel 34:6	Matthew 23:23	Leviticus 27:30; Micah 6:8
Matthew 10:35	Micah 7:6	Matthew 23:35	Genesis 4:8; 2 Chronicles 24:20–21
Matthew 11:5	Isaiah 35:5–6; 61:1	Matthew 23:38ff.	Jeremiah 12:7; 22:5

OLD TESTAMENT QUOTATIONS IN THE GOSPEL ACCOUNTS			
NEW TESTAMENT	*OLD TESTAMENT*	*NEW TESTAMENT*	*OLD TESTAMENT*
Matthew 11:10	Malachi 3:1	Matthew 24:15	Daniel 9:27; 11:31; 12:11
Matthew 11:15	Psalm 78:1; Ezekiel 3:10	Matthew 24:21	Daniel 12:1
Matthew 11:23	Isaiah 14:13–15	Matthew 24:24	Deuteronomy 13:1–3
Matthew 11:24	Genesis 19:24	Matthew 24:29	Daniel 8:10; Amos 8:9; Isaiah 13:10
Matthew 11:29ff.	Jeremiah 6:16	Matthew 24:30	Isaiah 13:9–10; Ezekiel 32:7–8;
Matthew 12:2	Exodus 20:10; Deuteronomy 5:14		Daniel 7:13; Zephaniah 1:14–16
Matthew 12:3	Leviticus 24:9; 1 Samuel 21:1–6	Matthew 24:37	Genesis 6:11–13; 7:7, 21–23
Matthew 12:5	Numbers 28:9–10	Matthew 25:31	Zechariah 14:9
Matthew 12:7	Hosea 6:6	Matthew 25:46	Daniel 12:2
Matthew 12:18–21	Isaiah 42:1–4	Matthew 26:28	Exodus 24:8; Leviticus 4:18–20;
Matthew 12:40	Jonah 1:17; 2:1–2		Jeremiah 31:31; Zechariah 9:11
Matthew 13:14–15	Isaiah 6:9–10	Matthew 26:31	Zechariah 13:7
Matthew 13:32	Daniel 4:9–22	Matthew 26:64	Psalm 110:1; Daniel 7:13
Matthew 13:35	Psalm 78:2	Matthew 26:65	Leviticus 24:16
Matthew 13:43	Daniel 12:3	Matthew 27:6	Deuteronomy 23:18
Matthew 15:4	Exodus 20:12; 21:17; Leviticus 20:9	Matthew 27:9–10	Jeremiah 18:2; 19:2; 32:6–10;
Matthew 15:8–9	Isaiah 29:13		Zechariah 11:13
Matthew 27:24	Deuteronomy 21:6–9	Mark 14:64	Leviticus 24:16
Matthew 27:34	Psalm 69:21	Mark 15:24	Psalm 22:18
Matthew 27:35	Psalm 22:18	Mark 15:34	Psalm 22:1
Matthew 27:46	Psalm 22:1		
Mark 1:2	Malachi 3:1; Isaiah 40:3	Luke 1:15	Numbers 6:3; Judges 13:4–5
Mark 1:3	Isaiah 40:3		
Mark 1:11	Psalm 2:7; Isaiah 42:1	Luke 1:17	Malachi 3:1; 4:5–6
Mark 1:24	Isaiah 41:14, 16, 20	Luke 1:19	Daniel 8:16; 9:21
Mark 1:44	Leviticus 13:13; 14:2–32	Luke 1:31	Isaiah 7:14
Mark 2:24	Exodus 20:10; Deuteronomy 5:14; 23:25	Luke 1:32	2 Samuel 7:12–17
Mark 2:25	Leviticus 24:9; 1 Samuel 21:1–6	Luke 1:35	Isaiah 11:2; 61:1–2
Mark 4:12	Isaiah 6:9–10	Luke 1:38	Psalm 31:14–16
Mark 4:29	Joel 3:13	Luke 1:46	1 Samuel 2:1–10
Mark 4:32	Daniel 4:10–12	Luke 1:48	1 Samuel 1:11; Psalm 138:6
Mark 6:18	Leviticus 18:16; 20:21	Luke 1:49	1 Samuel 2:2
Mark 7:6–7	Isaiah 29:13	Luke 1:50	Psalm 103:17
Mark 7:10	Exodus 20:12; 21:17; Leviticus 20:9;	Luke 1:51	1 Samuel 2:4; Psalm 89:10; 98:1
	Deuteronomy 5:16	Luke 1:52	1 Samuel 2:7; Job 5:11; 12:19
Mark 8:18	Isaiah 6:9–10; Jeremiah 5:21;	Luke 1:53	1 Samuel 2:5; Psalm 107:9

OLD TESTAMENT QUOTATIONS IN THE GOSPEL ACCOUNTS			
NEW TESTAMENT	*OLD TESTAMENT*	*NEW TESTAMENT*	*OLD TESTAMENT*
	Ezekiel 12:2	Luke 1:54	Isaiah 41:8–9; Genesis 17:7; Micah 7:20
Mark 8:38	Psalm 62:12; Proverbs 24:12	Luke 1:59	Leviticus 12:3
Mark 9:7	Deuteronomy 18:15; Isaiah 42:1;	Luke 1:68	Psalm 72:18; 111:9
	Psalm 2:7	Luke 1:69	1 Samuel 2:10; Psalm 18:2
Mark 9:12	Malachi 4:5	Luke 1:71	Psalm 18:3; 106:10
Mark 9:48	Isaiah 66:24	Luke 1:72	Genesis 17:7; Leviticus 26:42; Psalm
Mark 9:49	Leviticus 2:13		105:8; Micah 7:20
Mark 10:4	Deuteronomy 24:1	Luke 1:76	Malachi 3:1
Mark 10:6	Genesis 1:27; 5:2	Luke 1:78	Malachi 4:2
Mark 10:7–8	Genesis 2:24	Luke 1:79	Isaiah 9:2; 59:9
Mark 10:19	Exodus 20:12–17; Deuteronomy 5:16–21	Luke 2:21	Genesis 17:12; Leviticus 12:3
Mark 10:27	Genesis 18:14; Job 42:2	Luke 2:23	Exodus 13:2; Leviticus 12:1–8
Mark 11:9	Psalm 118:26	Luke 2:30	Isaiah 52:10
Mark 11:17	Isaiah 56:7; Jeremiah 7:11	Luke 2:32	Isaiah 42:6; 49:6
Mark 12:2	Isaiah 5:1ff.	Luke 2:41	Exodus 23:14–17; Deuteronomy 16:1–8
Mark 12:10–11	Psalm 118:22ff.	Luke 2:52	1 Samuel 2:26
Mark 12:19	Genesis 38:8; Deuteronomy 25:5–6	Luke 3:4–6	Isaiah 40:3–5
Mark 12:26	Exodus 3:6	Luke 3:22	Psalm 2:7; Isaiah 42:1
Mark 12:29	Deuteronomy 6:4, 6	Luke 3:23–38	1 Chronicles 1:1–4, 24–28; 2:1–15; 3:17;
Mark 12:31	Leviticus 19:18		Ruth 4:18–22
Mark 12:33	1 Samuel 15:22	Luke 4:4	Deuteronomy 8:3
Mark 12:36	Psalm 110:1	Luke 4:8	Deuteronomy 6:13
Mark 13:12	Micah 7:6	Luke 4:10, 11	Psalm 91:11
Mark 13:14	Daniel 9:27	Luke 4:12	Deuteronomy 6:16
Mark 13:19	Daniel 12:1	Luke 4:18ff.	Isaiah 58:6; 61:1ff.
Mark 13:24	Daniel 8:10; Ecclesiastes 12:2; Joel 3:15	Luke 4:25–27	1 Kings 17:1, 8–9; 18:1–2; 2 Kings 5:1, 14
Mark 13:26	Daniel 7:13		
Mark 14:12	Exodus 12:18–20	Luke 4:34	Isaiah 41:14, 16, 20
Mark 14:18	Psalm 41:9	Luke 5:14	Leviticus 13:12–14; 14:2–32
Mark 14:24	Exodus 24:8; Leviticus 4:18–20;	Luke 6:2	Exodus 20:10; Deuteronomy 5:14; 23:25
	Jeremiah 31:31	Luke 6:3	Leviticus 24:9; 1 Samuel 21:1–6
Mark 14:27	Zechariah 13:7	Luke 6:21	Isaiah 55:1–2; 61:2–3
Mark 14:34	Psalm 42:6	Luke 7:22	Isaiah 35:5–6; 61:1
Mark 14:62	Psalm 110:1; Daniel 7:13	Luke 7:27	Malachi 3:1

OLD TESTAMENT QUOTATIONS IN THE GOSPEL ACCOUNTS			
NEW TESTAMENT	*OLD TESTAMENT*	*NEW TESTAMENT*	*OLD TESTAMENT*
Luke 8:10	Isaiah 6:9ff.		
Luke 10:12ff.	Genesis 19:24		
Luke 10:15	Isaiah 14:13–15		
Luke 10:27	Leviticus 18:5; 19:18;	John 1:23	Isaiah 40:3
	Deuteronomy 6:4–5	John 1:29, 36	Isaiah 53:7
Luke 11:29	Jonah 1:17		
Luke 11:32	Jonah 3:5 10	John 1:49	2 Samuel 7:14–16; Psalm 2:7
Luke 11:42, 51	Leviticus 27:30; Genesis 4:8;	John 1:51	Genesis 28:12
	2 Chronicles 24:20–21; Micah 6:8	John 2:17	Psalm 69:9
Luke 12:53	Micah 7:6	John 3:14	Numbers 21:8–9
Luke 13:14, 19	Exodus 20:8–11; Deuteronomy 5:12–15;	John 4:5	Joshua 24:32
	Daniel 4:10–12, 20ff.	John 5:10	Nehemiah 13:15–22; Jeremiah 17:21
Luke 13:27, 29	Psalm 6:8; 107:3; Isaiah 49:12	John 6:14	Deuteronomy 18:15
Luke 17:12	Leviticus 13:45–46	John 6:31	Exodus 16:4; Nehemiah 9:15;
Luke 17:13	Leviticus 13:39; 14:1–3		Psalm 78:24
Luke 17:26	Genesis 6:11–13; 7:7, 21–23		
Luke 17:28, 33	Genesis 18:20–22; 19:24–26	John 6:45	Isaiah 54:13
Luke 18:20	Exodus 20:12–17; Deuteronomy 5:16–21	John 7:22	Genesis 17:9–14; Leviticus 12:1–3
Luke 19:8, 10	Exodus 22:1; Numbers 5:6–7;	John 7:38	Proverbs 18:4; Isaiah 58:11
	Ezekiel 34:16	John 7:42	2 Samuel 7:12; Isaiah 11:1; Micah 5:2
Luke 19:38	Psalm 118:26		
Luke 19:46	Isaiah 56:7; Jeremiah 7:11	John 8:5	Leviticus 20:10; Deuteronomy 22:22–24
Luke 20:9	Isaiah 5:1ff.	John 8:17	Deuteronomy 17:6; 19:15
Luke 20:17	Psalm 118:22ff.	John 8:39	Isaiah 6:9ff.
Luke 20:18	Isaiah 8:14	John 9:16	Ezekiel 20:11, 12; Daniel 6:26, 27
Luke 20:28, 38	Genesis 38:8; Deuteronomy 25:5ff.;	John 10:34	Psalm 82:6
	Exodus 3:6	John 12:13	Leviticus 23:40; Psalm 118:26
Luke 20:42	Psalm 2:7; 110:1	John 12:14, 15	Zechariah 9:9
Luke 21:20	Daniel 9:27	John 12:27	Psalm 42:6
Luke 21:22	Daniel 12:1	John 12:38	Isaiah 53:1
Luke 21:25	Daniel 8:10; Joel 3:15; Isaiah 13:9ff.;	John 12:40	Isaiah 6:9ff.
	Ezekiel 32:7ff.; Amos 8:9;	John 13:18	Psalm 41:9
	Zephaniah 1:14ff.	John 15:25	Psalm 35:19; 69:4; 109:3
Luke 21:27–28	Daniel 7:13; Isaiah 27:12ff.	John 16:22	Isaiah 66:14; Jeremiah 31:10–12

OLD TESTAMENT QUOTATIONS IN THE GOSPEL ACCOUNTS			
NEW TESTAMENT	*OLD TESTAMENT*	*NEW TESTAMENT*	*OLD TESTAMENT*
Luke 22:37	Isaiah 53:12	John 17:12	Psalm 41:9; 133:1
Luke 22:46	Psalm 31:5		
Luke 22:69	Psalm 110:1; Daniel 7:13	John 19:24	Psalm 22:18
Luke 23:30	Hosea 10:8	John 19:29	Psalm 69:21
Luke 23:46	Psalm 31:5	John 19:36	Exodus 12:46; Numbers 9:12;
Luke 23:56	Exodus 12:16; 20:8–11;		Psalm 34:20
	Deuteronomy 5:12–15	John 19:37	Zechariah 12:10
Luke 24:46	Hosea 6:2	John 19:42	Deuteronomy 21:22–23

Appendix B

MIRACLES OF CHRIST				
NATURE OF MIRACLE	WHERE RECORDED			
	Matthew	Mark	Luke	John
Water turned to wine				2:1–11
Healing of official's son				4:46–54
Large catch of fish			5:1–11	
Demoniac healed on Sabbath		1:21–28	4:31–37	
Healing of Peter's mother-in-law	8:14–17	1:29–31	4:38–39	
Healing of a leper	8:2–4	1:40–45	5:12–15	
Paralytic healed	9:2–8	2:3–12	5:17–26	
Invalid man healed				5:1–15
Shriveled hand healed	12:9–14	3:1–6	6:6–11	
Centurian's servant healed	8:5–13		7:1–10	
Widow's son resurrected			7:11–15	
A blind and dumb man healed	12:22–24		11:14	
Storm stopped on Galilee	8:23–27	4:35–41	8:22–25	
Gadarene demoniacs delivered	8:28–34	5:1–20	8:26–39	
Woman with bleeding healed	9:20–22	5:25–34	8:43–48	
Jairus' daughter resurrected	9:23–26	5:35–43	8:41–56	
Two blind men healed	9:27–31			
A dumb demoniac delivered	9:32–34			
Feeding of five thousand	14:15–21	6:34–44	9:12–17	6:5–13
Jesus walks on water	14:22–33	6:45–52		6:17–21
Syrophoenician woman's daughter healed	15:21–28	7:24–30		
A deaf and dumb man healed		7:31–37		
Feeding of four thousand	15:32–38	8:1–9		
A blind man healed		8:22–26		
Jesus transfigured	17:1–8		9:29–33	
A demoniac boy delivered	17:14–21	9:14–29	9:37–43	
Coin found in mouth of fish	17:24–27			
Healing of a man born blind				9:1–41
Woman healed after 18 years of infirmity			13:10–17	
A man healed of dropsy			14:1–14	
Lazarus resurrected				11:1–44
Ten lepers healed			17:11–19	
Blind Bartimaeus and companion healed	20:29–34	10:46–52	18:35–43	

MIRACLES OF CHRIST				
NATURE OF MIRACLE	*WHERE RECORDED*			
	Matthew	*Mark*	*Luke*	*John*
Barren fig tree cursed	21:18–21	11:12–14, 20–22		
Malchus' ear healed			22:50–51	
Christ's resurrection	28:1–7	16:1–13	24:1–35	20:1–18
Christ's appearance to disciples through closed doors		16:14–18	24:36–49	20:19–31
Another large catch of fish				21:3–11
Christ's ascension		16:19–20	24:50–52	
Healing of all manner of sickness*	4:23ff.			
Healing of every sickness*	9:35ff.			
Many made whole*		6:56		
Many sick brought to Christ for healing*			4:40ff.; 5:15ff.	
All are healed*			6:17–19	
Christ healed many of sicknesses*			7:21ff.	
Miracles*				2:23; 3:2
Christ did many things*				4:45

* References to general (rather than specific) healings and miracles

Appendix C

PRAYERS OF CHRIST *(In Their Probable Chronological Order)*		
WHERE RECORDED	*WHERE OFFERED*	*THE LESSON WE SHOULD LEARN*
Luke 3:21–22	Jordan River	We must not attempt to fulfill righteousness without prayer—God answers promptly and unmistakably
Mark 1:35; see Isaiah 26:9; Psalms 5:3; 63:1	Solitary place— Capernaum	The duty of early morning prayer—we should enter upon the discharge of duties with prayer
Luke 5:16; see Matthew 6:5	Chorazin— wilderness	To withdraw from the multitude and pray in secret
Luke 6:12; see 1 Thessalonians 5:17; Colossians 4:2; Psalm 55:17	Capernaum— mountain	Every work designed to advance to God's glory should open with prayer—we should not limit the time
Matthew 11:25–26; see Isaiah 25:9; Matthew 15:36	A city	We must be as babes if we would receive divine light—we should be thankful for what seems good in God's sight
Luke 9:16; Matthew 26:26–27	Sea of Galilee, Jerusalem,	The duty of giving thanks at our meals
Luke 24:30	Emmaus	
Matthew 14:23; John 6:15; see Psalm 55:17	Bethsaida— mountain	The duty of closing the day's work with prayer in secret
Psalm 55:17		
Luke 9:18	District of Caesarea Philippi	The duty of frequent secret prayer
Luke 9:28–29	Mount Tabor	The duty of prayer
John 11:41–42; see Psalm 123:1–2	Bethany	We should recognize God's power—God hears prayer at all times
Luke 11:1–4; see Matthew 6:7–8	Gethsemane (probably)	We should learn how to pray
Matthew 19:13–14; see 1 Peter 2:1–2;	Borders of Judaea	"Of such is the kingdom of heaven"
Matthew 18:5; Psalm 8:2		
John 12:27–28; see John 13:31–32; Philippians 1:20–21	Jerusalem— temple	Not to pray for deliverance, even from the severest sufferings, when such lie in the course of our duty, but to seek God's glory in all things
John 17	Jerusalem— upper chamber	We should remember first, in all our prayers, God's glory—we should so live that we may at death say with Jesus, "I have finished the work which thou gavest me to do"—it is our duty to pray for others

PRAYERS OF CHRIST (In Their Probable Chronological Order)		
WHERE RECORDED	*WHERE OFFERED*	*THE LESSON WE SHOULD LEARN*
Luke 22:32	Jerusalem— upper chamber	The duty of intercessory prayer
Matthew 26:36–44; Mark 14:32–41; Luke 22:40–46; note carefully, Luke 22:40, 43–44, 46	Gethsemane	The thrice uttered prayer of Jesus' agony should teach us: a higher sense of His sufferings for us—it is not wrong to be "exceeding sorrowful"—while we pray to be delivered from evil, we should ever say from the heart, "Not as I will but as thou wilt"
Luke 23:34; see Matthew 5:44	Calvary	We must pray even for our bitterest enemies
Matthew 27:46; Mark 15:34; see John 19:30	Calvary	The love that induced our Savior to bear such sufferings for us should teach us to love Him more and more each day.
Luke 23:46	Calvary	May we be able to utter the same glorious prayer
Luke 24:50–51	Bethany	May we share therein

Appendix D

	INTRODUCTION TO NEW TESTAMENT LITERATURE AT A GLANCE					
Book	Date Written (Approximate)	Place Written	Author	Emphasis	Written to	Theme
James	AD 45–50	Jerusalem	James, Jesus' brother	Doctrinal	Jewish Christians of the Dispersion	Christian ethics
Galatians	AD 48, 49	Antioch	Paul, apostle	Doctrinal	Christians in Antioch, Iconium, Lystra, and Derbe, South Galatia	Justification by faith
1 Thessalonians	AD 51	Corinth	Paul, apostle	Doctrinal	Christians in Thessalonica	Christ's return
2 Thessalonians	AD 52	Corinth	Paul, apostle	Doctrinal	Christians in Thessalonica	Christ's return
1 Corinthians	AD 55	Ephesus	Paul, apostle	Doctrinal	Christians in Corinth	The application of the gospel
2 Corinthians	AD 55	Macedonia	Paul, apostle	Doctrinal	Christians in Corinth	The Christian ministry
Romans	AD 56	Corinth	Paul, apostle	Doctrinal	Assembly at Rome	The righteousness of God and man
Matthew	AD 56–70	Antioch in Syria	Matthew, apostle	Historical	Jews in Syria	Christ's rnessiahship
Luke	AD 60	Rome	Luke, Gentile	Historical	Gentiles	Christ's manhood
Colossians	AD 60	Rome	Paul, apostle	Doctrinal	Christians in Colossae	The Christ of the church
Philemon	AD 60	Rome	Paul, apostle	Personal	Philemon and Colossians	Forgiveness and reconciliation
Ephesians	AD 60	Rome	Paul, apostle	Doctrinal	Christians around Ephesus	Christ's church
Philippians	AD 60	Rome	Paul, apostle	Doctrinal	Christians in Philippi	Thanksgiving for the gospel
Acts	AD 63	Rome	Luke, Gentile	Historical	Gentiles	The birth and growth of the church
Hebrews	AD 64	Unknown	Paul, apostle	Doctrinal	Jewish Christians in Rome and Jerusalem	Superiority and finality of Christianity
1 Peter	AD 63	Rome	Peter, apostle	Doctrinal	Assemblies in North Asia Minor	Grace of God in suffering
Jude	AD 67–68	Unknown	Jude, Jesus' brother	Doctrinal	Christians everywhere	Defending the faith

INTRODUCTION TO NEW TESTAMENT LITERATURE AT A GLANCE						
Book	Date Written (Approximate)	Place Written	Author	Emphasis	Written to	Theme
1 Timothy	AD 62	Macedonia	Paul, apostle	Personal	Timothy	Church administration
Titus	AD 62, 63	Macedonia	Paul, apostle	Personal	Titus	Challenge for Christian ministry
2 Timothy	AD 63, 64	Rome	Paul, apostle	Personal	Timothy	Instructions for Christian ministry
2 Peter	AD 64	Rome	Peter, apostle	Doctrinal	Assemblies in North Asia Minor	Truth versus error
Mark	AD 50–70	Rome	John, Mark	Historical	Romans	Christ's servanthood
John	AD 90	Ephesus	John, apostle	Historical	Persons around Ephesus	Christ's divinity
1 John	AD 90	Ephesus	John, apostle	Doctrinal	Christians near Ephesus	To know eternal life
2 John	AD 90	Ephesus	John, apostle	Personal	An assembly near Ephesus	Christian love and truth
3 John	AD 90	Ephesus	John, apostle	Personal	Gaius	Church administration
Revelation	AD 96	Ephesus	John, apostle	Prophetic	Pastors of seven assemblies in Asia	Revelation of Christian triumph

Appendix E

MAP OF DISTANCES

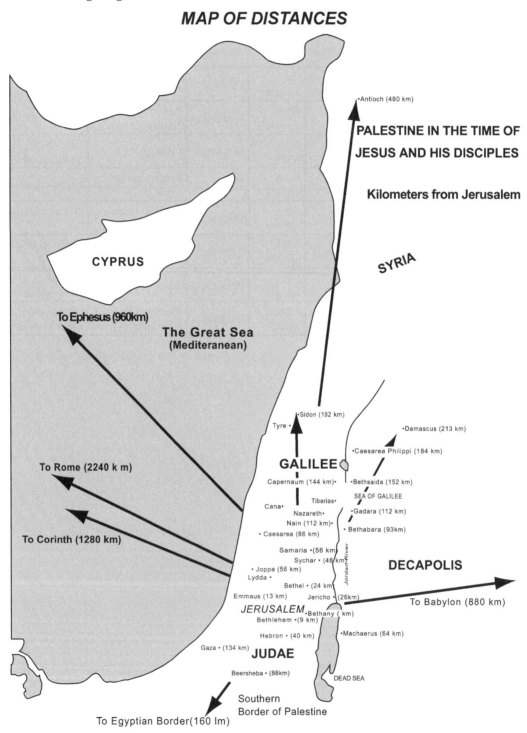

PALESTINE IN THE TIME OF JESUS AND HIS DISCIPLES

Kilometers from Jerusalem

CYPRUS

To Ephesus (960km)

The Great Sea (Mediteranean)

SYRIA

•Antioch (480 km)

•Sidon (192 km)

Tyre •

•Damascus (213 km)

•Caesarea Philippi (184 km)

GALILEE

Capernaum (144 km)•   •Bethsaida (152 km)

SEA OF GALILEE

Cana•   Tiberias•

Nazareth•   •Gadara (112 km)

Nain (112 km)•

• Caesarea (86 km)   • Bethabara (93km)

Samaria •(56 km)

Sychar • (48 km)

To Rome (2240 k m)

To Corinth (1280 km)

• Joppa (56 km)

Lydda •

Bethel • (24 km)

DECAPOLIS

Emmaus (13 km)   Jericho • (26km)

JERUSALEM•Bethany (km)   To Babylon (880 km)

Bethlehem •(9 km)

Hebron • (40 km)   •Machaerus (64 km)

Gaza • (134 km) **JUDAE**

Beersheba • (88km)

DEAD SEA

Southern Border of Palestine

To Egyptian Border(160 lm)

Jordan River

Appendix F

THE PARABLES OF CHRIST					
	Where Recorded				
Parable	*Matthew*	*Mark*	*Luke*	*John*	*Lesson*
About temple				2:19–22	Christ's death and resurrection
Acceptable prophet		6:4–6	4:24		One's acceptance at home
A physician	9:12–13	2:15–17	5:29–32		Christ's mission to the needy
The bridegroom	9:14–15	2:18–19	5:33–35		Christ, our bridegroom
New material on old garment	9:16–17	2:21	5:36		The Holy Spirit will not dwell in the unregenerate
The speck and the plank	7:1–5		6:41–42		Not judging others
Pearls and pigs	7:6				Not wasting the sacred on the profane
Wise and foolish builders	7:24–27		6:47–49		Building spiritual on solid foundation
Narrow and broad ways	7:13–14		13:24		Christ's way and Satan's way
The dancing children	11:16–19				Unresponsive hearers
The two debtors			7:36–50		Gratitude for forgiveness of sin
Satan's kingdom	12:22–32	3:22–30	11:14–23		Blasphemy against the Holy Spirit
Sign of Jonah	12:38–41				Symbolic of Christ's death and resurrection
The sower	13:3–23	4:2–20	8:5–15		Different types of hearers
The seed growing of itself		4:26–29			Manner of the Kingdom's growth
The lighted candle	5:14–16	4:21–25	8:16–18		Influence of Christian living
The weeds	13:24–30				Good and evil grow together till judgment
The mustard seed	13:31–32	4:30–32	13:18–19		Extent of the Kingdom's growth
The yeast	13:33		13:20–21		The influence of the gospel
The hidden treasure	13:44				The value of Christian experience
The pearl of great price	13:45–46				The value of Christian experience
The net	13:47–50				The work and consummation of the Kingdom
The householder	13:51–52				The variety of lessons in the Kingdom
The unmerciful servant	18:23–35				Lack of mercy
The good shepherd				10:7–18	The loving provision of God for His own
The good Samaritan			10:25–37		Christian compassion

THE PARABLES OF CHRIST					
	Where Recorded				
Parable	Matthew	Mark	Luke	John	Lesson
The bold, persistent friend			11:5–13		Perseverance in prayer
The rich fool			12:16–21		The foolishness of materialism
The waiting servants			12:35–48		Need for readiness for Christ's return
The unfruitful fig tree			13:6–9		Necessity of bearing fruit
The feast			14:7–11		The necessity of humility
The feast for the poor			14:12–14		The necessity and reward of benevolence
The great supper			14:15–24		Many are called, but few accept
The tower and king			14:25–35		The cost of serving Christ
The lost sheep	18:10–14		15:3–7		The love of God
The lost coin			15:8–10		The love of God
The lost son (prodigal)			15:11–32		The love of God
The unjust steward			16:1–13		The importance of faithfulness in all things
The rich man and Lazarus			16:19–31		Necessity of preparation for eternity
The unjust judge			18:1–8		Perseverance in prayer
The Pharisee and publican			18:9–14		Pride and repentance
The pounds			19:11–27		The reward of good and bad stewardship
The laborers	20:1–16				The reward of works
The two sons, repentance	21:28–32				Pretense and repentance
The wicked husbandmen	21:33–46	12:1–12	20:9–19		The Jews' rejection of God's messengers
The rejected stone	21:42	12:10	20:17		Christ's supremacy
The marriage of the king's son	22:2–14				Readiness for Christ's return
The fig tree	24:32–35	13:28–32	21:29–31		Sign of Christ's return
The porter / watching servants		13:34–37	12:35–38		Readiness and watchfulness for Christ's return
The master of the house	24:42–45		12:39–40		Readiness and watchfulness for Christ's return
The wise servants	24:46–51				Readiness and watchfulness for Christ's return
The ten virgins	25:1–13				Readiness and watchfulness for Christ's return
The talents	25:14–30				Reward of good and bad stewardship
The sheep and goats	25:31–46				Separation of good and evil at the Judgment

Appendix G

PERSONS MENTIONED IN THE GOSPEL ACCOUNTS					
NAME	*OTHER INFORMATION*	*MATTHEW*	*MARK*	*LUKE*	*JOHN*
Alexander	Son of Simon of Cyrene		15:21		
Andrew	Apostle	10:2	1:16	6:14	1:40
Anna	Prophetess in Jerusalem			2:36–38	
Annas	High priest			3:2	18:13
Barabbas	Robber and murderer	27:16–26			
Bartholomew	Apostle	10:3	3:18	6:14	
Bartimaeus	Blind beggar		10:46		
Caesar Augustus	First Roman emperor			2:1	
Caesar Tiberius	Son-in-law of Augustus			3:1	
Caiaphas	High priest	26:3		3:2	
Chuza	Steward of Herod			8:3	
Cleopas	Disciple of Christ			24:18	
Cyrenius	Roman governor of Syria			2:2	
Elizabeth/ Elisabeth	Mother of John the Baptist			1:5–57	
Herod Antipas	Son of Herod the Great	14:1–6	6:14–29	3:1–2	
Herod Archelaus	Son of Herod the Great	2:22			
Herod the Great	Roman governor, son of Antipater	2:1–19			
Herod Philip	Son of Herod the Great		6:17		
James	Apostle, brother of John	4:21	1:19	5:10	
James	Apostle, son of Alphaeus & Mary	10:3	3:18	6:15–16	
James	Son of Joseph and Mary	13:55	6:3		
Joanna	Wife of Chuza			8:3; 24:10	
John	Apostle, brother of James	4:21; 17:1	1:19–20	5:10	
John the Baptist	Forerunner of Christ	3:1–14	1:2–8	1:13–17	3:23–30
Joseph	Husband of Jesus' mother	1:18–25		2:4–5; 3:23	
Joseph	Member of Sanhedrin, from Arimathaea	27:57–60	15:43–46		
Joses (Joseph)	Son of Joseph and Mary	13:55	6:3		
Jude	Son of Joseph and Mary	13:55	6:3		
Judas	Apostle, called Thaddaeus	10:3	3:18	6:16	14:22
Judas	Apostle, Iscariot	10:4		6:16	12:4
Lazarus	Of Bethany				11:1–44; 12:1–17
Malchus	Servant of high priest				18:10
Martha	Sister of Mary and Lazarus			10:38–42	11:1
Mary	Sister of Martha and Lazarus			10:38–42	11:1
Mary	Mother of Jesus	1:18–25			19:25

PERSONS MENTIONED IN THE GOSPEL ACCOUNTS					
NAME	*OTHER INFORMATION*	*MATTHEW*	*MARK*	*LUKE*	*JOHN*
Mary	Wife of Cleophas (Clopas)				19:25
Mary	Of Magdala	27:56	16:9	8:2	
Matthew	Apostle, called Levi	9:9	2:14	5:27–29	
Nicodemus	Pharisee, member of Sanhedrin				3:1–21
Peter	Apostle, called Simon	10:2	3:16		1:40–42
Philip	Apostle	10:3			1:43–48
Pilate	Roman procurator of Judea	27:2, 11–26	15:2–15	23:1–6, 24	18:28–40; 19:1–16
Rufus	Son of Simon of Cyrene		15:21		
Salome	Woman who ministered to Jesus		15:40		
Salome	Daughter of Herodias	14:6	6:22		
Simeon	Worshipped baby Jesus in temple			2:25–35	
Simon	Father of Judas Iscariot				6:71
Simon	Brother of Jesus	13:55	6:3		
Simon	A leper of Bethany	26:6	14:3		
Simon	Pharisee, entertained Jesus			7:36–50	
Simon	Bore Jesus' cross	27:32	15:21	23:26	
Simon	Apostle, the Zealot	10:4	3:18	6:15	
Susanna	Woman who ministered to Jesus			8:3	
Thomas	Apostle, called Didymus	10:3	3:18	6:15	11:16

Appendix H

PLACES MENTIONED IN THE GOSPEL ACCOUNTS					
Place	*Description*	*Matthew*	*Mark*	*Luke*	*John*
Aenon	Town				3:23
Bethabara	Town				1:28
Bethany	Town	21:17	11:1	19:29	11:1
Bethesda	Pool				5:2
Bethlehem	Town	2:1		2:4	7:42
Bethphage	Town	21:1	11:1	19:29	
Bethsaida	Town	11:21	6:45	9:10	1:44
Caesarea Philippi	Town	16:13	8:27		
Calvary	Hill			23:33	
Cana	Town				2:1
Capernaum	Town	4:13	1:21	4:31	4:46
Cedron (Kidron)	Ravine				18:1
Chorazin	Town	11:21		10:13	
Dalmanutha	Town		8:10		
Decapolis	District	4:25	5:20		
Egypt	Country	2:13–15			
Emmaus	Town			24:13	
Ephraim	City				11:54
Gadara	Town	8:28	5:1	8:26	
Gennesaret	Plain	14:34	6:53		
Gennesaret	Lake			5:1	
Gergesa	Town		5:1	8:26, 37	
Gethsemane	Garden	26:36	14:32		
Golgotha	Hill	27:33–50	15:22		19:17
Gomorrah	Destroyed City	10:15	6:11		
Jericho	Town	20:29	10:46	10:30	
Jerusalem	City	20:18	11:11	2:41–43	4:45
Jordan	River	3:5–6, 13	1:5	3:3	1:28
Magdala	Town	15:39			
Nain	Town			7:11	
Nazareth	City	2:23	1:24	2:39	1:45
Nephtali	Town	4:13			
Nineveh	City	12:41		11:32	
Olivet (Mount of Olives)	Mountain	24:3		21:37	8:1
Sarepta	Town			4:26	

PLACES MENTIONED IN THE GOSPEL ACCOUNTS					
Place	*Description*	*Matthew*	*Mark*	*Luke*	*John*
Sidon	Town	11:21	3:8	4:26	
Siloam	Pool				9:7
Sodom	Destroyed City	10:15	6:11	10:12	
Sychar	Town				4:5
Tiberias	Town				6:1, 23
Tyre	Town	15:21	7:24		

Appendix I

OTHER RECORDED NEW TESTAMENT MIRACLES			
Where Recorded	*Location*	*By Whom*	*Nature of the Miracle*
Luke 1:11–23, 57–78	Jerusalem—temple	Angel Gabriel	Zacharias is punished for unbelief by being deprived of speech for a season.
John 5:2–4	Jerusalem	An angel	Curative properties are imparted to the pool of Bethesda.
Mark 6:7–13	Throughout Galilee	The apostles	Devils are cast out and many sick persons cured.
Mark 9:38–40	Place not recorded	One not a disciple	Devils are cast out.
Luke 10:17	Galilee	The 70 disciples	Devils are subject to them through the name of JESUS.
Acts 2:1–43	Jerusalem—upper room	The Holy Spirit	The power of speaking languages they had not learned is bestowed on the Apostles and disciples.
Acts 2:43; 5:12–16; Mark 16:20		The apostles	Their commission is attested by many signs and wonders.
Acts 3:1–4:16	Jerusalem—Beautiful Gate	Peter (with John)	A man lame from his birth is enabled to "walk and leap."
Acts 5:l–11	Jerusalem	Peter	Ananias and Sapphira are struck dead for lying to the Holy Spirit.
Acts 5:15–16	Jerusalem	Peter	Many healings take place.
Acts 5:17–24	Jerusalem	The angel of the Lord	Some of the apostles, having been cast into prison are delivered without the doors being opened or the guard disturbed.
Acts 6:8	Judea	Stephen, the deacon	Being "full of faith and power" he does wonders and miracles among the people.
Acts 8:6–13	A city of Samaria	Philip, the deacon	Unclean spirits are cast out, and many cases of palsy, lameness, etc., are cured.
Acts 8:39–40	Near Gaza	Spirit of the Lord	Philip, having baptized the eunuch, is "caught away" and taken to Azotus.
Acts 9:3–18	Near Damascus	The glorified Jesus	A series of miracles are connected with the conversion of Saul of Tarsus.
Acts 9:33–35	Lydda	Peter	Aeneas, who had been confined to his bed with palsy for eight years, is "made whole."
Acts 9:36–42	Joppa	Peter	Dorcas (or Tabitha) is raised from the dead.
Acts 12:4–17	Jerusalem	The angel of the Lord	Peter, being in chains and in prison, is delivered.
Acts 12:21–23	Caesarea	The angel of the Lord	Herod Agrippa I dies because he fails to rebuke impious flattery.
Acts 13:6–12	Paphos	Paul, the apostle	Elymas, the sorcerer, trying to prevent the conversion of Sergius Paulus, is stricken with temporary total blindness.
Acts 14:8–11	Lystra	Paul	A man who had been a cripple from birth so that he "never had walked" is enabled to "walk and leap."

OTHER RECORDED NEW TESTAMENT MIRACLES			
Where Recorded	*Location*	*By Whom*	*Nature of the Miracle*
Acts 16:16–18	Philippi	Paul	A spirit of divination is cast out.
Acts 16:23–33	Philippi	By an earthquake	Paul and Silas having been cast into prison, their feet fast in stocks, the prison doors are opened, the stocks loosened.
Acts 19:11–12	Ephesus	Paul	Special miracles are wrought without his seeing the objects.
Acts 20:9–12	Troas	Paul	Eutychus, killed by a fall from a window is restored to life.
Acts 28:3–6	Island of Melita	Paul	A deadly viper proves harmless.
Acts 28:7–9	Island of Melita	Paul	The father of Publius and many other sick persons are cured.

Glossary

The right-hand column lists the lesson in the Independent-Study Textbook in which the word is first used.

Lesson

adoption — action of God in taking a person into a new relationship with Him as His child and heir with Christ, when the person is saved — 10

advent — coming of Christ at His incarnation (birth) — 4

antidote — anything that will counteract or remove the effects of error, evil, poison, or disease — 13

antinomianism — the belief that faith frees the Christian from the obligations of the moral law (you could do as you pleased and it would make no difference); denial of the Lordship of Christ — 13

apocalyptic — genre of literature usually produced in times of persecution or oppression as a means of encouraging those who were suffering for their faith; including the judgment of the wicked and the deliverance of the righteous — 14

Apocrypha — non-authoritative religious works — 2

apocryphal — not included in the New Testament canon — 2

apologetic — offered in vindication or defense of — 7

apologist — a person defending an idea or belief — 6

apostolic — pertaining to or descending from the apostles — 5

aristocracy — hereditary, privileged class of high station — 1

avaricious — greedy for riches, grasping — 1

---

canonical — accepted as belonging to the authoritative list of Scriptures composing the Bible and known as the canon — 15

canonical Gospels — relating to, established by, or conforming to a canon (model, standard); those Gospels included in the canon of Holy Scripture — 3

capstone — final or crowning point, stroke, or culmination — 14

casuistic — based on case histories or cases — 10

cerinthianism — an advanced form of Gnosticism: the belief that the Christ-spirit did not actually inhabit the human Jesus until His baptism and left Him before His death on the cross, making a strange contradiction out of the personality of Jesus; blurred the nature of Jesus so that one would not know if the human Jesus or Divine Christ-spirit were speaking and acting — 13

christological — pertaining to theological interpretations of the work and person of Christ — 9

Christology — the study of the person and attributes of Christ; theory or doctrine concerning Christ — 11

Lesson

clairvoyant	— person professing to have insight into what is distant, hidden, or beyond moral perception	9
climactic	— relating to the culmination or major turning point in the action	5
constituency	— persons making up the church	8
consummation	— fulfillment, completion, conclusion, end	7
corroborative	— tending to confirm or strengthen	15
cosmopolitan	— person having worldwide interests, concerns, and attitudes in contrast to a local, provincial, regional or national orientation without the wider concern and activities	6
coterminous	— having the same scope or extent in space or time; identical with	14
credence	— belief, especially as based on the evidence or reports of others; mental acceptance as real or true	14
credentials	— that which entitles a person to exercise a certain authority or position	5
credo	— strongly held belief, system of tenets to guide action	10

---

declension	— a sinking into an inferior or lower condition	12
deified	— made a god, worshiped as a god	2
demagoguery	— spirit, principles, conduct, or methods of leaders of the plebeians who sought personal gain by extravagant claims	1
denouement	— final revelation of an event which clarifies the nature or outcome of a plot	4
Diaspora	— Jews living outside Palestine, dispersion of the Jews into the world	2
didactic	— instructional	4
didactic purposes	— teaching purposes, purposes of instruction	3
docetism	— a heresy which held that Christ was not historically real but a phantom that appeared in human guise and then vanished; a form of Gnosticism	13
dynamic	— power	15

---

ecclesiastical	— pertaining to the church as an organization with governing power	15
ecclesiological	— pertaining to study of the doctrine of the church	12
egregious	— conspicuously bad, glaring, flagrant, apostate	13
encyclical	— a letter intended for general circulation among several churches	11
epigram	— brief, clever, pointed, witty remark or observation	1
epilogue	— concluding section of a literary work that summarizes and comments on the principal action	5
epithet	— descriptive word used in place of a name, especially a disparaging, qualifying word	1

Lesson

errorists	— those who hold beliefs or opinions contrary to the established doctrines of their religion	13
eschatological	— related to belief in or about the end of the world or the last things (such as the second coming of Christ, resurrection, judgment)	4
Ethic	— set of values or moral principles	9
evangelistic	— pertaining to winning individual commitments to Christ	5
explicitly	— in a clear manner without obscurity or vagueness	9
futurist school	— interpreters who hold that the first three chapters of Revelation apply only to the day in which the book was written, or who interpret the seven churches of Asia as representing seven eras of church history from the apostolic age to the return of Christ; those who hold that the events from Revelation 4:1 onward belong to the future period called the Great Tribulation	14
genealogy	— descent of a person, family, or group from an ancestor in the direct line	4
gladiator	— paid freedman, slave, or captive in ancient Rome who fought men or animals with weapons as public entertainment	1
harbinger	— one who, or that which, goes before and announces the coming of something or someone; herald	13
Hellenism	— assimilation of Greek culture, speech, styles, manners, ideals as by the Romans or Jews of the Diaspora; Greek civilization especially as modified by oriental influences in the period of Hellenism	1
Hellenist	— a person who was not Greek by ancestry, yet lived in Hellenistic times and adopted the Greek language, customs, ideas	1
Hellenistic	— relating to the spread of Greek influence as far as India and Egypt between the periods of Alexander the Great and the conquest of Rome	1
heresies	— beliefs or opinions contrary to the established doctrines of the church or religious system	13
heyday	— prime; time of greatest success or vigor	9
hierarchy	— that which is organized into orders or ranks each subordinate to the one above it; a graded or ranked series	1
historicist school	— interpreters who think that Revelation outlines the entire course of the history of the church from Pentecost to the advent of Christ	14
hortatory	— advisory, characterized by giving of encouragement or advice	12
idealist school	— interpreters who focus on the ethical and spiritual truth of Revelation and thus view the book as only a symbolic picture of the enduring struggle between good and evil, between Christianity and paganism	14

		Lesson
importunate	— persistent in requesting	7
imputation	— act by which God ascribes Christ's righteousness to those who believe He paid the penalty for their sin, so that they are justified	10
incarnated	— divinity embodied in humanity; God manifested in the human body and personality of Jesus Christ, who experienced humanity while still being God	3
incarnation	— union of divinity and humanity in Jesus Christ, who had the bodily form, personality, nature, and experiences of a human while still being God	4
inherent	— related to the essential character of something	2
internecine	— of, relating to, or involving conflict within a group; mutually destructive or harmful, involving slaughter and destruction	1
intrinsic	— pertaining to the fundamental nature of something	15
justification	— acceptance of those who respond in wholehearted faith to God as revealed in Jesus Christ; His regard of them as free from sin, as righteous, and as reconciled with Him	9
legalism	— practices, deeds, observances, principles, or characteristics of a code such as the Law or oral law of Judaism	9
legalistic	— condition of observing strict, literal, or excessive conformity to the practices, observances, or principles of a code such as the Law and oral law of Judaism	9
libertine	— one completely lacking in moral restraint, especially a habitually unchaste person; one who has unconventional or unorthodox religious opinions	13
libertinism	— licentious disregard of moral restraints; unusual freedom from standard patterns of behavior	10
lingua franca	— any one of various languages used as a commercial or common language by people whose languages are diverse	1
malfeasance	— official misconduct	1
manumitted	— freed from slavery	1
mark (of God)	— seal of the living God on the foreheads of those saved from judgment by God's sheltering grace	14
mark (of the beast)	— badge of followers of the Antichrist, on the forehead or the right hand (Revelation 13:16–17); token of apostasy; spiritual state subjecting men to the wrath of God and to eternal torment	14
metaphorically	— using a word for one object in place of another to suggest a likeness between them	15
milieu	— environment, setting, surroundings	2

Lesson

Millennium	— the thousand years of peace, prosperity, and prevailing holiness during Christ's reign on earth following His second coming after the Tribulation Period and while Satan is in the bottomless pit (Revelation 20)	14
mime	— ancient Greek or Roman farce characterized by mimicry or burlesque	1
normative	— relating to the standard	8
omniscient	— possessing complete knowledge of all things (past, present, future) not from human intellect or any mental process but because the basis of reality is in Him (God)	14
parenthetical	— pertaining to a digression or added passage	14
patent	— readily visible or obvious, not hidden	1
patristic	— of or relating to the church fathers or their writing (especially in the first six centuries after Christ)	4
pedagogy	— the practice of teaching	3
philosophy	— the attempt to correlate all existing knowledge about the universe into systematic form and to integrate human experience with it; the general beliefs, concepts, and attitudes of an individual or group	2
precedents	— teachings to determine or guide subsequent living	12
predilection	— mental attitude or tendency to take a stand without having full knowledge about the subject	7
prerogative	— a special right or privilege that no one else has	7
presbyter	— official leader or overseer of a local congregation in the early Christian church	7
preterist school	— interpreters who hold that the symbolism of Revelation relates only to the events of the day in which it was written	14
pristine	— extremely pure, unspoiled, relating to the earliest condition	10
proletariat	— the lowest class of people in Roman society, the propertyless, the working class	1
propitiation	— refers to sacrificial death of Jesus Christ on the cross as a sin offering to atone for the offenses of those who repent, believe, and thus restored to fellowship with God the Father	10
proscriptions	— condemnations to death	1
rapture	— refers to the doctrine that members of the true church will be caught up suddenly by Christ at His return in the air	14

Lesson

sanctification	— experience of the Christian believer by which he is freed from sin and enabled by the Holy Spirit to realize the will of God in his life, and to share God's love as a redeemed person who is entirely acceptable to God	10
schismatic	— guilty of separating from or rivaling the true worship of God	8
self-authenticating	— that which independently convinces readers of its genuineness, truth	15
soteriological	— pertaining to the theological doctrine of salvation by divine activity	10
supernatural	— attributed to or relating to God, transcending the laws of nature	5
synchronized	— happened at the same time; joined together	8
syncretistic	— having the characteristics of two opposing beliefs fused or joined together	9
Synoptic	— of or relating to the first three Gospel accounts of the New Testament, affording a general view of a whole, manifested or characterized by comprehensiveness or breadth of view	3

tacitly	— in a silent manner, without speaking, in a manner expressed by action rather than speech	7
tenaciously	— tending to adhere or cling to; holding fast	9
tenet	— belief or doctrine generally held to be true, especially by a group	2
transcended	— excelled, went beyond the limits of, separated from	8
transcendence	— existence apart from the material universe	2
transfiguration	— refers here to the experience in which Jesus was transformed on the mountaintop in the presence of three of His disciples (Matthew 17:1–8)	5
transition	— a change from one condition to another	8
Tribulation	— coming period of suffering and terrible affliction never before known, many believe it will occur between the Rapture and the second coming of Christ to earth; also known as the "time of Jacob's trouble" (Jeremiah 30:7)	14

universality	— quality or state of being universal, applying to all people rather than only to a select group	8

Essential Course Materials

Contents

Materials to Be Submitted to the Enrollment Office

Pages to be submitted are marked with this symbol:

After Taking Unit Progress Evaluations

- ❏ Student's Request to Take Final Examination
- ❏ Service Learning Requirement Report
- ❏ Project

The address of your local enrollment office is:

Global University
1211 South Glenstone Avenue
Springfield, Missouri 65804
USA

Instructions

LIT1303 New Testament Literature, Sixth Edition

COMPLETING THE TIME SURVEY

This course has been selected for a special review that involves your cooperation. To participate, you are asked to note the time you spend in completing various tasks throughout the course. Then you will log the total times on the Time Survey response form in these Essential Course Materials. Submit the form to your enrollment office with your SLR report.

Studying for Maximum Learning

Use the following forms to improve your study methods and use of study time:

- *Checklist of Study Methods*
- *Student's Planner and Record*

Asking Your Adviser a Question

Use the *Question/Response Form* to send any questions you may have to your adviser.

Completing Your Service Learning Requirement

This course requires you to do a service learning requirement (SLR) assignment and submit a report. You must submit the SLR report before or at the time you take the final examination. The SLR instructions are found before the project instructions in these Essential Course Materials.

Undergraduate Writing Assignment Guidelines

Guidelines for the undergraduate writing assignments are provided to assist you in properly completing course assignments and understanding how Global University faculty members will evaluate and grade them. Carefully following these guidelines can improve the quality of your written work and elevate your grade.

Completing Your Project

This course requires you to complete a project. Project instructions are included in these Essential Course Materials. You must submit the project before taking your final examination. Submit your project by e-mail attachment. A template is available for download at http://libguides.globaluniversity .edu/templates. If e-mail is not available, submit by mail or fax.

Correcting the Self-Test in Your Independent-Study Textbook (or Study Guide)

Answers to the self-tests are included in these Essential Course Materials.

Taking Your Unit Progress Evaluations

1. Review the chapters in each unit before you take the unit progress evaluation (UPE). Study and understand the objectives that highlight key concepts of the course. Refer to the form *Checklist of Study Methods*.

2. Answer the questions in each UPE without referring to your course materials, Bible, or notes.

3. Look over your answers carefully to avoid errors.

4. Check your answers with the answer keys provided in these Essential Course Materials. Review chapter sections pertaining to questions you may have missed. Note: The UPE scores do not count toward your course grade, but they may indicate how well you will perform on the final examination.

5. On your *Student's Planner and Record* form, enter the date you completed each UPE.

6. When you are ready to complete the next to the last UPE, submit the form *Student's Request to Take Final Examination* to your enrollment office. If you do this, you will be able to take the final examination without delay when you complete the course.

Submitting Your Assignments

Submit to your enrollment office the items listed on the Essential Course Materials table of contents page in the section *Materials to Be Submitted to the Enrollment Office*. Submit your project assignment by e-mail attachment. If e-mail is not available, submit by mail or fax. Record on your *Student's Planner and Record* form the date you submitted each item.

Taking Your Final Examination

1. You will take the final examination in the presence of an approved examination supervisor. You may be asked to suggest the name of an appropriate examination supervisor if your enrollment office does not already have one in your area.

2. Review for the final examination in the same manner in which you prepared for the UPEs. The final examination covers material drawn from the chapters, self-tests, and UPEs. Refer to the form *Checklist of Study Methods* under "End-of-Unit Review" for further helpful review hints.

3. After you have completed your examination, your examination supervisor will send your final examination booklet and answer sheets to the appropriate office for forwarding to the International Office in Springfield, Missouri. It may take a number of weeks for you to receive your final grade report from your enrollment office.

Checklist of Study Methods

- If you carefully follow the study methods listed below, you should be able to complete this course successfully. As you complete each lesson, mark a ✓ in the column for that lesson beside each instruction you followed. Pace yourself so you study at least two or three times a week. Study the step-by-step procedure in the Course Introduction to see how each component organizes course content.

LESSON STUDY METHODS	1	2	3	4	5	6	7	8	9	10	11	12	13	14	15	16	17	18
1. Read each introduction to be aware of new concepts presented and review the previous lesson. Study the highlights or learning activities to know what to expect in the lesson.	✓																	
2. Study the objectives carefully to make sure you understand and master the key concepts of the course.																		
3. Study the outline to identify each main topic and how it relates to each subtopic.																		
4. As you study each lesson, note the defined words in the margin (and repeated in the glossary) for the definitions of words whose meanings may be unfamiliar to you. Use a dictionary to clarify other difficult words.																		
5. Underline, mark, and write notes in your study materials as you read through the lesson content. Use a notebook to write additional notes and comments.																		
6. Answer the interactive questions, guiding questions, or study questions as you read through the lesson to identify key concepts and relevant perspectives.																		
7. Complete the learn-by-doing activities (if included).																		
8. Review the lesson content (explanations, questions, answers) before taking the self-test.																		
9. After taking the self-test, check your answers with those provided and review the materials related to any questions you answered incorrectly.																		
10. Read Scripture references in more than one translation of the Bible for better understanding. Take any opportunities you may have to discuss with others what you are learning.																		
11. Apply what you have learned in your spiritual life and ministry.																		
END-OF-UNIT REVIEW																		
Review for each unit progress evaluation by rereading the																		
a. lesson outlines to recall what you learned under each topic.																		
b. lesson objectives to be sure you know the key concepts to be able to answer a question on them.																		
c. questions you answered incorrectly in the lesson content or the self-test.																		
d. lesson content for topics you need to review.																		

- Use the *Student's Planner and Record* on the back of this page for an up-to-date record of your progress in this course.

- These charts are for you to record your personal progress in this course. Be sure to keep them up-to-date for quick reference.

LESSONS

- In the boxes below, record the unit number, the date you expect to complete each lesson, the date you do complete the lesson, and the date of review.

Unit Number	Lesson Number	Expected Completion Date	Actual Completion Date	Date Reviewed

FINAL EXAMINATION

Be sure to mail your request in time to receive your appointment before you finish studying and reviewing the course.

Appointment for Final Examination

Date _____

Hour _____

Place _____

Examiner _____

UNIT PROGRESS EVALUATIONS

- Record below the date you complete each unit progress evaluation.

	Date Completed
Unit Progress Evaluation 1	
Unit Progress Evaluation 2	
Unit Progress Evaluation 3	
Unit Progress Evaluation 4	
Unit Progress Evaluation 5	
Unit Progress Evaluation 6	

WRITTEN ASSIGNMENTS/FORMS

- Record below the date you submit each assignment and other requested forms to your enrollment office. Also record your score for each graded item.

	Date Submitted	Score
Service Learning Requirement (if required)		❑ Satisfactory ❑ Unsatisfactory
Project		
Collateral Reading Assignment (if required)		
Student's Request to Take Final Examination		
Final Examination		

Use the *Checklist of Study Methods* on the previous page to help you develop good study habits.

Question/Response Form

LIT1303 New Testament Literature, Sixth Edition   Date.......................................

Your Name .... Your Student Number.......................................

If you have a question concerning your course or academic policies, use this form to write to your adviser. Write your question clearly in the space provided. Your adviser will respond in the space reserved for this. Send this form to the office that is supervising your study program.

Your Question:

For Your Adviser's Response:

PN 06.14.01

Question/Response Form

LIT1303 New Testament Literature, Sixth Edition   Date.....................................

Your Name .... Your Student Number......................................

If you have a question concerning your course or academic policies, use this form to write to your adviser. Write your question clearly in the space provided. Your adviser will respond in the space reserved for this. Send this form to the office that is supervising your study program.

Your Question:

For Your Adviser's Response:

PN 06.14.01

Question/Response Form

LIT1303 New Testament Literature, Sixth Edition   Date..

Your Name .... Your Student Number......................................

If you have a question concerning your course or academic policies, use this form to write to your adviser. Write your question clearly in the space provided. Your adviser will respond in the space reserved for this. Send this form to the office that is supervising your study program.

Your Question:

For Your Adviser's Response:

PN 06.14.01

SLR TIME SURVEY INSTRUCTIONS

Make a note of the time it takes you to complete the SLR and fill out the SLR report. When you have completed the SLR, record the total time spent on the Time Survey response form in these Essential Course Materials. Submit the form to your enrollment office with your SLR report.

Service Learning Requirement

The purpose of the SLR is for you to apply and present principles learned from each course to people in your life or community during the course enrollment period.

The SLR report must be submitted with your project and CRA (if required) before you take your final examination.

The SLR will be assessed by a faculty member as satisfactory or unsatisfactory.

Course credit will be granted ONLY after the SLR report is submitted and assessed as satisfactorily completed.

The SLR assessment will be returned to you.

Service Learning Requirement

Connecting the Course with the Church and the Community for the Kingdom
LIT1303 New Testament Literature, Sixth Edition

The Service Learning Requirement (SLR) will help you apply principles you learned from the content of this course to people in your life or ministry. (1) It must be a planned, intentional activity, and (2) it must be course-content related. (More flexibility will be given to General Education courses for content relatedness.)

The SLR

- May be completed in a ministry or nonministry setting.
- May be completed in conjunction with a student ministry program or classroom presentation in your school or study group.
- Should consist of any valid and meaningful ministry experience that incorporates this specific course's content and interacts with other people.
- Will be assessed by a faculty member as satisfactory or unsatisfactory. The following constitute an unsatisfactory SLR: incomplete or incorrect assignment, inadequate information on the report, failure to complete the assignment during the course enrollment period, failure to present the assignment to one or more persons, or an illegible report. In such cases, the SLR will be returned and the student will be requested to redo the assignment and/or resubmit the report.
- Must be submitted with your project and CRA (if required) before you take your final examination. Course credit will be granted only after the SLR report is submitted and assessed as satisfactorily completed.
- Will be assessed by a faculty member and his or her comments will be returned to you.

Assignment

The following suggestions are given to help you understand the possible activities that fulfill this requirement. Choose an activity that will connect well with your course material. You may also develop a ministry activity that is not on this list or incorporate content from this course in ministry you are actively involved in at this time. **However, for an activity not on this list, you must obtain advance approval from the faculty member.**

- Preach a sermon to any size group.
- Teach a class or small group.
- Intervene or give counsel to help resolve personal conflicts.
- Share the gospel with nonbelievers. (Be prepared to develop new relationships to open doors for this ministry.)
- Interview pastors, missionaries, or other leaders on a course-related topic. (Do not post or publish interview content.)
- Lead a prayer group or mentor an individual over an extended period.
- Personally share encouragement and resources with those in need (outreach).
- Organize and/or administer an event in a church program such as leading youth ministry, feeding homeless people, transporting shut-ins, conducting nursing home services, and similar ministries.
- Publish an online blog or article in a church newsletter. (Include a link in your report to the content of your article or blog.)

1. Consider using any School for Evangelism and Discipleship materials from our GlobalReach website: www.globalreach.org. These proven tools are available for free and in many languages.
2. Have someone observe you, or at least share with someone what you did. Then ask that person to provide feedback by answering the questions in Point 5 of the SLR report.
3. Complete the SLR report. Use additional paper if needed. (Note: You need to submit only one report, even if, for example, you witnessed to several people at different times.) Submit the SLR report to your enrollment office along with your project and CRA (if required) before you take the final examination for this course.

Service Learning Requirement Report
LIT1303 New Testament Literature, Sixth Edition

Please print or type your responses on this form, and submit the form with your project and CRA (if required). If you need to use additional paper, print your name, student number, course number, and course title at the top of each page. Be sure to use correct spelling and write neatly and legibly using complete sentences where possible. Summarize points logically.

Student Name .... **Student Number** ....

Date: ....

1. Description of assignment: Describe what you did. ....

....

....

Where (location/s)? ....

To whom (person/s)? ....

....

What were the ministry results? Use only **NUMBERS** in the appropriate spaces below.

....	Witnessed to	....	Baptism(s) in the Holy Spirit
....	Decision(s) for Christ	....	Church(es) planted
....	Taught/preached to recipient(s)	....	Baptism(s) in water

List other results with numbers (such as 8 healings, 3 deliverances, 5 calls to ministry, 9 rededications).

....

2. Content: Summarize in the space below the content of your sermon, lesson, or witness. State the theme and main points or principles. If your assignment was another type of event, summarize the highlights.

....

....

....

....

3. Application: Explain how you applied the course content to yourself and to others. If you preached, taught, or witnessed, explain how you illustrated and applied your presentation.

....

....

....

....

4. Reflection: From this assignment, what did you learn from or about

Yourself? ....

....

....

....

The Lord?..

....

....

....

The Ministry?..

....

....

....

Others?...

....

....

....

Time: State how much time you spent in prayer .... and preparation .... for this assignment.

Evaluate your time. ....

For Student: By signing below I freely give permission to Global University (and affiliate agencies) to publish my SLR Report to promote the work of God through Global University.

....
                    Student Signature   Date

5. Required feedback from an independent observer (pastor, teacher, or colleague).

What did you like best about the student's presentation? ....

....

....

How could the student improve in the way he or she participated? ....

....

....

What other words of encouragement do you have for the student? ....

....

....

Name of person commenting and his or her relation to the student: ....

....

SLR Time

Hr_____ Min_____

TIME SURVEY

LIT1303 New Testament Literature

Check the appropriate box:
I am enrolled in this course for ☐ 2 credits ☐ 3 credits

In the space provided below, write in the *total time* (hours and minutes) it took you to complete each component or task.

COMPONENT / TASK	TOTAL TIME	
	Hours	*Minutes*
Reading all IST lessons (Add up the time spent on every IST lesson and submit the total.)		
Completing the learn-by-doing activities (Add up the time spent on every set of learn-by-doing activities and submit the total.)		
Completing and checking the self-tests (Add up the time spent on every self-test and submit the total.)		
Writing the project		
Preparing and completing the SLR		
Completing and grading the UPEs (Add up the time spent on every UPE and submit the total.)		
Reviewing weak areas in regard to the UPEs		
Time studying for final exam		
For 3-credit version:		
Reading the CRA textbook		
Writing the CRA or CWA		
TOTAL		

Submit this form with your Service Learning Requirement report.

ATTENTION

Undergraduate Writing Assignment Guidelines (UWAG)

These Undergraduate Writing Assignment Guidelines are provided to assist you in properly completing course assignments and understanding how Global University faculty members will evaluate and grade them. Carefully following these guidelines can improve the quality of your written work and elevate your grade.

Undergraduate Writing Assignments (CRA and Project)
Guidelines, Expectations, and Grading

Global University's *Undergraduate Form and Style Guide* defines the form, style, and documentation system for completing undergraduate writing assignments. The guide can be downloaded for free at http://www.globaluniversity.edu/PDF/UG-FormAndStyleGuide.pdf. The guide is also available as a stand-alone document.

Writing for Academic Quality and Other Conceptual Issues
- Follow instructions carefully. Failure to follow instructions will reduce the assignment grade.
- Develop thoughts logically.
- Do not merely repeat the author's position—evaluate the author's position.
- You are encouraged to both agree and disagree with the authors of course materials. Explain why you agree or disagree.
- Avoid using Hebrew, Aramaic, and Greek for most undergraduate CRAs and projects.
- Write at a college level, using appropriate vocabulary, grammar, and spelling. Avoid using the second person (you). Avoid generalizations, idioms, and slang.
- Consult reference works, including theological and Bible dictionaries, to accurately define terms.
- Express concepts in your own words as much as possible. Document all quotations, paraphrases, and important ideas that are not your own, even if they are from course materials.
- Clearly identify CRAs and projects on a title page.
- Reference list. See the *Undergraduate Form and Style Guide* for documenting sources correctly.

Grading

This grading rubric represents a transition in grading guidelines for all Global University undergraduate writing assignments, effective January 1, 2014. **Note: Not all the following indicators may apply to a particular written assignment.**

Content and Organization	40%	(40 points)
Following instructions		
Organization of assignment and logical thought progression		
Subject matter content quality and accuracy		
Critical Thinking Skills	30%	(30 points)
Accurate understanding and evaluation of author's position		
Statement of student's position with supporting rationale		
Application and Research	20%	(20 points)
Appropriate plans for applying course concepts		
Contextualization of course concepts to the student's culture or setting		
Inclusion of research using a minimum of three references from the		
GU Library Course Guides or other academic/scholarly resources		
Style, Grammar, Spelling, and Documentation	10%	(10 points)
Syntax (word choice and arrangement), spelling, and grammar		
Appropriate form and style, including source documentation		
TOTAL	*100%*	*(100 points)*

Academic/Scholarly Resources

When writing course papers, students are asked to include at least three academic/scholarly sources in their research. Generally, *scholarly* refers to original research found in books, magazines, and journals written by professional and credentialed experts. This is not to say that "popular" sources or authors cannot be used; however, such sources must be evaluated and found to be authoritative.

Students may contact course faculty members for source evaluations. Also, a tutorial explaining the difference between popular and academic/scholarly resources can be found with the GU Library Course Guides. To access the tutorial, go to the home page of any undergraduate course guide under "Research & Writing Helps."

To Ensure Your Assignment Is Graded Accurately

1. Respond to questions and their subparts in the exact order they appear in the instructions.
2. Type (or copy) each question and its number. Below it type (or write) your response.
3. Respond to all components, clearly labeling and separating your answers to each. Your grader must be able to easily match responses to the corresponding component.

General Directions

Please type your CRA/project using double-spaced lines. If you are unable to type your assignment, you may neatly write it with an ink pen, but DO NOT USE A PENCIL.

Valuable resources to help with your writing assignments can be accessed through the Global University Library Course Guides at http://libguides.globaluniversity.edu. To access licensed resources, you will be asked to log in with a user ID and a password. You can also log in from the main Library website for recurrent access to licensed resources. For your user ID, type in your Global University student ID number. For your password, type in the first two letters of your first name, the first two letters of your last name, and the last four digits of your GU student ID number. (Use lowercase letters; do not type spaces within the password.)

You can access a Course Research Guide for each undergraduate course that provides links to scholarly, academic resources compiled by GU librarians and faculty. Here you will find links to full-text journal articles in databases, reference articles in encyclopedias, scholarly articles, and websites and other web-based articles as well as project templates and a link to Global University's *Undergraduate Form and Style Guide*. Interactive tutorials are available on the Course Research Guides to help you navigate the website.

Document any resources you use in course assignments (or other written work) according to GU's *Undergraduate Form and Style Guide*. The style guide can be downloaded at http://www.globaluniversity .edu/PDF/UG-FormAndStyleGuide.pdf, or you can contact the university to purchase a hard copy.

Submitting Assignments

Submit your assignments by e-mail attachment. Templates for the project and CRA are available for download at http://libguides.globaluniversity.edu/templates. If e-mail is not available, submit assignments by mail or fax.

Terms

The following definitions help you give a better answer to each inquiry within your CRA/project:

- **Analyze** means to divide a complex whole into its individual components for the purpose of revealing how each works together and contributes to the whole.
- **Apply** means to put, or to show how to put, specific principles or concepts to practical use.
- **Compare** means to identify similarities.
- **Contrast**, **differentiate**, and **distinguish** mean to identify differences.
- **Critical thinking** is a reflective and systematic process in which you gather information, study it from every angle, and then exercise your best judgment to draw conclusions.
- **Describe**, **discuss**, and **explain** mean to give details, examples, illustrations, implications, and/or reasons to support your answer.
- **Evaluate** means to determine the significance, worth, or condition of something by careful study. This includes identifying the strengths and weaknesses of whatever is being evaluated, whether it is a concept, principle, application, idea, event, opinion, object or product.

Quick Guide to Referencing

Q   Where do I document sources—inside the paper or at the end of the paper?

A   Both. Author, date of publication, and page number must be included as parenthetical references within the text. Titles are not listed in the parenthetical references. A reference list at the end of the paper should list full publication details. Page numbers are not included in the reference list.

Book in Print

In-Text Documentation

When quoting from a book, quotation marks are required at the beginning and end of the quotation. Immediately after the quote and before ending punctuation, insert a parenthetical reference including author's last name, most recent date of publication, and page number(s).

> Biblical context is one of the key factors in interpreting Scripture correctly and there are "three kinds of
>
> context: immediate context, remote context, and historical context" (Arnold and Beyer 1999, 29).

A quote longer than four lines is single spaced without quotation marks and indented from the left margin. Insert a parenthetical reference at the end of the quote, following ending punctuation.

> Note the verbs describing God's concern: I have seen . . . have heard . . . I am concerned . . . I have come down. Three of the verbs with *God* as subject are repeated from 2:24–25 (*see, hear, know*), with a closer specification as to just what it is God sees and knows. God truly sees their affliction. God knows their sufferings. For God to know the people's sufferings testifies to God's experience of this suffering, indeed God's intimate experience. God is here depicted as one who is intimately involved in the suffering of the people. (Fretheim 1991, 36)

When the author's name is stated in the text, the parenthetical reference lists only the date and page number. The author's name is not repeated.

> Arnold and Beyer note that there are "three kinds of context" (1999, 29). *OR*
>
> Arnold and Beyer (1999) note that there are "three kinds of context" (29).

Reference List Documentation

Works used in the paper are also listed at the end of the paper in the reference list.

> Arnold, Bill T., and Bryan E. Beyer. 1999. *Encountering the Old Testament*. Grand Rapids, MI: Baker Book House.

NOTE: In this referencing system, only works actually cited in your paper are to be included in the reference list. (See the Global University *Undergraduate Form and Style Guide* 2013, page 7.)

Book on the Internet

In-Text Documentation

A full book accessed from the Internet is referenced in the text the same as a printed book.

> Scripture attributes varying ministries to each person of the Trinity. "The different functions that we see the
>
> Father, Son and Holy Spirit performing are simply outworkings of an eternal relationship" (Grudem 1994, 251).

Reference List Documentation

In the reference list, both the website and date of access are listed after the other information.

> Grudem, Wayne A. 1994. *Systematic Theology: An Introduction to Biblical Doctrine*. Grand Rapids, MI: Zondervan. http://books.google.com/books (accessed February 2, 2006).

Consult the Global University *Undergraduate Form and Style Guide* for other examples (journal or magazine articles, books with more than one author, and so forth).

Cover and Page Design

Example cover pages for your project and CRA are included in this packet. **It is very important** that you place your name, student number, course number, course title, course PN (located on the copyright page), and page number at the top of **each additional page**. (See sample pages below.) You are required to clearly mark each part of the answer. Be sure to write legibly, using a computer printer, typewriter, or pen. DO NOT USE A PENCIL.

SAMPLE PROJECT COVER PAGE

PROJECT TITLE

By
Your Name
Student Number

A Project
Submitted to the Faculty
In Partial Fulfillment of the Requirements for

Course Number
Course Title, Edition
Course PN

Global University
Month Year

SAMPLE CRA COVER PAGE

CRA TITLE
By
Student Name
Student Number

A Collateral Reading Assignment
Submitted to the Faculty
In Partial Fulfillment of the Requirements for

Course Number
Course Title, Edition
Course PN

COLLATERAL READING ASSIGNMENT

TEXTBOOK:

CRA Textbook Title
by CRA Textbook Author
Publisher Location: Publisher Name, Year

Global University
Month Year

SAMPLE SECOND PAGE

Student Name, Number	Course Number, Title, PN Number
	2

Project/CRA Title

Part 1

....
....
....
....
....
....
....
....
....
....
....
....
....
....

SAMPLE THIRD PAGE

Student Name, Number	Course Number, Title, PN Number
	3

....
....
....
....
....
....
....
....
....
....
....
....
....
....

Project Instructions

This project is worth 25 percent of your final course grade and must be submitted to your enrollment office before you may take the final examination.

You will be graded on your ability to apply the principles that are taught in the course as well as your ability to follow instructions.

PROJECT TITLE

By

Your Name

Student Number

A Project

Submitted to the Faculty
In Partial Fulfillment of the Requirements For

Course Number

Course Title, Edition

Course PN

Global University

Month Year

SLR TIME SURVEY INSTRUCTIONS

Make a note of the time it takes you to complete the SLR and fill out the SLR report. When you have completed the SLR, record the total time spent on the Time Survey response form in these Essential Course Materials. Submit the form to your enrollment office with your SLR report.

Project Instructions

LIT1303 New Testament Literature, Sixth Edition

In This Project You Will

Summarize the primary messages contained in (1) Matthew, (2) Romans, (3) 1 Corinthians, and (4) 2 Timothy, and assess how these messages are relevant to contemporary society.

Your Project Should Include

1. A summary of the primary message each author is trying to impress upon his readers.
2. An assessment of how the primary message of each book is relevant to contemporary society.

Project Instructions

Your project should be divided into four parts, one part each for Matthew, Romans, 1 Corinthians, and 2 Timothy. For each part, provide the following:

1. A summary of the primary message the author is trying to impress upon his readers. In two or three paragraphs tell what you believe to be the theme of the book. Use one brief Scripture passage that illustrates why you believe this is the book's theme.

2. An assessment of how the primary message of each book is relevant to contemporary society. Tell in two or three paragraphs why you believe it is relevant. Give one brief Scripture passage that shows the importance of the book's message for today.

An example would be 2 Timothy whose theme is the instructions and exhortations the aged apostle Paul gave his young protégé, Timothy. The message is as relevant today as when it was written since the task of communicating the gospel is continuously being entrusted to the new generation by the old.

This project is worth 25 percent of your course grade and should be submitted to your enrollment office before you take the final examination.

Writing Instructions

If you have not already done so, read the Undergraduate Writing Assignment Guidelines (found in the Essential Course Materials) and the *Global University Undergraduate Form and Style Guide.*

Your total word length should be approximately 1,200–1,500 words (5 to 6 double-spaced, typewritten pages). The addition of the cover and reference list could make the completed project 7 to 8 pages. You may use your Bible, IST or Study Guide, notes, and research material.

In completing the writing assignments, a minimum of three scholarly sources (in addition to the course textbooks) must be included.

- All sources (excluding Bibles and general reference books such as dictionaries) must be cited properly in the text and entered into a REFERENCE LIST at the end of your project.

- Acceptable academic resources may be acquired from personal research or obtained through accessing the Global University Library website and the Course Research Guides.

- The references must relate logically to the project; and you must explain, describe, interact with, or react to each reference as part of your written responses.

Instructions for accessing the Library website are given in the UWAG. If you have a legitimate reason for **not** having access to the Internet or other academic sources, you must include a statement explaining why you are unable to do so.

Submitting Your Assignment

Submit your project by e-mail attachment. A template is available for download at http://libguides .globaluniversity.edu/templates. If e-mail access is not available, submit by mail or fax with the project title page (a model is provided) on the front of your project.

This project is worth 25 percent of your course grade and should be submitted to your enrollment office before you take the final examination.

Total Project Time

Hr_____ Min_____

Answers to Self-Tests

LIT1303 New Testament Literature, Sixth Edition

Lesson 1

1 d) Alexander's conquest.

2 i) Titus.

3 a) Greek Empire.

4 m) Pilate.

5 o) Aramaic.

6 b) Roman Empire.

7 e) Priests.

8 c) Maccabean revolt.

9 h) Nero.

10 j) Domitian.

11 g) Claudius.

12 k) Tiberius.

13 f) Augustus.

14 p) Latin.

15 n) Morality.

16 l) Roman emperor.

17 b) Augustus.

18 a) Claudius and Nero.

19 b) Greek.

20 c) Hebrew.

21 b) Aramaic.

22 d) Greek.

23 a) Romans.

24 d) Greeks.

25 b) Romans.

Lesson 2

1 True.

2 True.

3 False.

4 True.

5 False.

6 True.

7 True.

8 False.

9 False.

10 True.

11 True.

12 True.

13 False.

14 True.

15 False.

16 True.

17 False.

18 True.

19 True.

20 False.

21 f) Cynicism.

22 d) Epicureanism.

23 a) Platonism.

24 g) Scepticism.

25 e) Stoicism.

26 c) Neo-Platonism.

27 b) Gnosticism.

28 d) The Day of Atonement.

29 a) The Passover.

30 g) The Feast of Purim.

31 b) Pentecost.

32 f) The Feast of Lights.

33 c) The Feast of Trumpets.

34 e) The Feast of Tabernacles.

35 The Pharisees.

36 The Essenes.

37 The Sadducees.

Lesson 3

1 r) Emmaus.

2 g) The New Testament.

3 b) Bethany.

4 m) "Q"

5 k) Ephraim.

6 t) Kidron.

7 i) Secular literature.

8 q) Jerusalem.

9 e) Jesus.

10 l) New.

11 c) Parables.

12 p) Testamentum.

13 h) Question-and-answer method.

14 f) Synoptic.

15 s) Epigram.

16 n) Synoptic problem.

17 o) Discussion.

18 d) Documentary hypothesis.

19 j) Object.

20 a) Argument (or reasoning).

21 c) Geographical.

22 a) The Old was preparation, the New was realization.

23 d) Christ is the central and uniting theme for both the Old and New Testaments.

24 b) Christ is presented historically in the Gospel accounts and Acts, doctrinally in the Epistles, and prophetically in Revelation.

25 d) Inception, (6 BC–AD 29); expansion, (AD 29–60); consolidation, (AD 60–100).

26 Luke

27 Paul

28 John

29 Paul

30 Jude

31 James

32 Peter

33 Peter

34 Paul

35 Paul

36 Paul

37 Paul

Lesson 4

1 a) Matthew 5:3–12.

2 j) Matthew 6:9–13.

3 h) Matthew 7:12.

4 f) John the Baptist.

5 g) Matthew 6:12, 14–15.

6 c) Matthew 28:19–20.

7 i) Matthew 19:3–12.

8 d) Peter.

9 b) Matthew 24–25.

10 e) Matthew 22:37–40.

11 c) by Matthew Levi, a tax collector.

12 b) He is shown by the book of Acts to have been active in the church until AD 95.

13 d) Antioch in AD 50–70.

14 a) Mark, Matthew, Luke, John.

15 a) Jewish audience.

16 d) Law and gospel.

17 b) Biographical and topical.

18 d) He concludes his book with a reference to the Mosaic Law.

19 a) It is didactic, messianic, and biographical.

20 b) The faithful servant.

21 a) A major key to understanding the relation between law and gospel.

22 a) The Passion of the Messiah Accomplished.

23 c) Advent, miracles, parables, conflict, cross.

24 c) Nazareth and Cana are small towns, close together, between the Great Sea and the Sea of Galilee.

25 d) 11, 12, and 13, with chapter 13 having the greatest collection.

Lesson 5

1 a) a Christian family in Jerusalem.

2 d) John the Baptist.

3 c) They were simultaneously authored under the inspiration of the Holy Spirit.

4 d) The genealogy of Christ.

5 a) Action, reaction, vividness, evangelistic.

6 c) Turned water into wine.

7 a) Mary Magdalene.

8 d) had a wife named Joanna.

9 c) Jesus asked the man to dip seven times in the Jordan River.

10 a) Mark records little about Jesus' ministry in Jerusalem prior to the Passion.

11 b) It was about 115 miles (184 kilometers) north of Jerusalem at the foot of Mt. Hermon.

12 b) The Value of Life and the Cost of Discipleship.

13 d) The Power of Faith and Forgiveness in Prayer.

14 c) The Great Commission.

15 a) The Institution of the Lord's Supper.

16 c) Mark 1:1–13.

17 a) Mark 14:1–15:47.

18 b) Mark 16:1–20.

19 d) Mark 1:14–13:37.

Lesson 6

1 c) He was a Jew.

2 b) Matthew.

3 d) The Messiahship of Christ

4 d) Luke concentrates on Jesus' fulfillment of messianic prophecies.

5 a) The Good Samaritan

6 c) He was a Zealot.

7 b) He was exalted because he humbled himself.

8 c) It was about 8.1 miles (13 kilometers) west of Jerusalem.

9 d) The twelve apostles named

10 j) Seek heavenly treasure

11 h) The Father's desire to give the Holy Spirit

12 g) AD 60

13 b) The Magnificat.

14 e) Is introduced in Luke only

15 l) The Great Commission and Great Enablement

16 c) The book of Acts

17 i) Jesus' criteria for ministry

18 m) The parable of the Good Samaritan

19 f) Is named in Matthew, Mark, and Luke

20 a) Jesus the Son of Man

Lesson 7

1 True.

2 True.

3 False.

4 True.

5 False.

6 False.

7 False.

8 True.

9 True.

10 True.

11 d) love.

12 b) believe.

13 a) divine life that God gives to one who believes in Christ.

14 d) followed descriptions of events or miracles with related discourses.

15 c) fill in or add to what was recorded in the other Gospel accounts.

16 b) The seven "I AMs" of Christ

17 a) Like an eagle, spiritual, the Lord, the Branch

18 b) Parables

19 a   the Messiah.

   b   the Servant.

   c   the Son of Man.

   d   the Son of God.

20 signs, belief, life.

Lesson 8

1 e)   Rome

2 g)   Stephen

3 i)   AD 63

4 a)   Luke's first volume

5 b)   The book of Acts

6 f)   Peter

7 d)   Antioch

8 h)   Paul (or Saul)

9 k)   AD 61

10 l)   Conversion of Saul (Paul)

11 n)   Samaritans

12 m)   Universality

13 j)   Pentecost

14 o)   Jerusalem

15 c)   Gentiles

16 p)   Resurrection of Jesus

17 b)   Second

18 d)   Stephen

19 c)   seven years

20 a)   organization.

21 d)   five years.

22 b)   resurrection.

23 d)   democratic.

24 a)   missionary witness.

25 b)   Rome.

Lesson 9

1 f)   James.

2 d)   2 Thessalonians.

3 b)   South Galatian Theory.

4 e)   Troas.

5 c)   1 Thessalonians.

6 a)   Galatians.

7 True.

8 False.

9 True.

10 False.

11 True.

12 False.

13 True.

14 False.

15 True.

16 True.

17 False.

18 True.

19 False.

20 False.

21 False.

22 Luke.

23 Rapture (or Parousia).

24 Revelation (or Apocalupsis).

25 fruit.

Lesson 10

1 Because their major concern is the doctrine of salvation through the cross of Jesus Christ.

2 Liberty from the Law and justification by grace through faith.

3 Your answer may be similar to this one: We are no longer bound by the Law because Christ has set us free. We love Him because He gave Himself for us, and we choose to serve Him and obey Him because of our love for Him.

4 Because their background was so immoral.

5 Paul chose spiritual solutions based on a personal relationship with Christ and a desire to obey Him.

6 I would say yes. Perhaps you have faced similar problems in your ministry. I believe Paul's solutions were the correct ones.

7 He wanted to defend himself against those

who were attacking him. He wanted to ask the Corinthian church to give an offering for the Jerusalem assembly.

8 He reveals deeply personal things about himself.

9 ministry.

10 You may list the following in any order:

a It gives an insight into the life of Paul and into the sufficiency of God's grace.

b It reveals to us that the early church had to deal with sin and problems.

c It provides positive teaching on subjects such as the ministry, giving, and life after death.

11 True.

12 False.

13 False.

14 True.

15 True.

16 True.

Lesson 11

1 True.

2 False.

3 False.

4 True.

5 True.

6 True.

7 False.

8 True.

9 True.

10 False.

11 b) wanted to stop rumors that he was against Jewish customs.

12 b) the need for forgiveness and reconciliation.

13 a) The letter was preserved and shared by its owner.

14 d) reproduced and sent to several churches to whom Paul wanted the message given.

15 c) A specific call to a specific ministry.

16 a) show Christ's relationship to His church universal.

17 d) deal with the problem of heresy.

18 b) knowledge.

19 a) Philemon, Ephesians, Colossians, Philippians.

20 c) thanksgiving, joy.

Lesson 12

1 f) Second Timothy 4:6–8.

2 g) Babylon.

3 a) Hebrews.

4 b) Jewish Christians.

5 j) Second Timothy 4:1–5.

6 i) Apollos.

7 h) Second Timothy.

8 e) First Timothy 3:1–13.

9 d) Grace.

10 c) 1 Peter.

11 d) 1 Timothy, Titus, and 2 Timothy.

12 a) ecclesiological.

13 d) the pastoral Epistles.

14 c) from Macedonia in AD 62.

15 b) 1 Timothy, Titus, and 2 Timothy.

16 d) Titus.

17 a) There is no doctrine in Titus.

18 b) 1 and 2 Timothy.

19 c) a pioneer movement to an organized institution.

20 d) Secret Christian meetings in the catacombs to plot Caesar's death.

21 Jewish.

22 Paul.

23 Organizational.

24 Titus.

25 Romans, faith.

Lesson 13

1 j) 2 Peter 1:15–21.

2 g) Theological value.

3 a) 2 Peter.

4 d) Antinomianism.

5 c) Jude.

6 f) Gnosticism.

7 e) Historical value.

8 i) AD 64.

9 b) True knowledge.

10 h) AD 90.

11 False.

12 True.

13 True.

14 True.

15 False.

16 True.

17 True.

18 False.

19 False.

20 True.

21 backsliding.

22 world.

23 humanity.

24 Gaius.

25 soul.

Lesson 14

See chart on page 329.

Lesson 15

1 c) authorship, general acceptance, inspiration.

2 b) 2 Timothy 3:16–17.

3 b) Theological effect.

4 d) formal lists or canons.

5 a) informal witnesses to canonicity.

6 b) fourth century.

7 d) Private individuals and professional scribes.

8 a) Content of a private nature.

c) Brief and without enough general interest.

9 b) Different in style than another book by the same author.

10 d) Content of more interest to Jews than to Greeks.

11 a) Content of a private nature.

c) Brief and without enough general interest.

12 c) Brief and without enough general interest.

13 a) Content of a private nature.

c) Brief and without enough general interest.

14 (Any of these.) Treatment of the central subject matter: Jesus Christ. Claims within the text that it is the Word of God and produces effects in those who believe it. Acceptance by some New Testament writers of other books.

15 (Either of these.) Informal witness: casual use of the books in the early church. Formal lists or canons: lists accepted as authoritative, or decisions of special councils.

16 Resources for reconstructing the text are greater than for any other documents of its period, and some date back to within half a century of the lifetime of the author. Examination of these texts proves that translations are still intact.

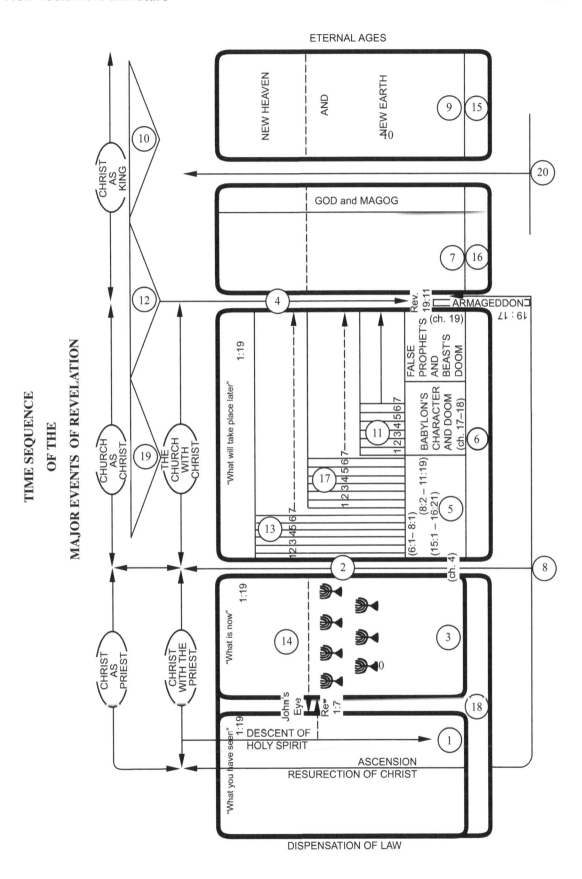

TIME SEQUENCE OF THE MAJOR EVENTS OF REVELATION

Unit Progress Evaluations

The Unit Progress Evaluations (UPEs) are designed to indicate how well you learned the material in each unit and how well you may do on the final examination.

Answer the UPE questions without referring to your course materials, Bible, or notes.

When you have completed each UPE, compare your answers with those in the UPE answer keys in the next section of the Essential Course Materials. Review any items you may have answered incorrectly.

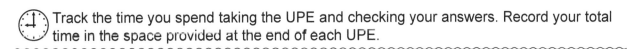

Start Time

_____

Unit Progress Evaluation 1

LIT1303 New Testament Literature, Sixth Edition

(Unit 1—Lessons 1–2)

Multiple Choice Questions

Select the best answer to each question.

1 Who was the emperor of Rome during the ministry and death of Jesus Christ?
 a) Augustus
 b) Claudius
 c) Julius Caesar
 d) Nero
 e) Tiberius

2 Roman provinces that were peaceful and loyal to Rome were under
 a) praetors responsible to regional military commanders.
 b) tetrarchs directly responsible to the Roman people.
 c) ethnarchs under the appointment of the emperor.
 d) proconsuls responsible to the Roman Senate.

3 The emperor often had armies stationed in provinces that were rebellious which were governed by
 a) committees of magistrates.
 b) military tribunes.
 c) preconsuls.
 d) procurators.

4 While Roman proconsuls were in office for one year, procurators, prefects, and propraetors held office
 a) for from three to five years based upon ability to govern.
 b) for life based upon good behavior and intelligent administration.
 c) as long as the emperor chose to leave them in a given position.
 d) for as long as the emperor who appointed them was in office.

5 According to Tenney, administrators in the provinces followed what kind of policy toward the worship practices of their subjects? They were
 a) intolerant as a rule, but on occasion they granted some local customary worship.
 b) quite tolerant and never interfered with the religious freedom of their subjects.
 c) indifferent, because their primary concern was tribute and security.
 d) officially against all religions that would not incorporate emperor worship into their own system.

6 Which statement concerning Roman administration in the provinces is NOT true?
 a) A majority of proconsuls and procurators were guilty of crime and poor administration.
 b) A system of first-class roads was constructed.
 c) Public buildings were built that were both beautiful and practical.
 d) Commerce was developed rapidly throughout the empire.

7 The expansion of the Greek Empire moved forward rapidly
 a) as a result of the campaigns of Alexander the Great.
 b) following the collapse of the Roman Empire.
 c) while the Seleucids and Ptolemies fought for control of the Eastern Mediterranean area.
 d) as a result of the general collapse of the Babylonian Empire.

8 According to Tenney, the rule of the Ptolemies
of Egypt and the Seleucidae of Syria had a
tremendous effect
  a) spreading the Greek language widely
     throughout the Eastern Mediterranean area.
  b) distributing Greek literature throughout the
     Eastern Mediterranean area.
  c) making the Greek language and literature a
     common medium of culture for oriental and
     western peoples.
  d) all of the above.

9 Two very important contributions that Jewish
exiles in Babylon made to Judaism were
  a) a renewed emphasis on keeping the Law and
     quickly renouncing idolatry.
  b) the development of the synagogue and the
     beginning of the order of the scribes.
  c) the beginning of the public reading of the
     Law and renewal of some animal sacrifices.
  d) admitting Gentiles into the synagogue
     worship and development of a structure
     of worship.

10 The Jewish exiles in Babylon responded to the
destruction of the temple and the end of their
state by
  a) studying the Law and the prophets, and
     continuing their worship of God during
     the exile.
  b) appointing teachers who diligently taught
     the exiles to revere and obey the Law.
  c) substituting the study of the Law for animal
     sacrifices and ethical observances in place
     of ritual.
  d) only a) and c) above.
  e) all three: a), b), and c) above.

11 During the Persian and Greek periods, the
two prominent aspects of Jewish life that
disappeared were the
  a) monarchy and the prophetic office.
  b) priesthood and the offering of sacrifices.
  c) emphasis on oral tradition and books that
     interpreted the Law.
  d) temple worship and feasts.

12 Under the Ptolemies, the high priest, was
aided by the council of priests and elders in
administering the law in the national life which,
at this time, was centered around the
  a) synagogue.
  b) provincial council.
  c) temple.
  d) local council under the control of
     the scribes.

13 What significant achievement made under the
Ptolemies aided both Jews of the Dispersion
and writers of the New Testament?
  a) A great research library was founded in
     which the chief literary treasures of antiquity
     were preserved.
  b) Alexandria became an outstanding center of
     commerce and education.
  c) Jewish Scriptures were translated into
     Greek, and the finished work was called
     the Septuagint.
  d) The wars between the Seleucidae of Syria
     and the Ptolemies of Egypt so weakened
     both kingdoms that Israel was able to gain
     her independence.

14 The effect of the Seleucidae on the Jewish
people in Palestine was tremendous. The
Hellenizing pressure of the Seleucid rulers
  a) forced Judaism into a "Gentile" mold
     with customs that were no longer
     exclusively Jewish.
  b) consolidated the Jews into a resistance group
     intensely loyal to its faith and distinctive
     way of life.
  c) signaled the end of Judaism as a "national"
     religion because most Jews apostatized.
  d) forced a total way of life on Jews as a
     whole, and this included religion, language,
     education, and even thought patterns.

15 Herod the Great ruled over Judea from 37 to 4
BC. In spite of some internal problems his rule
was considered successful; nevertheless, he did
not succeed in winning the friendship of the
Jews because
  a) his Idumean blood made him a foreigner in
     their eyes.
  b) he openly supported heathen cults with royal
     funds.
  c) his loyalty to Judaism was doubted.
  d) all of the above.
  e) both a) and c) above.

16 According to Tenney, the Jewish people generally regarded all the foreign rulers as illegal rulers; therefore, the people never gave them full support. The real controlling power of the Jewish mind, he says, was the
a) political power of the Great Synagogue.
b) priesthood.
c) order of new professionals, the scribes.
d) underground military order.

17 Prior to the Jewish War in AD 66, the group of patriots from Galilee that openly called for a holy war to get rid of the hated foreigners was called the
a) Zealots.
b) Assassins.
c) Herodians.
d) Bar-Cochbites.

18 Which of the following was NOT a part of Jewish society at this time?
a) A sense of moral equality prevailed as well as a sense of responsibility to the Law.
b) There was an abundance of slavery.
c) There was a priestly hierarchy.
d) The majority of the people were poor.

19 Which one of the following statements does NOT correctly describe a social class in pagan society in the Roman Empire?
a) The aristocracy profited from exploitation of the conquered provinces.
b) Slaves made up a large proportion of the population of the Roman Empire.
c) The middle class was thriving on the benefits of the tax system.
d) The lot of the plebes was pitiful, and since they lacked employment they were worse off than slaves.

20 According to Tenney, the restless hordes of the unemployed—the cheats and robbers, the despairing and desperate—all made a fertile ground for the breeding of criminals which indicated that
a) there was no internal standard in paganism to check the downward trend.
b) crime prevailed everywhere and in all levels of society.
c) the picture of the heathen world in Romans 1:18–32 was accurate.
d) all of the above.
e) both a) and c) above.

21 Music and drama, in the early stages of the Roman Empire, were committed to
a) stimulating the thought of intellectuals through the presentation of the great Greek tragedies.
b) entertaining the wealthy middle class.
c) amusing the royal court and government officials.
d) entertaining the mobs through degenerating and degrading farces and mimes.

22 Emperors and public office seekers, according to Tenney, promoted bloody contests between men and beasts or between men and men in which most of the participants died in the arena in a shocking and gruesome manner, glorifying
a) brutality.
b) obscenity and lust.
c) human bravery and physical skill.
d) the competitive spirit common to all peoples of the empire.

23 Three of the four major languages in the Roman Empire that gave Christianity a means of universal expression were
a) Greek, Hebrew, and Aramaic.
b) Aramaic, Latin, and Greek.
c) Latin, Hebrew, and Aramaic.
d) Latin, Greek, and Hebrew.

24 Which statement below best represents the economic and commercial picture of the early empire that Tenney presents?
a) Caravans moved goods throughout the empire quickly, cheaply, and safely.
b) Although good roads existed, carts and wagons drawn by animals moved slowly and the cost was great for transported goods.
c) Shipping was limited to the navigable rivers and to the ocean during the summer months.
d) both a) and c) above
e) both b) and c) above

25 The spread of the gospel within the Roman Empire was affected by which of the following?
a) Frontiers between countries were governed by different rules, and this caused much delay in travel and communications.
b) One could travel with ease and relative safety anywhere within the empire. Communications could be maintained by means of an efficient imperial postal system.
c) Only citizens of Rome could move freely on imperial roads and waterways.
d) Because of the many different languages spoken, travel and communications were made difficult from country to country within the empire.

26 The worship of the Graeco-Roman pantheon, which originally involved the worship of the gods of nature, had begun to decline by the time of Christ because
a) of the gross immoralities and petty squabbles of these deities.
b) worship was semipolitical, and one worshiped a certain deity simply because he happened to live where that deity was worshiped.
c) when a city was overthrown by Roman armies, people questioned "why" their deity could not protect them.
d) all of the above.
e) both b) and c) above.

27 Emperor worship had great value for the state as noted in all of the statements below EXCEPT one. It did not have value for
a) arousing feelings of patriotism.
b) meeting the supposed needs of worship.
c) making subjects conform to the support of the state as a religious duty.
d) meeting the individual needs of worshipers.
e) meeting ego needs in the lives of emperors.

28 Mystery religions drew considerable support from the people who wanted immediate contact with deity. These religions
a) satisfied the desire for personal immortality and for social equality.
b) offered an outlet for emotion in religion and made religious experience very personal.
c) were based on objective sets of rules that governed all mystical experiences.
d) all of the above.
e) both a) and b) above.

29 We have seen that occultism was widespread in the early Roman Empire and that all of the following are true of occultism EXCEPT which one?
a) Occultism was an acceptable form of direct revelation for those who were not professional prophets.
b) Jew and Gentile alike shared a superstitious belief concerning the spirit world.
c) The Babylonian captivity brought Jews into contact with the mystic lore of the East, and many became professional exorcists and necromancers.
d) The biblical attitude toward occultism was always hostile.

30 Which philosophy promotes a fatalistic attitude toward life?
a) Platonism
b) Epicureanism
c) Stoicism
d) Skepticism
e) Gnosticism

31 Which philosophy taught that only spirit was good and matter was evil and promised salvation by knowledge?
a) Platonism
b) Epicureanism
c) Stoicism
d) Skepticism
e) Gnosticism

32 Christianity was built upon the foundation of Judaism that, unlike other religions, was based on
a) subjective experience.
b) spiritual phenomena.
c) a revelation from God.
d) tradition.

33 Which one of the following was fundamental to the beliefs of Judaism?
a) Its followers were forbidden to worship any other god than Jehovah God.
b) There was an absolute denial of moral freedom; people were forced to be obedient.
c) Revelation was encouraged by means of ritual, righteous works, and supplication.
d) Its followers asserted that there were many roads to truth, and all of them somehow achieved the same goal.

34 The synagogue fulfilled all of the following needs of Judaism EXCEPT which one?
   a) It served a social function, for the members met here weekly for fellowship with each other.
   b) The needs of education for the community were served here.
   c) The sacrificial offering, the substitutionary function, was served here.
   d) The religious function of the community was accomplished here.

35 Synagogue worship procedure exerted a strong influence on the worship pattern of the early church that is seen in the church's emphasis on
   a) the reading of Scripture and preaching sermons.
   b) free access to synagogue worship for all people—Jews and Gentiles alike.
   c) the role of the priest as leader of the people.
   d) observance of the Law and sacrifices for the atonement of sin.

36 Which Jewish feast celebrated the anniversary of the deliverance of the Jews from Egypt and their establishment as an independent people by the redemptive act of God?
   a) Pentecost
   b) Feast of Trumpets
   c) Feast of Tabernacles
   d) Feast of Lights
   e) Passover

37 Which statement below best describes the particular educational emphases of the Jewish people?
   a) Education consisted of a broad exposure to ancient literature with special emphasis on tradition and the Law.
   b) It emphasized a narrow but very precise knowledge of interpreting the Law and manual training in some vocational skills.
   c) Jewish students were encouraged to think critically and creatively and to pursue scientific research for a well-rounded educational experience.
   d) The only emphasis for Jewish students was on theology because they were first and foremost "people of the Book."

38 The body of works (books) called the Apocrypha, is most accurately described as
   a) works of a secular and entertaining nature much like epic poetry.
   b) a body of teaching literature that paralleled the Decalogue.
   c) an expansion of the original body of wisdom literature.
   d) works that had a religious flavor, but which were not generally accepted as authoritative.
   e) the writings of Josephus, the Jewish Roman historian

39 The collection of Jewish traditions together and the commentary on them by the early rabbis, which regulates the faith and practice of the orthodox Jew, constitute the
   a) Apocrypha.
   b) Torah.
   c) Talmud.
   d) Midrash.

40 Which statement is NOT true of the Pharisees as a sect of Judaism?
   a) The Pharisees accepted the entire Old Testament as a basis for their theology.
   b) The Pharisees attempted to practice complete obedience to both the written and oral Law.
   c) The Pharisees believed in angels and spirits.
   d) The Pharisees believed in the resurrection and immortality.
   e) Most of the disciples of Jesus had been practicing Pharisees.

Part 2—True-False Questions

Indicate whether each statement is TRUE or FALSE.

41 Although Nero persecuted Christians and probably martyred Paul and Peter, in the last years of his life, he publicly accepted Jesus Christ and became a Christian.

42 Two kinds of provincial government existed at the same time in the Roman Empire: government under the senate and government under the emperor.

43 At the time of Jesus and later Paul, the Jewish high priest was elected to his office by vote of the Jewish Sanhedrin.

44 Aramaic was the predominant spoken language of the Eastern Mediterranean area.

45 Emperor worship began in the Roman Empire by vote of the Roman Senate.

46 Jews wrote all but one of the New Testament books.

47 The largest and most influential sect in New Testament times was that of the Pharisees, who were the separatists or Puritans of Judaism.

48 The Sadducees were less numerous than the Pharisees; however, they possessed political power and were the governing group in the civil life of Judaism under the Herods.

49 The religious practice of the Pharisees involved a cold legalism and was much more open to Hellenizing influences than was the religious practice of the Sadducees.

50 The moral and spiritual standards of the Pharisees may have tended toward self-righteousness, but their standards were high when compared with the standards of other people of their day.

After answering all of the questions in this UPE, refer again to points **3–6** under the heading *Taking Your Unit Progress Evaluations.* You will find these on the Essential Course Materials **INSTRUCTIONS** page.

Total UPE Time

Hr_____ Min_____

Unit Progress Evaluation 2

LIT1303 New Testament Literature, Sixth Edition

Start Time

(Unit 2—Lessons 3–7)

Multiple Choice Questions

Select the best answer to each question.

1 What does the word Testament in the expression New Testament literally mean?
 a) A decree issued by the Jewish Sanhedrin and carried to all parts of the then known world by Jewish apostles.
 b) The contract agreed upon and signed by individual historians and the early Jerusalem church for the writing of the individual books of the New Testament.
 c) An arrangement made by one party that might be accepted or rejected by another party, but the second party could not alter it; and that when accepted, both parties are bound by its terms.
 d) The word refers to archives dug up near Caesaria. These archives were written agreements between Roman military officers and businessmen traveling through Palestine in camel caravans.

2 Which books are NOT classified as doctrinal?
 a) 1 and 2 Timothy
 b) Romans and Galatians
 c) 1 and 2 Corinthians
 d) 1 and 2 Peter

3 Which of the following were books written by Paul?
 a) Acts and Luke
 b) Acts and Revelation
 c) Colossians and John
 d) Titus and Philippians

4 Which of the following indicates the correct chronological order of New Testament time periods and books written during those periods?
 a) Inception, expansion, and consolidation
 b) Inception, consolidation, and expansion
 c) Refutation, inception, and consolidation
 d) Consolidation, expansion, and refutation

5 The mutual interdependence, oral tradition, Formgeschichte, and documentary hypothesis theories fail to emphasize the
 a) people's ability to retain content after hearing it preached.
 b) importance of John Mark's eyewitness accounts of Jesus.
 c) common inspiration by God.
 d) interaction of the various writers of the Gospels.

6 Secular literature at the time of Jesus and the early church revealed several facts about Jesus and Christianity. Which item below was NOT found in secular literature?
 a) Christianity was widespread by the second century.
 b) The historical existence of Christ was acknowledged even by those who were against Him.
 c) Some secular authors considered Jesus a fanatic whose cult had grown unexpectedly.
 d) A very brief statement of the crucifixion of Jesus was included in an annual report of Pontius Pilate to Emperor Tiberius.

7 Which statement below is a true statement?
 a) The Gospel writers are more concerned with the significance of events in the life of Jesus than giving a complete chronological arrangement of His life.
 b) Three of the four Gospels give a detailed account of the birth of Jesus.
 c) Only three of the four Gospels give a detailed account of the death of Jesus.
 d) Each Gospel writer gives a chronological report of the events in the life of Jesus.

8 Which numbers and cities below correctly correspond to the numbers on the map at the right?
   a) 2-Dead Sea, 3-Cana, 4-Nazareth, 5-Jerusalem.
   b) 1-Dead Sea, 2-Sea of Galilee, 3-Jerusalem, 4-Nazareth.
   c) 1-Sea of Galilee, 2- Dead Sea, 3-Bethlehem, 4-Samaria.
   d) 2-Sea of Tiberias, 3-Jerusalem, 4-Bethlehem, 5-Cana.

9 What method of teaching did Jesus employ when He talked of the seed that fell in different types of soil?
   a) Epigram
   b) Argument
   c) Allegory
   d) Parable

10 We accept Matthew as the author of the Gospel of Matthew because
   a) he was the most prominent apostle.
   b) early church writers credited him as the author.
   c) he had been a close friend of orthodox Jews.
   d) he was the most orthodox apostle.

11 Evidence regarding the time of the writing of Matthew indicates that it was written
   a) after the reign of the Emperor Domitian.
   b) prior to the overthrow of Jerusalem.
   c) before Paul went to Rome.
   d) before the accession of Emperor Nero.

12 What kind of audience was Matthew writing to?
   a) Jewish
   b) Greek Gentile
   c) Roman Gentile
   d) Spanish Gentile
   e) Church

13 A main purpose for writing the Gospel of Matthew was to
   a) record the special miracles of Christ to inspire people to believe in Christ's deity.
   b) form a bridge between the old covenant and the new covenant.
   c) record an account of the life of Jesus primarily for the Gentiles.
   d) recount some incidents and some commentary about the life of Jesus.

14 What is the theme of the Gospel of Matthew?
   a) God reveals Himself through signs that produce belief, which results in new life.
   b) The revelation of the fulfillment of the messianic promise through Jesus Christ the Messiah.
   c) The refusal of the nation of Israel to accept Jesus Christ as the prophesied Messiah.
   d) A systematic biography of the life of Jesus Christ and its influence on human history.

15 How does Tenney explain law and gospel from the book of Matthew?
   a) The gospel does not do away with the Law, but adds the Law as a requirement to be kept in addition to faith in Jesus Christ.
   b) The gospel does away with the Law as a means to know human sin, reveals the holiness of God, and leads to Christ.
   c) The gospel does not do away with the Law, but rather through the power of Jesus Christ, enables believers to keep the Law and the teaching of Jesus.
   d) The gospel does not do away with the ceremonial Law of Moses. At the end of history, the Jews must again perform animal sacrifices in a rebuilt temple.

16 Which of these statements does NOT describe the content of Matthew?
   a) It is a didactic Gospel.
   b) It has numerous discourses.
   c) It emphasizes individual action.
   d) It is a messianic Gospel.

17 Matthew has special features that are not found in the Synoptic Gospels. Which of the following statements is NOT one of those special features?
   a) Matthew contains more of Jesus' teaching than any other Synoptic Gospel.
   b) Matthew is the only Gospel in which Christ speaks of the church.
   c) Matthew is the Gospel of the King; the royalty of Christ is emphasized.
   d) Matthew is the only Gospel that shares Christ's ministry among the Gentiles in Syria.

18 Clement of Alexandria and Eusebius suggest that John Mark
a) was an eyewitness of most of the events of the life of Christ.
b) really never wrote the Gospel that bears his name.
c) wrote the Gospel of Mark as Peter explained it.
d) wrote the Gospel of Mark as Paul dictated it.

19 The Gospel of Mark was most likely written from
a) Rome.
b) Ephesus.
c) Antioch.
d) Jerusalem.
e) Caesarea.

20 Which set of words characterizes Mark's Gospel?
a) Straightway, immediately, activity, servant
b) That it might be fulfilled, explanation, discourses
c) Faith, hope, love, power
d) Abstract, philosophical, heavenly

21 How does Tenney describe the Gospel of Mark?
a) Mark is a theological book. Mark gives more space to theology than any other Gospel.
b) Mark is a book of contemplation and praise. Mark is to the New Testament what Psalms are to the Old Testament.
c) Mark is a Gospel of action. Mark gives more space to the miracles of Christ than any other Gospel.
d) Mark is a prophetic book. Mark gives more space to the second coming of Christ than Daniel and Revelation combined.

22 One of Mark's main purposes in his Gospel was to
a) provide an adequate genealogy of Jesus.
b) provide philosophical discourses on the servanthood of Christ.
c) minimize the supernatural element in Christ's life.
d) evangelize the Gentiles with a gospel of action.

23 Which Bible character(s) are not mentioned in the Gospel of Mark?
a) Alexander and Rufus
b) Simon the leper
c) Peter
d) The twelve disciples
e) Luke

24 Which statement describes Luke, the author of Acts?
a) The "we" sections of Acts suggest that Luke was a close associate of the Apostle Paul.
b) Luke was a retired officer-secretary of a high ranking officer in the Roman Army by the name of Theophilus.
c) Luke was the adopted son of Theophilus, a Roman senator.
d) Luke was one of the seventy disciples that Jesus sent out two-by-two.

25 The author of Luke-Acts was
a) a Gentile whose literary skill defended Christianity.
b) employed as a tax collector and political activist.
c) an eyewitness to nearly all of the events in Luke-Acts.
d) a close associate of Peter, wealthy, a native of Jerusalem, and inclined toward skepticism.

26 The purpose of the Gospel of Luke was to
a) prove that Jesus is the promised Messiah.
b) challenge the readers to believe that Jesus is the Christ, the Son of God, through the signs recorded, so that the readers might have eternal life.
c) write an organized, complete, historically accurate account of the gospel.
d) prove through the life of Jesus Christ that Christianity is superior to all other religions and philosophies.

27 Which subject did Luke emphasize?
a) Women
b) Children
c) The poor
d) All of the above
e) Both b) and c) above

28 What doctrine does the parable of the Pharisee and the publican illustrate?
a) Sanctification
b) Justification
c) Adoption
d) The Holy Spirit

29 Luke portrayed which doctrine through Elizabeth, Zacharias, Mary, John the Baptist, and Simeon?
a) Salvation
b) Justification
c) The Holy Spirit
d) Eschatology

30 Which is a characteristic of Luke's writings?
a) Presenting his subjects in an abstract way
b) Portraying Jesus as a real person in history
c) Portraying Jesus as the Divine One
d) Expressions that reveal an extremely close association with Peter

31 According to Tenney, the best evidence that John, the son of Zebedee, was the author of the Gospel of John is
a) the independent witness of the synoptic writers.
b) the Gospel of John and the writings of the early church fathers.
c) eastern tradition.
d) extensive archaeological evidence.

32 Because the Gospel of John was included in Tatian's Diatessaron, it would indicate that this Gospel was written prior to
a) AD 80.
b) AD 100.
c) AD 140.
d) AD 180.

33 The Gospel of John was most probably written from
a) Antioch.
b) Jerusalem.
c) Rome.
d) Ephesus.

34 Which Gospel account would you tell a friend to read if he had problems of unbelief and thought of Jesus as only a common man?
a) Matthew
b) Mark
c) Luke
d) John

35 Which word or phrase is NOT characteristic of John?
a) I am
b) Word of God
c) Believe
d) Straightway

36 Which is NOT characteristic of the Gospel of John?
a) Confirmation of Christ by the "I am" sayings
b) Emphasis on the personal relationships of Jesus
c) Emphasis on the deity of Christ
d) Emphasis on Christ as a man of action

37 The Gospel of John presents Jesus as
a) the divine Son.
b) the perfect Man.
c) the obedient Servant.
d) the prophesied King.

38 Which statement is NOT true?
a) The Gospel of John points out the biological relationship of Jesus to the priestly family in Jerusalem.
b) The Gospel of John stresses the personal relationship of Jesus with man.
c) The Gospel of John emphasizes the humanity of Jesus Christ.
d) The Gospel of John emphasizes the deity of Jesus Christ.

39 What is the purpose of the Gospel of John?
a) John wrote his Gospel because he thought that Roman emperor Nero had destroyed all the copies of the Synoptic Gospels.
b) John wrote his Gospel as an apologetic, a defense of Christian beliefs, and also as a supplement to the Synoptic Gospels.
c) John wrote his Gospel as a defense document for his court trial prior to his banishment to the Island of Patmos.
d) John wrote his Gospel at the request of his trusted disciple Polycarp.

40 Which statement of Jesus does NOT appear in the Gospel of John?
a) "I am the Bread of Life."
b) "I am the Light of the World."
c) "I am the Good Shepherd."
d) "I am the Resurrection and the Life."
e) "I am the Alpha and Omega."

Part 2—True-False Questions

Indicate whether each statement is TRUE or FALSE.

41 In the Sermon on the Mount, Jesus commands the keeping of every aspect of the law of Moses.

42 A major emphasis of the parables in Matthew 11–13 is to portray the nature and program of the kingdom of heaven, particularly in reference to the future.

43 The Gospel of Matthew is didactic in emphasis. It contains the largest block of discourse material found in the four Gospels.

44 John Mark, the author of the Gospel of Mark, traveled with Paul, Barnabas, and Peter on each of their missionary journeys.

45 The Gospel of Mark shows Jesus as He hurried toward some unseen goal which He alone envisioned and revealed only in part to His disciples.

46 The Gospel of Mark very clearly answers why so marvelous a person as Jesus, with such tremendous authority, should come to so untimely an end.

47 The Gospel of Luke is the only Gospel which shares Jesus' parable of the Good Samaritan.

48 Luke says very little about the Holy Spirit in his Gospel, but a great deal about the Holy Spirit in Acts.

49 The purpose for which John wrote his Gospel is that the readers would believe that Jesus is the promised Messiah and the Son of God and that by believing they would receive eternal life in His name.

50 The outline of the Gospel of John is structured around the key word belief. In this context "belief" implies a total commitment of oneself to Jesus Christ.

After answering all of the questions in this UPE, refer again to points **3–6** under the heading *Taking Your Unit Progress Evaluations.* You will find these on the Essential Course Materials **INSTRUCTIONS** page.

Total UPE Time

Hr_____ Min_____

Unit Progress Evaluation 3

LIT1303 New Testament Literature, Sixth Edition

Start Time

(Unit 3—Lessons 8–11)

Multiple Choice Questions

Select the best answer to each question.

1 What are the three primary features of the book of Acts found in Acts 1:8?
   a) The ministry of Peter, the ministries of Stephen and Philip, and the ministry of Paul.
   b) The ministry of Jerusalem, the ministry of Palestine, and the ministry of the world.
   c) The name of Jesus, the power of the Holy Spirit, and the preaching of the word of God.
   d) The purpose: witness of Jesus; the power: Holy Spirit; and the plan: Jerusalem and outward.

2 Acts 1:8 provides a logical outline of the
   a) geographical development of the church.
   b) numerical development of the church.
   c) transition from the leadership of one apostle to that of another.
   d) doctrinal emphasis of the early church.

3 The general plan of evangelization the early missionaries followed was to
   a) minister in small villages where people had no temple to worship in.
   b) instruct leaders of Judaism in the synagogues in an effort to reach the people through their spiritual leaders.
   c) preach in key cities from which the gospel could flow out in ever-widening circles.
   d) stress one-to-one evangelization, ministering to individuals rather than multitudes.

4 The purpose of the book of Acts was to present the continuation of the acts and teaching of Christ through his church. Which of the Disciples was NOT involved in that work?
   a) Judas
   b) Paul
   c) John
   d) Peter

5 We can assume that the account of the growth and expansion of the church northward to Rome as recorded in Acts is
   a) a complete account of all the events that took place and the areas that were reached with the gospel during that time.
   b) simply a report of that part of the development of the church with which the writer was most familiar.
   c) an effort of the writer to record only the travels of the apostle Paul.
   d) a comprehensive survey of the missionary growth of the early church.

6 The book of Acts primarily stresses the
   a) impact of the gospel on the lives of individual men.
   b) messiahship of Jesus and the establishment of His kingdom.
   c) gradual decline of the Jewish church and the rise of Gentile Christianity.
   d) suffering and persecution of the early church.

7 Scripture describes in Acts 2:1–4, Acts 8:17, Acts 10:44–46, and Acts 19:6 the
   a) miracles performed by Peter and the resultant persecution of believers.
   b) outpouring of the Holy Spirit upon four representative groups of people.
   c) Old Testament prophesies concerning the outpouring of the Spirit.
   d) conversions of large numbers of people following the preaching of the gospel.

8 Which of the following statements best explains the comment, "The birthday of the church was Pentecost"?
a) When the disciples began to speak in unknown tongues, they were able to minister to people who had never been reached.
b) The day of Pentecost was an important Jewish event that carried over into Christianity.
c) Before the outpouring of the Holy Spirit, believers were not able to live victorious Christian lives.
d) The outpouring of the Holy Spirit gave impetus to the spread of the gospel by empowering the disciples.

9 How does the baptism of the Holy Spirit in the first century compare with the baptism of the Holy Spirit today? The experience
a) brought about the birth of the church in the first century but it is unnecessary today.
b) in the first century was considered normative, but its occurrence today is considered unnecessary because the church is established and does not need it.
c) was and is the same as salvation.
d) is considered normative for believers in the twentieth century just as it was in the first century.

10 Why did the ministry of Philip in Samaria became a spiritual transition in the advancement of the early church?
a) Peter and John had to go ahead of Philip and get permission for Philip to minister from the chief priest of the Samaritan temple in Mt. Gerizim.
b) The united evangelistic effort of Philip and Simon of Samaria was a pilot project that would be copied by future missionaries in using existing religious leaders for the spread of Christianity.
c) The Samaritans were not pure Jews. They were a cultural and racial mixture of Jews and Gentiles dating back to the captivity of the Northern Kingdom by Assyria.
d) Philip was not a Hebrew Jew like the twelve apostles; rather, he was a Hellenistic Jew. Thus he became the first Hellenistic Jew used by the Holy Spirit.

11 Apart from the Lord Jesus Christ, which individual had the greatest influence upon the advancement of the Christian church?
a) Apostle Peter
b) Apostle Paul
c) Emperor Constantine
d) Martin Luther

12 Which of the following changes did NOT occur in the period of transition from the era of the Law to the Church Age?
a) Forgiveness of sins was the message stressed.
b) Believers included Samaritans and foreigners.
c) The leaders emphasized the restoration of the Kingdom.
d) The church faced the problem of applying the Law to Gentile believers.

13 Which statement is NOT true of the Antioch church?
a) The disciples were first called Christians at the Antioch church.
b) The Antioch church sent out missionaries and mothered Gentile churches.
c) The controversy over whether Gentiles must keep the Law of Moses was started in the Antioch church.
d) The first early church council, which included speeches by Paul, Peter, and James, took place in Antioch.

14 Which was NOT a benefit of Paul's first missionary journey to Cyprus, Pisidian Antioch, Iconium, Lystra, and Derbe?
a) Paul emerged as the apostle to the Gentiles.
b) The theology of justification by faith came to the attention of the churches.
c) The church was forced to deal with the issue, "To what extent must Gentiles keep the Law?"
d) Peter emerged as the first bishop of the church in Rome.

15 The crucial question of the Council in Jerusalem was whether
a) Gentiles should be allowed to take communion without knowledge of the Law.
b) the Law had a place in the plan of God for the church.
c) circumcision was necessary to be saved.
d) there would be a resurrection of the dead.

16 In his Epistle, the apostle James argues that
   a) faith in Jesus Christ is not sufficient, obedience to the Law must be added to faith.
   b) if faith in Jesus Christ is genuine, it will lead to a life of obedience to the moral law of Moses.
   c) equality of race, equality of gender (sexes), and equality of rich and poor is important.
   d) faith in Jesus Christ is not sufficient, it must be supplemented with wisdom, knowledge, and education.

17 What was Paul's main purpose for writing the book of Galatians?
   a) Paul and Barnabas had just planted the church in Galatia. Paul wrote the Epistle as a manual for local church government in the newly planted churches.
   b) Paul primarily wrote it to promote the doctrine of justification by faith. Paul wrote it as a protest against the teaching and practices of the Judaizers.
   c) Paul wrote Galatians as a defense document after being reprimanded by Peter and James at the Council in Jerusalem.
   d) Paul wrote Galatians primarily to teach on the fruit of the Holy Spirit versus the "works of the flesh."

18 Paul and Barnabas parted company after a disagreement over whether
   a) Gentiles should be circumcised before they became Christians.
   b) Peter should be placed in charge of the church at Antioch.
   c) John Mark should accompany them on their second mission to Asia Minor.
   d) the Law should be permanent in the early church.

19 What special event took place in Troas?
   a) The Holy Spirit called Paul in a vision to go into Macedonia.
   b) Paul added Timothy to his missionary team.
   c) Paul was stoned and cast out of the city.
   d) Luke became Paul's constant companion.

20 The greatest result of Paul's ministry in Macedonia was that it
   a) added many new converts to the church.
   b) introduced the doctrine of justification by faith.
   c) added deacons to the administration of the church.
   d) introduced the gospel into Europe where it made a profound impact upon western civilization.

21 The main doctrinal theme in both 1 and 2 Thessalonians is the
   a) Lordship of Jesus Christ.
   b) second coming of Christ.
   c) adoption of the believer.
   d) place of works in the plan of salvation.

22 The main reason for the instability of the church at Corinth was the
   a) lack of experienced leaders in the church.
   b) pagan background of new Christians who lacked the foundational teaching of Old Testament Scriptures.
   c) lack of Spirit-filled believers.
   d) lack of harmony between the church at Jerusalem and the apostle Paul.

23 What two important problems did Paul face when he came to Ephesus?
   a) (1) The continuation of the teachings of John the Baptist by those without a knowledge of Jesus Christ, and (2) Ephesus was a stronghold for the occult.
   b) (1) The Jewish synagogue in Ephesus had received a decree from the Sanhedrin in Jerusalem that Paul was a false prophet. (2) Judaizers from Jerusalem had preceded Paul to Ephesus and had alienated the Jews and God fearers against Paul before his arrival.
   c) (1) The Cayster River at Ephesus was filling up with sand and ships could no longer navigate on the river. (2) The residents of Ephesus were moving away as import income diminished.
   d) (1) The arrival of Gnostic teachers and their secret initiations. (2) The declining financial support from the mother church in Antioch.

24 Who was Apollos?
a) Apollos was one of the seventy disciples that Jesus sent out two-by-two.
b) Apollos had thoroughly studied the Greek philosophies of his time and thus could integrate Christian theology with Greek philosophies.
c) Apollos attracted many Corinthians by his learning and his polished presentation of truth.
d) He was one of the seven deacons and also a disciple of Peter.

25 Paul's main purpose in his first letter to the Corinthian church was to
a) raise money for the Jerusalem church.
b) provide teaching regarding the second coming of Christ.
c) defend his testimony and his right to be the spiritual leader.
d) treat serious problems within the church and to answer questions raised by the converts.

26 We can summarize the value of 2 Corinthians by saying that it
a) provides positive teaching.
b) shows that the early church had its struggles and yet survived.
c) gives insight into the life of Paul.
d) all of the above.

27 Paul's plan to go to Rome can be compared with Christ's plan to go to Jerusalem because each plan
a) involved moving resolutely toward a predetermined goal.
b) followed three years of intensive missionary activity.
c) led to the spread of the gospel into unreached areas.
d) was accepted by the followers of its leader.

28 The book of Romans treats all of the following doctrines EXCEPT
a) salvation.
b) the Holy Spirit.
c) eschatology.
d) faith versus works.

29 From his description of events following Paul's return to Jerusalem, Luke indicates his desire to show Theophilus that
a) Christianity would overtake the world whatever the cost might be.
b) no political organization could bring harm to a servant of God.
c) Paul, because of old age, found it necessary to limit his activities.
d) Christianity was not a political threat to imperial Rome; rather, its relations with the Roman government had always been friendly.

30 When Paul returned to Jerusalem at the end of his third mission, his reception by the Jews indicated the
a) general acceptance of Christianity by the Jews.
b) ever-widening breach between Christianity and Judaism.
c) indifference of the general population to the Christian message.
d) love and appreciation of the Jews for Paul and his ministry.

31 Paul was imprisoned in Jerusalem because
a) Jews from Asia said he took a Gentile friend with him into the forbidden sanctuary of the temple.
b) he preached a fiery sermon against Jews from the castle steps.
c) Paul, being a Roman citizen, took a Nazarite vow.
d) he refused to worship in the temple.

32 The hearings that followed Paul's arrest in Jerusalem showed that
a) Paul was innocent of any political or criminal offense.
b) Paul favored the Gentile Christians, and this turned the Jewish converts against him.
c) Paul's judges were unmoved by his testimony and sought to kill him.
d) Paul faced certain death and the existence of the church was endangered.

33 Paul's vision in Jerusalem and the appearance of the angel at the time of shipwreck confirmed to him that
a) he would die a martyr's death.
b) God would punish his accusers.
c) it was God's will for him to go to Rome.
d) his ministry was drawing to an end.

34 Which statement is correct concerning the assemblies to whom Paul wrote his Epistles?
  a) The earlier Epistles went to a strong, aggressive church whose converts readily accepted the teachings of Christianity.
  b) The prison Epistles addressed a maturing church whose members were complacent rather than confused and unstable.
  c) Members of the churches which received the prison Epistles were unorganized and easily misled by false teachers.
  d) The prison Epistles were written to churches whose members needed basic instruction.

35 Describe the four prison Epistles.
  a) The four prison Epistles are primarily christological, because they are centered around Christ.
  b) The four prison Epistles are primarily historical, because they describe how four churches were started.
  c) The four prison Epistles are primarily prophetical, because Paul foretells future events.
  d) The four prison Epistles are primarily theological, because Paul gives a systematic presentation of the gospel in each epistle.

36 What do the following six words describe: offense, compassion, intercession, substitution, restoration, and elevation?
  a) The cycles of apostasy
  b) The steps to salvation
  c) The elements of forgiveness
  d) The progressive nature of sin

37 The Greek word Paul uses in Ephesians for church is ekklesia, which means
  a) the called out ones.
  b) people who loved each other.
  c) people who responded in faith to the gospel.
  d) those prepared to die as martyrs.
  e) people who have the seal of the Holy Spirit.

38 In his Epistle to the Colossians, how did Paul combat the "Colossian Heresy"?
  a) Paul gave a systematic presentation of the involvement of God in Hebrew history.
  b) Paul gave a very thorough dissertation on the order and ranks of angels in heaven, demons under Satan in hell, and animal and nature spirits on this earth.
  c) Paul gave a systematic theology on justification, and glorification of Christians.
  d) Paul gave a positive presentation of the preeminence of Christ.

39 Why did Paul write his Epistle to the Philippians?
  a) Paul wrote to correct immoral practices in the church that came from the involvement of prostitutes in the worship of the goddess Diana.
  b) Paul primarily wrote the Epistle as preventive maintenance; he had heard that the Judaizers were starting to promote legalism among the Philippians.
  c) Paul wrote to thank the Philippians for a very generous gift and to share his personal joy in Jesus.
  d) The Philippians had concerns about their members who had died, so Paul wrote a letter of spiritual comfort and shared about life in heaven.

40 The results of Paul's prison years are remarkable because
  a) he won many of Caesar's household to Christ and brought Christianity to the attention of public officials.
  b) he utilized his time to strengthen the church through his Epistles.
  c) he demonstrated that one can experience great joy in Christ even in difficult circumstances.
  d) both b) and c) above.
  e) all of the above.

Part 2—True-False Questions

Indicate whether each statement is TRUE or FALSE.

41 The preaching of the apostles in the early church interpreted Old Testament Scriptures and emphasized the resurrection of Jesus Christ.

42 All of the case examples in the book of Acts infer or clearly reveal that the baptism in the Holy Spirit follows personal conversion and is evidenced with speaking in other tongues.

43 Paul already had a conversion experience through watching the martyrdom of Stephen; the encounter with Jesus on the Damascus Road merely made public what had already happened in the spiritual life of Paul.

44 God still requires complete obedience to the Law as a requisite to salvation.

45 We are justified by faith, but our good works demonstrates our faith.

46 The customs and rituals of the Law are unchanging and still apply to us today.

47 If we accept Jesus Christ as our Savior, we are His children no matter how much we continue in sin.

48 Complete surrender to Christ would naturally result in a life of moral and ethical purity.

49 First and Second Thessalonians clearly reveal that the return of Jesus Christ and the seven years of tribulation come before the rapture of the saints.

50 One reason Paul wrote the Epistle to the Romans was to prepare the Church in Rome to become a financial supporting church for a future church, planting ministry in Spain.

After answering all of the questions in this UPE, refer again to points **3–6** under the heading *Taking Your Unit Progress Evaluations.* You will find these on the Essential Course Materials **INSTRUCTIONS** page.

Total UPE Time

Hr_____ Min_____

Student's Request to Take Final Examination
LIT1303 New Testament Literature, Sixth Edition

We are pleased that you are nearing the completion of this course. At this point you will want to make arrangements to take your final examination. You may do so by filling in this form and sending it to your enrollment office. In this way, your adviser can make an appointment for you to take the final examination.

Please print in block (capital) letters, one letter or number per box.

Your name:

Your student number:

Your current address (if changed since enrolling in this course):

If you are taking this course as a part of a school class, what is the name of the school?

Name, address, and phone number of examination supervisor:

Unless the time and date for your examination have already been arranged, use this box to request an appointment.

	DATE	MORNING	AFTERNOON	EVENING
First Choice				
Second Choice				
Third Choice				

FOR OFFICE USE ONLY

Director:	Signature or stamp
1. Sign or stamp. 2. Make a copy of this information for your files. 3. You have already received a final examination for this student. If you do not have the exam, please send this form to the IO.	

Note: The final grade for this course cannot be computed or recorded until the subject enrollment card (SEC) for this course and the grade for any required projects have been received by the International Office.

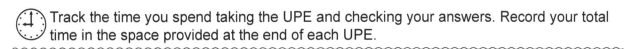

Unit Progress Evaluation 4

LIT1303 New Testament Literature, Sixth Edition

Start Time

(Unit 4—Lessons 12–15)

Multiple Choice Questions

Select the best answer to each question.

1 The pastoral Epistles seem to support the theory that
   a) Paul was acquitted after his first imprisonment.
   b) the apostle was never released from his house arrest in Rome.
   c) they were written from prison.
   d) in point of time they precede the prison Epistles.

2 Which organizational changes listed below were emerging in the church when the Pastoral Epistles were written?
   a) Offices had become fixed and were desired as a way to win recognition.
   b) Bishops, elders, and deacons served the church, and widows enrolled by the church were responsible for the church's social welfare program.
   c) Services in the church had certain regular features (that is, a structure was emerging).
   d) All of the above.

3 In which Epistle does Paul deal with matters of organization in the church that might be considered "advice to a young preacher"?
   a) 2 Timothy
   b) Titus
   c) 1 Timothy
   d) 1 Peter

4 Paul's charge to one of the young ministers under his supervision is classic. The man of God, he counsels, is to flee, follow, fight, and keep. In which Epistle is this found?
   a) 2 Timothy
   b) Titus
   c) 1 Timothy
   d) 1 Peter

5 The major emphasis of Titus centers on advice to a
   a) fellow missionary who was struggling with the basic doctrines of salvation.
   b) pioneer missionary who represented a church that had advanced to the place of settled policies and established doctrines.
   c) young minister who was weak, timid, and struggling in his ministry.
   d) novice in the ministry who needed instruction concerning the Second Coming and other important end-time events.

6 Which of the following statements does NOT accurately describe the conditions that existed in Crete?
   a) The church was unorganized, and its members were quite careless in their behavior.
   b) The church members' actions and attitudes seemed to imply that salvation by faith was unrelated to honest work and clean living.
   c) Hymenaeus and Alexander opposed Paul's moral standard, and their example was affecting others in the church.
   d) A Judaizing group there spent its time arguing about Jewish fables.

7 Which of Paul's Epistles might very well be called his "Farewell address"?
   a) 2 Timothy
   b) Hebrews
   c) 1 Timothy
   d) Titus

8 The Epistle written to encourage the church, which faced government hostility and threat of persecution in a hostile world, was
   a) 1 Peter.
   b) Hebrews.
   c) 2 Timothy.
   d) Titus.

9 The purpose of the main theme of 1 Peter would be to show the
   a) response of the church to the oppressive measures of a dictatorial government.
   b) need to persevere as indicated by the "Let us" exhortations.
   c) role of the Christian church in society.
   d) sufficiency of God's grace in suffering.

10 The question posed to Jewish Christians who were confronted with the issues of patriotism for their country versus loyalty to Christ and of grace versus legalism is dealt with in
   a) 1 Peter.
   b) 2 Timothy.
   c) Hebrews.
   d) 1 Timothy.

11 Tenney believes that the single greatest value of the book of Hebrews is its teaching on the
   a) present ministry and priesthood of Christ.
   b) perils which give us direction in the area of Christian responsibility.
   c) exhortations given to the recipients in the "Let us" passages.
   d) theme of salvation by faith in the sacrifice of Christ.

12 The five short Epistles, 2 Peter, Jude, 1, 2, and 3 John, were written to cope with the trends toward
   a) the spirit of secularism, which glorified the state and emperor.
   b) false doctrine within the church.
   c) a greatly stepped-up program of official government persecution.
   d) differences between Judaism and Christianity which meant that they were now less compatible than ever.

13 The chief contribution of 2 Peter to the teaching of the New Testament is its
   a) detailed analysis of end-time events, including judgment and the new heaven and new earth.
   b) statement concerning the inspiration of the Scriptures.
   c) carefully worded statement concerning the policies and procedures which the church should follow in a hostile world.
   d) well-developed Christology.

14 In 2 Peter the writer attempts to show that the answer to false knowledge is
   a) true knowledge.
   b) strict discipline within each local assembly.
   c) more spiritual discrimination by church members.
   d) to de-emphasize knowledge and to stress the value of subjective spiritual experience.

15 Tenney says, "There can be no doubt that the two (Jude and 2 Peter) are separate Epistles, and yet the similarities of occasion, of thought, and of vocabulary between the two can hardly be accidental." Based upon the possibilities for these similarities, Tenney concludes that
   a) recipients of both letters faced the same problems.
   b) both Epistles borrowed from a common source.
   c) 2 Peter borrowed from Jude.
   d) Jude was stimulated by 2 Peter to write his own Epistle.

16 In style and vocabulary, in terseness and graphic expression, and in dependence on figures of speech from outdoor life, the Epistle of Jude resembles which of the following Epistles?
   a) 2 Peter
   b) 1 John
   c) 1 Timothy
   d) James

17 The Epistle of Jude shows that by the time it was written
   a) the battle against heresy had been fought and to a large extent lost.
   b) the threat to the church was primarily external and political rather than internal and spiritual.
   c) there was a recognized body of belief that could be called Christianity.
   d) there was a critical need for an ordered leadership in the church to direct its overall defense.

18 Jude addressed himself, among other things, to the problem of antinomianism, which
   a) denied the humanity of the Lord Jesus Christ.
   b) claimed that Christian grace and liberty entitled one to complete freedom in morals.
   c) dealt with the claims of the superiority of knowledge over faith.
   d) asserted the claims of legalism over faith.

19 Tenney says that 1 John differs from the Gospel of John in that the Gospel
  a) was written to arouse faith while the first Epistle was written to establish certainty.
  b) emphasizes the humanity of the Lord Jesus while the first Epistle stresses His divinity.
  c) arose out of the need to refute Gnosticism while 1 John deals with the heresy of antinomianism.
  d) was written at an early date to give the church an appropriate body of doctrinal teaching, while 1 John came later and was intended to serve as an apologetic for the faith.

20 In 1 John the writer insists that the Christ he preached was a person one could see, hear, and touch. He asserts specifically that any spirit in evidence in the church was not of God if it
  a) denied the necessity for knowledge in the body.
  b) refused to acknowledge the humanity of Jesus Christ.
  c) insisted that the church be subject to ungodly political powers.
  d) moved people to worship the Lord Jesus Christ as God.

21 Tenney shows that, based upon 3 John, much of the ministry toward the end of the first century was carried on by
  a) strong local pastors who were backed by good structural organization.
  b) itinerant preachers who made periodic rounds, staying a while in each church for home meetings.
  c) itinerant elders and bishops who exercised great power.
  d) lay leaders trained to serve under circuit-riding bishops who exercised real power.

22 Of the five characteristics of apocalyptic literature mentioned by your textbook, which one below is NOT true of the book of Revelation?
  a) Extreme despair of present circumstances and intense hope of future divine intervention
  b) Use of symbolic language, visions, and dreams
  c) Authorship unknown
  d) Celestial and demonic powers introduced
  e) Prediction of fearful judgment on the wicked and deliverance for the righteous

23 The conditions under which the book of Revelation was written suggest
  a) general tolerance, but some isolated cases of persecution existed.
  b) hostility and oppression of the church by the Roman state.
  c) general war, plagues, famine, and widespread bloodshed.
  d) a return to the status of general peace that had existed under Augustus.

24 The purpose of the writing of Revelation, as stated in Revelation 1:1, was to reveal
  a) in advance all the details of church history.
  b) the course of human history and the conflict between good and evil.
  c) to regional assemblies events which concerned only their immediate future.
  d) Christ in relation to events of the last days.

25 The millennial view which holds that Christ will return personally to initiate His kingdom, that the righteous dead will be raised, and that they will reign personally with Christ on earth for a thousand years, is called the
  a) premillennial view.
  b) postmillennial view.
  c) amillennial view.
  d) millennial view.

26 The school of prophetic interpretation which depends heavily on the literal interpretation of the events of the Apocalypse and regards most of them as yet remaining to be fulfilled is the
  a) Preterist School.
  b) Idealist School.
  c) Futurist School.
  d) Historicist School.

27 What, according the author of our study guide, is a major rule for interpreting prophecy?
  a) All prophecies in any book of the Bible classified as apocalyptic must be interpreted symbolically.
  b) Biblical prophecies can only be correctly interpreted through the spiritual gift of interpretation from the Holy Spirit.
  c) All biblical prophecies must be interpreted by the guidelines set forth in the Fundamental Doctrines of the Assemblies of God.
  d) Take the words of prophecy as literal, rather than figurative, unless the context and related prophecies indicate otherwise.

28 What particular significance has biblical prophecy and especially the message of Revelation to the life of the present day Christian? The Christian should
a) know completely the full calendar of prophetic events so that he may explain their significance to others.
b) recognize the value of these dreadful events in persuading people to join the church.
c) study the symbolism of prophecy in general and Revelation in particular, so that he may have some basis for interpreting the Revelation.
d) become more conscientious in his daily Christian ministry and be ready at all times for the return of the Lord Jesus Christ.

29 Which of the seven churches is the only one for whom no strengths are mentioned?
a) Philadelphia
b) Laodicea
c) Smyrna
d) Ephesus
e) Pergamos

30 The chart of time sequence of the major events of Revelation in your study guide follows which order?
a) Tribulation, Rapture, Revelation of Christ, New Heaven and New Earth
b) Rapture, Tribulation, Revelation of Christ, Millennium, Satan's Last Revolt, Perfect Age
c) Rapture, Revelation of Christ, Tribulation, Millennium, Satan's Last Revolt, Perfect Age
d) Tribulation, Revelation of Christ, Rapture, Millennium, Satan's Last Revolt, Perfect Age

31 The word canon as it relates to the New Testament documents, refers to the
a) books that were most generally accepted by each church council as being the ones of the most significant value for the church.
b) books that were accepted as divinely inspired, authentic, and agreed upon to become the standard for faith and practice, and thus to be included in the New Testament.
c) criterion or standard by which all works are either accepted into the New Testament or rejected solely on the basis of human authorship.
d) comprehensive standard by which a book is judged on its worthiness, literary qualities, and authenticity for inclusion into the body of sacred writings.

32 All of the principles of canonicity below helped influence the formation of the New Testament canon EXCEPT
a) authenticity.
b) the church's acceptance of the book.
c) infallibility.
d) inspiration.

33 Tenney notes that the writings of the New Testament have a self-authenticating quality that impart what he calls
a) internal testimony.
b) informal witness.
c) external testimony.
d) apostolic prerogative.

34 In ethical and spiritual effect the canonical books are different from all other literature in their greater power to
a) transform human thought and conduct.
b) influence human thought and sometimes conduct.
c) inspire lofty thoughts and desires in people.
d) reveal to people the truth of their message.

35 As far as we know, Clement, Ignatius, Polycarp, Justin Martyr, and several others wrote the earliest
a) canons in the formal list.
b) defense of the accepted New Testament canon.
c) apologetics for the methodology they used for determining canonicity.
d) documents in the informal witness to canonicity.

36 The role of church councils concerning canonicity of writings now in the New Testament was to
a) evaluate each book to determine the degree of its inspiration.
b) recognize and give an opinion concerning whether books were canonical or noncanonical.
c) examine the life and background of each author to see whether his work was deserving of recognition as being inspired (on the basis of his conduct).
d) determine the practicality, literary quality, and applicability of its message on a universal scale.

37 The New Testament was officially acknowledged as we now know it
a) at the end of the first century.
b) at about the middle of the second century.
c) near the end of the second century.
d) during the fourth century.

38 Of the books listed below, which one was NOT readily accepted as part of the New Testament canon?
a) Matthew
b) Romans
c) Revelation
d) Hebrews

39 All of the following are "Sources of the Text" EXCEPT the
a) Diatessaron of Tatian.
b) Rylands Fragment of John.
c) Chester Beatty papyri.
d) Bodmer Papyrus of John.

40 Because there were so many different Latin translations of the Bible, Pope Damascus commissioned Jerome to produce a new standard Latin version. This new corrected Latin text is known as the
a) Peshitta version.
b) Syriac version.
c) Vulgate version.
d) Syriac Vulgate version.

Part 2—True-False Questions

Indicate whether each statement is TRUE or FALSE.

41 The lack of correspondence between Paul's travels that are recorded in Acts and in the pastoral Epistles indicates that Paul continued to travel after his first imprisonment in Rome.

42 The internal evidence clearly reveals that Peter wrote his first Epistle from Babylon, a town on the Nile River in Egypt.

43 The second Epistle of Peter was actually written by Jude with the permission of Peter.

44 The first Epistle of John emphasizes the humanity of Jesus while the Gospel of John emphasizes the deity of Jesus Christ.

45 Docetism teaches that the Christ Spirit came upon Jesus at His water baptism and left Jesus just prior to His death.

46 Cerinthianism teaches that the Christ Spirit came upon Jesus at His water baptism and left Jesus just prior to His death.

47 The book of Revelation was not written by the apostle John, but by an elder John.

48 The Preterist Interpretation of Revelation claims that Revelation chapters 4 through 22 are prophecies of events still in the future.

49 Justin Martyr was the first early church father to include all twenty-seven books of the New Testament in the canon.

50 The Rylands Manuscript is the oldest complete copy of the Gospel of John in existence today.

After answering all of the questions in this UPE, refer again to points **3–6** under the heading *Taking Your Unit Progress Evaluations* and points **1–3** under the heading *Taking the Final Examination.* You will find these on the Essential Course Materials **INSTRUCTIONS** page.

Total UPE Time

Hr_____ Min_____

Unit Progress Evaluation Answer Keys

Unit Progress Evaluation (UPE) scores are not counted as part of your final course grade.

UPE scores indicate how well you learned the material and how well you may do on the final examination. Review lesson sections pertaining to any questions you miss.

The numbers following the answer represent the lesson number and the objective number.

Unit Progress Evaluation 1

1	E	1.1	14	B	1.4	27	D	2.1	40	E	2.7
2	D	1.2	15	D	1.4	28	E	2.1	41	F	1.1
3	D	1.2	16	B	1.4	29	A	2.1	42	T	1.2
4	C	1.2	17	A	1.4	30	C	2.2	43	F	1.4
5	B	1.2	18	B	1.5	31	E	2.2	44	T	1.5
6	A	1.2	19	C	1.5	32	C	2.3	45	T	2.1
7	A	1.3	20	E	1.5	33	A	2.3	46	F	2.3
8	D	1.3	21	D	1.5	34	C	2.3	47	T	2.7
9	B	1.4	22	A	1.5	35	A	2.3	48	T	2.7
10	E	1.4	23	B	1.5	36	E	2.4	49	F	2.7
11	A	1.4	24	E	1.6	37	B	2.5	50	T	2.7
12	C	1.4	25	B	1.6	38	D	2.6			
13	C	1.4	26	D	2.1	39	C	2.6			

Unit Progress Evaluation 2

1	C	3.1	14	B	4.3	27	D	6.4	40	E	7.7
2	A	3.2	15	C	4.4	28	B	6.4	41	F	4.4
3	D	3.2	16	C	4.4	29	C	6.4	42	T	4.4
4	A	3.2	17	D	4.5	30	B	6.4	43	T	4.4
5	C	3.3	18	C	5.1,2	31	B	7.1	44	F	5.1
6	D	3.4	19	A	5.2	32	C	7.2	45	T	5.3
7	A	3.5	20	A	5.3	33	D	7.3	46	F	5.3
8	B	3.6	21	C	5.4	34	D	7.3	47	T	6.3
9	D	3.7	22	D	5.4	35	D	7.3–7.7	48	F	6.4
10	B	4.1	23	E	5.5	36	D	7.3–7.7	49	T	7.3
11	B	4.2	24	A	6.1	37	A	7.5	50	T	7.3
12	A	4.3	25	A	6.2	38	A	7.5			
13	B	4.3	26	C	6.2	39	B	7.6			

The numbers following the answer represent the lesson number and the objective number.

Unit Progress Evaluation 3

1	D	8.1	14	D	9.2	27	A	10.3	40	E	11.8
2	A	8.2	15	B	9.3	28	C	10.4	41	T	8.3
3	C	8.2	16	B	9.4	29	D	11.1	42	T	8.3
4	A	8.2	17	B	9.5	30	B	11.2	43	F	8.6
5	B	8.2	18	C	9.5	31	A	11.2	44	F	9.4–5
6	C	8.2	19	A	9.6	32	A	11.2	45	T	9.4–5
7	B	8.3	20	D	9.6	33	C	11.2	46	F	9.4–5
8	D	8.3	21	B	9.7	34	B	11.3	47	F	9.4–5
9	D	8.3	22	B	9.8	35	A	11.3	48	T	9.4–5
10	C	8.5	23	A	9.9	36	C	11.4	49	F	9.7
11	B	8.6	24	C	10.1	37	A	11.5	50	T	10.4
12	C	8.7	25	D	10.2	38	D	11.6			
13	D	9.1	26	D	10.3	39	C	11.7			

Unit Progress Evaluation 4

1	A	12.1	14	A	13.2	27	D	14.3	40	C	15.5
2	D	12.1	15	D	13.3	28	D	14.4	41	T	12.1
3	C	12.2	16	D	13.4	29	B	14.5	42	F	12.5
4	C	12.2	17	C	13.4	30	B	14.6	43	F	13.2
5	B	12.3	18	B	13.4	31	B	15.1	44	T	13.5
6	C	12.3	19	A	13.5	32	C	15.1	45	F	13.5
7	A	12.4	20	B	13.5	33	A	15.2	46	T	13.5
8	A	12.5	21	B	13.5	34	A	15.2	47	F	14.1
9	D	12.5	22	C	14.1	35	D	15.3	48	F	14.2
10	C	12.6	23	B	14.1	36	B	15.3	49	F	15.3
11	A	12.6	24	D	14.2	37	D	15.4	50	F	15.5
12	B	13.1	25	A	14.2	38	D	15.4			
13	B	13.2	26	C	14.2	39	A	15.5			

Lightning Source UK Ltd.
Milton Keynes UK
UKOW07f1826240915

259201UK00015B/101/P